Choreography and the Specific Image

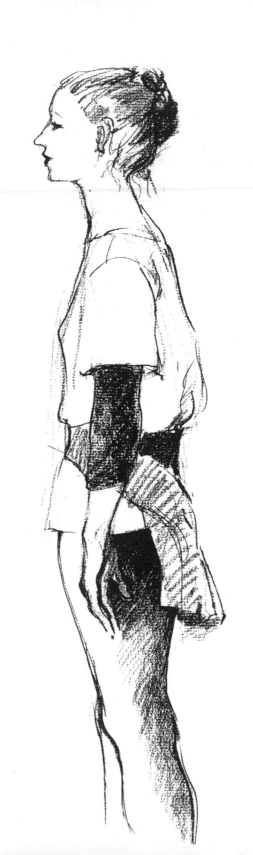

# Choreography and the Specific Image

## NINETEEN ESSAYS AND A WORKBOOK

Daniel Nagrin

*University of Pittsburgh Press*

Published by the University of Pittsburgh Press, Pittsburgh, Pa., 15261

Library of Congress Cataloging-in-Publication Data
Nagrin, Daniel.
    Choreography and the specific image : nineteen essays and a workbook /
Daniel Nagrin.
        p.  cm.
Includes index.
    ISBN 0-8229-4147-3 — ISBN 0-8229-5750-7
  1. Dance—Philosophy.  2. Choreography.  I. Title.
    GV1588.3 .N34 2001
    792.8'2—dc21

                                                    2001002663

Dedicated to CATHERINE MARSHALL
and
NIELS AABOE
whose editorial support, guidance
and sensitivity helped to bring
the Specific Image Series to life.

# Contents

## *The Workbook*

# Acknowledgments

My custom in writing these books has been to initially send the completed manuscripts of the Specific Image Series to a few of my friends, associates and colleagues rather than to the publisher. Their prime qualification, aside from a rich experience in dance, either as professionals or intense observers of dance, is the capacity to tell me exactly and eloquently what they think of what I write. I trusted their taste and am grateful for the time they invested in reviewing my manuscript. My gratitude to them is full and I take this space to thank them and absolve them for all responsibility for the final text. For this last volume they were: Christine B. Funsch, Professor Barbara Grubel, Katherine Longstreth, Meredith Monk, Phyllis Steele-Nagrin, Professor Meriam Rosen, Dr. Mel Rosenthal, Paul Taylor and Dr. Arthur Waldhorn.

Special attention is due to my wife, Phyllis Steele-Nagrin who not only read and astutely commented upon every page as it emerged from the computer but contributed the lovely, observant drawings decorating the pages of this book. The cover brush drawing is by Arthur Getz and is used by permission of Sarah Getz. A strategic piece of research information was performed by Katherine Krzys, a curator at the Hayden Library of Arizona State University. Thanks are also due to Elizabeth Keen, Cliff Keuter, Elina Mooney, Phoebe Neville and Marion Scott who participated in a panel on Tamiris's teaching; Edward Effron for his critique of my light plot; Tony Kramer for his interview; and, finally, to Donya Feuer, Elizabeth Keen and Susan Stroman for the remarkable essays.

A side note: The notes of my erstwhile neighbor, Paul Taylor, were as penetrating as they were hilarious.

# Choreography and the Specific Image

# Introduction

A book justifies its existence when it throws light upon what has been ignored or received scant attention. There are a number of good books on choreography. The major thrust of their analysis and exposition is structural, examining the trinity of Space, Time and Dynamics. Viewing the added factors of music, costume, lighting and content through the prism of these three elements supports a formal approach to choreography. The title of this book, *Choreography and the Specific Image*, points to a different perspective, one that is generally slighted. It seizes upon one of the factors that enters into the making of dances, *content*, and looks at all the others through that lens. Here, the idea and use of content in the creative act are contained in the key concept of "the specific image."

This is the third book in a series which revolves around this creative tool: "the specific image." Each book focuses on a different aspect of dance: improvisation, acting/performance technique and choreography.

*Dance and the Specific Image: Improvisation* (1993) describes 138 improvisation exercises, games and structures. Their development is traced through the life of a dance company called the Workgroup which I directed from 1971 to 1974. The text is directed primarily to teachers and choreographers of group or solo works. The exercises, games and structures delineate paths to individualized motion vocabulary, greater freedom in dance and seeds for choreographic works. The book in the hands of students and performers will draw in a collaborative energy that will facilitate exploration of the unexpected.

*The Six Questions: Acting Technique for Dance Performance* (1997) explores the ways by which dancers can perform with power, authority and the uninhibited outpouring of the total self. The technique allows for the physical dynamic and skill to serve the expression of the dancer's inner life. This volume presents an array of tools to elicit honest and rich expression in dance performance. It is designed for use and study by teachers, choreographers and particularly for dance performers and students. The approach asks for a new look at the act of dance.

Together, the three books offer a comprehensive map for creating and performing dance. Is the approach offered here better than others? Is this to be the one and true way? Answers: No and no. It is not better and it is not the only way. It is *a* way. I learned the bones of it from years of working with Helen Tamiris. The dances in my repertoire all blossomed out of "specific images." I have taught "Choreography and the Specific Image" since 1957 to a generation of dancers. For some that teaching proved useless to their temperaments, aesthetics and philosophies. For others, the doors opened and they rushed in to new found spaces that gave them the freedom to reach their deepest impulses. They did not *make* dances, they *found* dances and they emerged with individual profiles and personal identities as artists.

Another question: What is the point of *studying* choreography? When you are overflowing with an impulse, you don't need a method, you just do it. True, but the art of any artist who has produced a body of work is backed up by a method, an approach and a philosophy that were hammered out in study, apprenticeship with a master or in the lonely hours in the studio. The most inspired work of art has its bleak and barren moments. It is then, when the artist is clogged, blocked, uncertain, or when the impulse loses steam that he.she reaches into the bag of tools, trying this and that until something clicks within, until something says, "OK, this is it. We're back on the rails, back to the impulse or to a new impulse."

This book has a double concentration: the two sides of the creative process. One aspect aims to release the inner forces that fuel a dance. The other intellectually sharpens the conceptualizing tools that shape the dynamics and the direction of the work. Any choreographer who can keep his.her balance astride these contradictory and complementary forces will have the power to organically link the specifics of phrasing, counterpoint and relation to music that go into making the chains of movement, the use of space and the use of dancers.

More legitimate questions: Can one talk or write of choreography when the field of dance is afloat with dozens of styles, attitudes and philosophies? Will this book restrict itself to the problems of one style or does it try or pretend to embrace all of dance? The author is a modern dancer. Does what is said here preclude the interests and needs of ballet choreographers? Answers: If the heat of your ambition and aesthetic revolves about the tradition of Petipa and Balanchine, this may be alien territory. I myself have always been interested in and learned from observing alien territory. If you want to know how the other side thinks, come read and you may find something useful. If you consider yourself coming out of the Noverre-Tudor line of thinking and feeling about dance, you should feel at home.

Of what use can this book be for the abstractionists, the non-objective ones, those for whom movement and design are at the heart of their work? Again, most of these pages may appear as alien territory. Still, I suspect that some of the best choreographers who operate in this mode have at the heart of their movement invention and group orchestration specific images. Consider a classic formal concept for a dance: a chain of motions is derived from a single phrase. That too is indeed a specific image. To make a fine piece of choreography, all that is needed is a passion for exploring in depth that single phrase. If passion isn't the driving force, there's no point in making art at all and *the center of this book is locating the sources of passion.*

*Choreography and the Specific Image* comes with a hope that it will reach, among others, a generation of dancers who were schooled in the primacy of the structural concepts of choreography that supported the making of abstract and formal dance. So many of them are now turning to, for the lack of a better word, "content," as their focus. Why? The world outside has burst into the studio. It is unacceptable for the young to die, but the unacceptable is here. It is unacceptable for anyone to accept a lesser place because of not being a male, or not being white or not being straight. With courage and passion, many choreographers are confronting these concerns. Some achieve a degree of success, many are floundering. Their formalistic training never prepared them for what they now need to say. The hope is that one or more of these pages will help their work.

What about choreography for the entertainment industry? Musical comedy? Broadway? I spent the first years of my professional life working there, though I always yearned for the concert stage. I learned a great deal, much of it of significant value for the "art" stage and specifically from working with Helen Tamiris who never lost her integrity choreographing in that arena. She did recognize the pervasive demand for reaching a hyperbolic level in almost every piece of choreography for Broadway and/or films. She had the talent to succeed at that without transgressing the bounds of good taste.

In the end, that very pressure to make everything "boffo," "socko," turned me away from that way. The frustration was compounded by an oscillating creative process pushed about by producers, agents, authors, composers and stars. I opted to take the full responsibility for everything I did on stage. I decided never again to design my creative output to ensure the delight of any public. Rather I would pursue the mysteries and delights of the world as I experienced them, probe them and find a shape for them as my gift to whoever chose to see my work. Nothing here will be a guide to "knocking them dead," only to finding movement and dances that are important to you.

Nothing in this book can tell anyone how to phrase and shape a dance movement. Nothing can explicate the deftness and artistry by which the major masters of choreography spin out reams of movement which never lose our interest and which so often impact as a profound experiences.

The teaching of choreography as an art form is in its infancy compared to the teaching of the creative process in the other arts. Thus, it is not surprising that those who have been teaching and writing about choreography have often taken their lead from the highly structured syllabi of the more established arts, particularly music and painting. In both of these, there are at their very core a few inescapable "hard" elements. Music has harmony, melody, rhythm and dynamics. The scales contain between five and twelve notes. Painting has form, line and color. The latter, color, has at its heart but three colors, yellow, blue and red plus black and white. All the other colors come from blends of these five. The complexity of human movement is awesome. Some dance vocabularies make great efforts to reduce that complexity to an entity more easily grasped. Ballet, flamenco, the techniques of Martha Graham and of José Limon, tap dance, any ballroom dance are examples in which simplification becomes a condition of defining a style. Boundaries are set between what is considered dance and what is not. Obviously, there is a profound gap between a particular style of dance and the infinitely complex potential of human motion. The tendency is to generalize from a style to a universal philosophy about dance, which is a fallacy if there ever was one. The field of modern dance with its multiple choreographers and styles should have weakened any attempt to lay down rules. And yet, there are individual choreographers who do lay down rules for all and who judge all dance from their vantage points. Too bad. They might be able to learn from the others if they were not so sure they held the only truth.

The only truth I have ever been able to ascertain is the validity of a few telephone numbers. If I try to reach Jack by tapping out 123 1234 and I get an answering machine that says, "This is Jack's phone. Please leave a message," I have reached the pinnacle of certainty that is granted to me in this uncertain world. Beyond this, I am, and everyone else on this earth is, a squinty-eyed myopic babe stumbling around on a minuscule speck in an unfathomable universe. This book is offered with all of its guesses and hunches. It may help some choreographers, some of the time.

One final note: some of the text of this book will reflect my personal experience and beliefs. Can anyone write a book on choreography or on astronomy without placing upon it his.her personal stamp and prejudices? I admit mine. Most writers on dance theory and aesthetics make an implicit claim of authority by concealing their *opinions* behind the appearance of objectivity. Here, there will be no pretense at being objective.

I believe the best book that has ever been written on the history of dance is *Dance: A Short History of Classical Theatrical Dancing* by Lincoln Kirstein. Was there ever a more violently prejudicial work? The last chapter, "Postscript: Dancing in North America, 1519–1942" is a violent attack on the aesthetics and practitioners of modern dance (except for Martha Graham). For Kirstein, classical ballet is the ultimate and perfect expression of the dance art. For me, it is one form among many that has afforded me some great moments in the theatre and quite a few dreary ones. And yet, I have learned more from his writing about our dance history than any other source. I take what I need from the reading and distance myself from what I personally find unacceptable. Dear Reader, be you a publisher, a professional reviewer or just that, a reader, please grant this book the same intellectual courtesy. Is it asserted here that the approach to choreography given in this book is useful *or even necessary* for all choreographers, regardless of their style and philosophy? I think anyone involved in the work of creating dances may find something in here of value. Those whose creative concerns revolve about humans and things interacting and interweaving will find that the problems of their work are being directly addressed by this book. For those of a formalist bent, I believe they can find much herein that will either help or provoke useful thought, but then, am I being a snake oil salesman of dance?

⤙

In evocation after evocation, Ellington proves that he knew in his cells what William Carlos Williams meant when he observed in his classic *In the American Grain* that by truly exploring the specific, an artist will achieve the universal.

Stanley Crouch, "The Duke's Blues", *The New Yorker*, 6 May 1996, 164.

# THE ESSAYS

# 1 | Helen Tamiris and Her Teaching of Choreography

In the summer of my first year dancing, 1936, I saw Tamiris and her group perform *Salut Au Monde*, a suite of dances to the poetry of Walt Whitman. There is a hazy memory of dancers on boxes. Mostly, I recall waiting at the stage door when a friend pointed out Tamiris who was in conversation with someone. I was shocked to see this tall, slightly stooped and weary figure that just a little while before appeared as a towering, glorious, triumphant celebrant of Whitman's "I Sing the Body Electric". A year later, I was up out of my seat, clapping in rhythm with the rest of the audience at the Nora Bayes Theatre as Tamiris's dancers came charging across the stage to *Let's Go to the Buryin'*, the climax of her great work, *How Long Brethren?* This Works Progress Administration production which shared the evening with a delightful *Candide* by Charles Weidman may have been the most successful dance evening ever to appear on Broadway. Including a return engagement, it ran a total of thirteen weeks.

Two years later, I saw her *Adelante*, a full evening work of an hour and fifteen minutes, which gave a panoramic view of Spain, its people and its history as it drifted past the mind of a dying loyalist soldier cut down by an executioner's squad. Again, I was awed, impressed

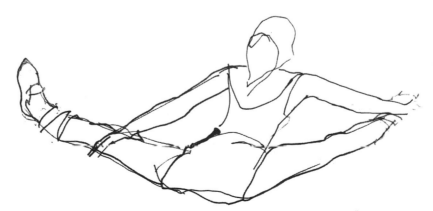

9

and moved by her conceptions, choreography and her own performance. That was in the spring of 1939. Two years later, in my second year working as a dancer, I auditioned for her. She hired me to be in a dance company that would be in residence for three summer months at Unity House, the vacation resort of the International Ladies Garment Workers' Union. Working for Tamiris was confusing. I was thrilled to get the job and yet I harbored hostility. Even though I'd been moved earlier by seeing her in concert several times , with a strong dose of prejudice, I had some way of shunting that awe aside. We were mono- gamists in those days and my loyalty was for the teachings and technique in which I was initially grounded—those of Martha Graham.

As the weeks went by, I began to melt. In various ways, Tamiris gave me a sense that she felt I had a certain strength and power as a dancer despite the fact that I was still quite raw. We hit it off very quickly, because I had received training as an actor and had the fa- cility to cope with the kind of problem she preferred entrusting to dancers. Instead of giv- ing me a phrase of dance, she would tell me who I was and what I was supposed to be doing. I'd say, "Oh." and then she'd say, "Well, you know what I want. Go work on it." That made all the sense in the world, particularly since I always had difficulty learning move- ment from others. I'd go off by myself, find the dance phrase I thought she needed, come back and ask, "Is this it?" She'd reject it, change it some or accept it whole.

It took me about a month to comprehend what was happening, to understand the process into which I had been drawn. She taught me that my skill and craft as actor could be, and in fact should be, an integral part of my work as a dancer. There was no need to separate them, since it wasn't so much that I was acting, but that I was a human being doing something and that in our art form we didn't talk, we danced. Of course, to develop successfully from doing and acting into doing and dancing demanded several complex poetic leaps.

Tamiris was brilliant in helping dancers find their way in this manner of working, which was as little known and understood then as it is now. Together, we did that until 1957 when I began to do solo concert work. Before that, we did many Broadway shows. I was her choreographic assistant for many of these and appeared in four of them. She cho- reographed many things on me and right up to the time that we stopped living and work- ing together in 1964, every solo I choreographed for myself was passed through the sieve of her brilliance and brutality.

We had a routine: she would watch what I was doing, then say something utterly dev- astating, I would react indignantly, we would then find ourselves in a terrible fight, she would then say that she would never again criticize any of my dances and I would say, "I hope not." A few hours later, she would rephrase what she had said. Then I would ask, "Well, why didn't you say that in the first place?" "I was trying to make a point." And so it went.

Like so many people whose living together makes a great deal of sense, there are certain scenes that make little sense yet are played over and over again. But I must have learned something about choreography that way.

She began to teach technique and choreography again in 1957. I often took her technique but never any of her choreography classes. In fact, as I write this, I realize I never did have a class in choreography with anyone, but certainly those rough sessions when she would observe and critique my newest efforts were a privileged apprenticeship as were all those years working with her in concert and on Broadway.

What did she do and what did she teach? Before rehearsals, she would spend hours thinking, visualizing and writing notes for herself. Her powers of visualization were strong. She told me that when she was performing on tour, she could rehearse in her mind as she traveled. In rehearsal, whether in the summer theatres, on Broadway or for the concert stage, she was a formidable force. She did not come into the studio with prepared phrases but conceptually her preparation was thorough. Most of her creative movement poured out of her on the spot. She would have us dance what had been choreographed over and over again, correcting the slightest deviation, but all the while she was sensing where the choreography was going. Right into her sixties she would suddenly rear up from her chair, explode into a fury of movement and pour out stunning sequences. These were usually fairly extended dance phrases. Desperately we would try to capture what we had just witnessed. Many times, as soon as we would get it, she would rise again and impatiently demonstrate *the correct way*. It was useless and ultimately stupid for us to insist that this was not what she had shown us at first. We learned that *the correct way* was just as often *her amendment of what she had first demonstrated*. There are times when it is petty to be "right."

Undoubtedly, the profoundest insight given me by Helen Tamiris was the *need to discover the inner life that fired up the motions*. The moment she opened that conceptual door, I walked right through it and found a technical freedom far beyond my years of training and an inexhaustible choreographic freedom. The foundation for this way of working in the theatre was uncovered by Constantin Stanislavski. Tamiris came by this at the very moment it was being introduced to America by the great actors and directors that formed the Group Theatre. She was the first to teach them body movement in their earliest two summer sessions. Among her students were Jules Garfield, Franchot Tone, Elia Kazan, Lee Strasberg, Harold Clurman, Cheryl Crawford, J. Edward Bromberg, Stella Adler, Luther Adler, Morris Carnovsky, Robert Lewis, Rohman Bohnen and Ruth Nelson. These were the people who reshaped the American theatre. Tamiris, in turn, brought Lee Strasberg in to teach her dancers. As I think back to all she told of that time, I never recall her telling me when and where she studied the Stanislavski technique. Did she absorb it from her contact with them? Did she participate in the classes at the summer workshops or in the classes that Lee gave to her dance group? I don't know.

By the time that I met her, that perspective had been absorbed into her entire creative process, both as a choreographer and as a dancer, for she was still performing. This was 1941. Working in those summer theatres was her preparation to enter the field of Broadway musicals, which was beginning to open up to creative choreographers. She was getting the feel of the musical revue form and a sense of musical comedies. She taught herself how to work quickly and best of all, how to absorb the style and rhythm of whatever songs or production numbers came her way.

Her speed in creative work was phenomenal. Of all the choreographers of that period, Agnes DeMille, Hanya Holm, Michael Kidd and Jerome Robbins, hers was the style that was the least easy to identify. She never tried to thrust her own agenda into a script. As Michael Todd, the producer of *Up in Central Park*, said at a production conference after a heated discussion about a major scene, "I can't believe what I am hearing. It's as if Helen is the only one of you who has read the book." This, with the authors and the composer present.

She learned to deal with the thorny egos and the vulgar tides that beat against the work on Broadway. In *Up in Central Park* the casting of the dancers took place when Mike Todd was out of town. The afternoon of the first day of rehearsal, he strode into the dance studio, sat himself on a chair in front of all, with his perennial, unlit cigar in his teeth. The rehearsal continued for a while until Todd abruptly rose and went to the door, waiting for Tamiris to come to him. (I am going to sanitize his remark.) "I wouldn't bed down with one of those women." Tamiris: "Mike, you don't really understand dancers. They look beautiful when they dance. We have five days. Come back then and if there are any you would rather not have in the show, we'll let them go." (In those days of a weak Chorus Equity, any dancer could be let go in the first five days without being paid a full two weeks' salary.)

Todd grunted between his teeth and left. Tamiris returned to us, "We have a lot of work to do." Five days later she had finished the complex Maypole dance and half of the famous Currier and Ives skating ballet. Came the crucial afternoon, Todd made the same bearish entrance, sitting before us, cigar and all. We danced—and did we dance! Finished, Todd made the same exit towards the door, stopped, turned and growled, "You're *all* beautiful," and was gone.

The complexity of Tamiris's career on Broadway is far beyond the scope of this book. Dr. Christena Schlundt, in a research paper entitled "Tamiris: A Chronicle of her Dance Career, 1927–1955"[1] blocks out Tamiris's time on Broadway within two dates, 1943, which marked the premier of *Oklahoma* choreographed by Agnes De Mille, and 1957, the year of Jerome Robbins's *West Side Story*. She writes:

In between the two demarcating dates, 1943 and 1957, she choreographed eighteen musical comedies, fourteen of which had runs on Broadway, six of which were long runs, among them *Up in Central Park, Annie Get Your Gun, Inside U.S.A., By the Beautiful Sea, Plain and Fancy* and *Touch and Go.*

Schlundt quotes John Martin discussing Tamiris's way of working in musical comedies:

She has no sense of using a show as a means for exploitation of the show. Her movement is always within the limits of the medium, expressive, inherent in the immediate content of the action, and again within the limitations of the medium, creative. She shows few displays of virtuosity as such, and no effort whatever to stop the show. Indeed quite the reverse: the effort is to keep the show going.

Briefly, it was difficult to define her style because whatever she did became the style of the particular show of the moment. I can pick out one pervasive quality. Almost everything she did was swept along by a propulsive rhythm, kept alive by her profound musicality and her passionate involvement in all she did. Finally, she drew vibrant performances from her dancers because many of them could meet the challenge she threw at me, "I need such and such. Go work on it," knowing that movement initiated by the dancer would draw rich performance—and yet always aware that it was within her to create the movement for that moment but choosing not to do so. Who did she cast in her shows? Valerie Bettis, Mary Anthony, Pearl Lang, Pearl Primus, Talley Beatty, Donald Saddler, Donald McKayle, Bertram Ross, Stuart Hodes, all of whom were established choreographers in their own right.

For me, the worst times on Broadway were the painful times of casting the shows, when hundreds of dancers would file into the cold theatres to audition for a dozen spots or less. It hurt to say the fateful words, "Thank you!" My best memories are of the rehearsals, making the dances. Being her choreographic assistant for the original Broadway productions of *Stovepipe Hat, Marianne, Up in Central Park, Show Boat, Annie Get Your Gun, Inside U.S.A., By the Beautiful Sea, Touch and Go* and *Plain and Fancy* was a constant charge.

Performing on the Broadway stage was a mixed experience. The challenge was enormous. The pressure was unrelenting. Everything had to be a blast. I recall coming off stage with my lip stuck to my upper gum from smiling non-stop for seven minutes. Worst of all, I remember the exquisite dances that were cut because they were not a blast. By the time of *Plain and Fancy*, 1956, both of us had had our fill of Broadway. A stunning ballet of an Amish ritual of shunning was to close the first act. It had a weakness which we were about to correct. We had allowed a spoken text to accompany it. The words sucked the intensity and pace of the work. We were in Boston, about three weeks from opening in New York, and poised to restructure it when the authors and the composer stepped into the process, cutting the dance altogether and making the closing of the first act a miniature operatic scene with no dance. Was it jealousy? Was it a revolt by the authors and the composers against the unexpected prominence and power of choreography in show after show?

Inasmuch as I worked with Tamiris from 1941 to 1963, and in that time evolved a way of working choreographically in a direct line with her methods and teaching, it is reasonable to ask: What is my contribution in this area? My only possible response to that question is that what I learned from her and what I worked through for myself make a seamless whole. First, I believe that in our working together I affected her thinking and teaching in ways that I cannot define precisely. Second, my teaching started the moment I left Broadway and embarked on a concert career in 1957. Third, in my creative work and teaching, I have been on my own from 1964 to the present. I truly do not know where her thinking stopped and where mine began. I never took a choreography class with her, though I witnessed some of them. I did show her my work in progress all the time that we were together and thus her thinking and influence was pervasive in my early work.

Knowing this book was waiting to be written, I felt the need to research what I had not experienced: What was it that Tamiris taught in her choreography classes? To this end, I summoned a conference to bring the five practicing choreographers who studied choreography with Tamiris to Arizona State University. They were among those who were inspired by her and went on to have substantial careers as choreographers and teachers: Elizabeth Keen, Cliff Keuter, Elina Mooney, Phoebe Neville and Marion Scott. The central question to be explored was "What and how did Tamiris teach choreography?" All the panelists agreed that her teaching in this area represents a significant departure from what the other founders of modern dance taught.

The conference was open to the public, to those who have studied with Helen Tamiris and to those interested in knowing more about one of the pioneers and founders of modern dance. I hoped also to address an oversight; in recent years, Tamiris has been neglected by scholars who saw little or nothing of her work.

In preparing for this conference, I had occasion to talk to Pauline Tish and Sidney Becker. Both had worked with Tamiris prior to the time I did—in May of 1941. I was startled to learn that in those early days, Tamiris did not have a very strong focus on teaching. There were some choreography classes but they do not seem to have been central to the work that was going on at the time, namely producing her new works and training the dancers. Even for that, her passion was not in the teaching. Helen's excitement then was in the making of dances and performing. When we formed the Tamiris-Nagrin Dance Company in 1960, teaching became every bit as important as her choreography. Her devotion to the classes was concentrated and fervent. The conference revealed much that was familiar and enough that I had never explored so that it justified the effort. About one hundred people attended the day and a half session. After we introduced ourselves, giving a brief description of our connection to Tamiris, Marion Scott led off:

*Marion Scott:* This is the sequence of her choreography classes, as I recall it. To her, a dance moved from action to action. She either gave us an action or asked us to choose our own. Taking an opening position, we were to fill ourselves with the impulse of that action. With that located internally, I can remember her saying, "Don't move at all," and finally she would say, "Now," and we would improvise movements from the action. The discipline was to hold onto that action and not be diverted from wherever it might go, giving the improvisation focus and direction. [Throughout this text, there are many references to the vitality of stillness, especially in Chapter 5, Rules for Choreography.]

The next step dealt with external and internal focus. I remember an early class when she had us falling while our action was to reach up to resist falling. This was called "contradiction." She had us concentrate on the problem of beginning a dance, either on stage or making an entrance. Another session was on transposing an action from greeting someone with the hand to doing it with the chest or an ear. We worked on rhythmic variety but I don't seem to have any details on that. All of these improvisations were given to us as tools for making a dance. We were learning to use improvisation in the making of a dance. Those are the steps that I have written down and the progression in which she gave them.

*Nagrin:* Thank you. Elina, what do you remember?

*Elina Mooney:* I remember "body contact." I think it was given the second summer I was at Maine.[2] It's a little hard for me to separate Helen's and Daniel's individual input. I don't always know what came from what because for me it was one experience. [In Workbook 10, there is a detailed description of the Workgroup's adaptation and use of Body Contact.]

*Nagrin:* I didn't teach choreography.

*Mooney:* No, in fact, but you did some of the improvisation. Before body contact and contact improvisation became such well-known techniques in modern dance it was already hinted at by Helen and Daniel. We would just start holding on to each other, hand to hand with our eyes closed and the demand was that nothing happen until it was ready to happen. You did not make up the movement, but in some unconscious way you gave birth to it without intention or planning. The physical necessity was just there. And you would begin moving with the dancer with whom you were in contact. Partly because of the age at which I began working with Helen, about eighteen, much of what she taught in composition was actually more relevant to me as a performer. I feel that I learned how to perform by studying composition with Helen. Only much later in my life were the lessons directly applicable to choreography because it was later that I began seriously choreographing. But what Marion says about the "inner and outer focus" has been one of the most important things to me as a performer. It is most exciting to me, and one of the things that I demand from people who work with me in either a class or performing situation.

"Body contact" was a wonderful thing for me, to be able to let go and let the movement have its own timing, its own necessity, its own strength, and also to work with my eyes closed was a revelation. We don't usually learn how to perform with our eyes closed. But here was the simple surprise to find that the movement existed even if I had my eyes closed. It wasn't like the tree which falls in the forest and nobody hears it. The movement happens whether or not my eyes are open, whether or not I was watching it, whether or not I was watching the person that was dancing it. So the undeniable reality of movement happening at its own pace and its own strength became very important to me as a performer.

*Phoebe Neville:* My memory of something we did that first summer was a study of "being in a confined place." [See Prison, in Workbook 9, a Workgroup structure that bears a relationship to "being in a confined place."] Also, we had a sense memory exercise which took the form of serving tea, "the tea ceremony." "Body contact" was not just starting from where we were, not just initiating but allowing the movement to go through to the other person. Also, if somebody else was initiating the movement, receiving it and taking it through your own body. It was very much about the sensitivity of give and take. We did it as couples, as groups, touching and not touching. The unsuccessful versions would be a messy tangle because of resistance and/or trying to control the results. The successful versions would be truly amazing. One of my important experiences was doing that with one of the other members, not touching and really having a sense of dancing with somebody else.

*Nagrin:* And now are there any more exercises that you can recall?

*Cliff Keuter:* I would like to add something about "texture." One time, Becky Arnold —a member of the Tamiris-Nagrin Dance Company—was doing dégagés to the back and they weren't working quite right. It was in a technique class, and Helen said, "Becky, I want you to be very aware that there's danger behind you, extreme danger, and I want you to think of your feet as daggers. And now do the dégagés to the back." Well, there were gashes in the floor.

*Scott:* Becky had powerful feet.

*Keuter:* But it took that image to bring out the power in them. [See Workbook 5 for a sequence of Workgroup sense memory exercises.]

*Mooney:* Phoebe talked about remembering the first assignment as "being in a confined space." Oddly enough, what I remember as being the first assignment is "breaking out of a small space."

*Nagrin:* Well, which of you would like to give the specifics of "being in a confined space"? I'm hearing two related actions involved. Being in a confined space, and the other is not accepting it, but trying to break out of the confined space.

*Mooney:* I remember very clearly, it was the very first thing I did in composition with her. I remember physically what I did and what the image was and what I perceived the instructions to be. I don't remember being confined, but I remember a small space. I remember the problem it caused me. This was a study that I never was able to go very far with because I was so excited by my own success—the first success—that I couldn't get to the second step to get out of there. Very quickly I knew that I was rocking and licking my wounds. I became a creature: part dog and part human. It was very exciting and to me it was so successful I could never take the next step. I never could stop and it was rocking and rocking for about six weeks.

*Neville:* The words that I remember Elina using were, "I am nursing a mental wound."

*Scott:* I remember that. You ended up doing a piece from that.

*Mooney:* Years later.

*Scott:* I don't know if we have emphasized enough the degree to which we were quizzed, "Who are you?" "Where are you?" "What are you doing?" We had to be specific although the dance could be very abstract in its final form. Helen was merciless in how we had to pin down those three questions.

*Nagrin:* Were you expected to articulate it?

*Scott:* Yes.

*Nagrin:* So that everybody could hear? [On this point Tamiris and I were diametrically opposed. See Chapter 17, The Criticism of Choreography.]

*Neville:* When Helen would talk about who we were, she would say, "You can't be Phoebe Neville. You're thousands of different people. You have to find a specific character: animal, vegetable, or mineral." It's like the image I take when I teach: It is like a Leko light. For those of you who don't know theatrical lighting, a Leko is a lamp with light source that is reflected so that its rays can create a sharply defined spot. Thus you focus on one aspect of the million aspects of yourself and you are that. And then there is the question: "Where are you?" You would move very differently in a cave than you would move in a meadow than you would move in the ocean. How you would move in space would be precisely qualified. That was point of dealing with a confined space for obviously you would move very differently in an open space.

*Nagrin:* Another question: What did Helen say when you did a literal gesture? Was that acceptable or did you have to do something with it? If you have a sense memory skill, you could easily create a confined space. If that is the only skill you have, you're stuck with the literal. How did she handle the literal? Did she say that it was acceptable? Did she ask you to modify it?

*Neville:* That's where transference would come in. [Workbook 3 contains two exercises, Circles and Each Alone, which fully explore the practice and use of transference.]

*Nagrin:* When she gave the exercises would she also say "transfer"?

*Neville:* Yes, if we hadn't found that as a solution ourselves. If she saw someone being literal she would ask, "Can you tell us the same thing by using another body part?"

*Keuter:* I also remember her specifically using the phrase, "Don't illustrate."

*Scott:* Right, or, "Take it out of the face and put it into the body," was a comment I remember. She said it to all of us and even to Daniel.

*Keuter:* She'd ask, "What are you doing? But don't illustrate."

*Nagrin:* I can remember standing in the doorway up in Sedgewick during one of your choreography classes and hearing her say to somebody, "That's too close to the bone," meaning it was too literal; that it was itself only. She saw no poem. She seemed to be implying that anyone can do the literal. Did she offer specific techniques for making the leap from the literal to a dance metaphor or did she just say, go do it?

*Scott:* Well, certainly transferring was one.

*Neville:* Yes. Could you weep with elbows? [This is a reference to metaphor, which is examined in Chapter 6, The Play of Metaphor.]

*Mooney:* There is another way that is less tangible, but again I can't find the words that she used, but I know I learned it from her. Instead of going out to the surface with the action you can go inside with it. It can move deep inside and it comes out in an unexpected way. So if I were going to touch Daniel, I wouldn't have to show that I was touching him, but I could feel the touch inside without actually touching him, and so my stomach might be reacting to the sensation of touching him and the whole body would respond to that experience in a subtle and non-literal way. The idea is to first take the action inward and then allow an outward manifestation.

*Nagrin:* As I hear you, I now realize I do that myself but I never heard her speak of it. Did she ever suggest in the transference that you change who's doing it?

*Neville:* The "who you are" could be an animal, vegetable, or mineral.

*Nagrin:* In other words, as long as you retained the action, you could shift from being a human to choosing an animal or a fantastic creature or anything. Thinking this way, the whole world in all of its variety lies before us from which we can find an evocative metaphor. All that is needed is imagination and taste.

*Neville:* If somebody produced a study that worked—that absorbed our full attention, she wouldn't discuss it. She would say, "That works." She would only ask those penetrating questions when she perceived fuzzy thinking and the lack of clarity of intent. Then she would wade in and demand that we really know what we were doing.

Her other comment was again and again, "You have to know more about what you're doing than anyone else. If anybody in the audience knows more than you about what you're doing, you're in trouble. You have to be really very, very clear in depth." The most interesting thing is that the result of this was not always dramatic dance. You could create something very abstract. In fact, the first pieces I saw of Marion Scott's which made a great impression on me were her *Three Energies.* She was working on them the first summer I was up there. She had a very definite who and where and what and yet the dance that emerged was abstract.

*At this point, there was a question from the audience concerning verbalization and its effect on intuitive thinking.*

*Scott:* Tamiris said that if the inspiration is flowing to go with it and don't ask questions. As Phoebe (Neville) said, it was when we got stuck and when we weren't clear that we had to ask the questions of "Who?" "What?" and "Where?" The questions would help us to clarify the moment of inspiration. When we were really connected, we knew. The struggle and effort had been done before, as preparation and exploration. Helen herself was both intuitive and brilliant analytically.

*Mooney:* Still when one is teaching, there is an obligation, I think, to present the material in a way that a student can hold on to it and to mirror back to the student what that student has accomplished. It would not be satisfactory if we had just created and then let it go and then come back the next day to create and then let it go without analysis.

Dance is so intangible. I think that there is a need to verbalize what is going on because we may not realize what we've learned if we can't put it into words. That's how we define our knowledge. Even those of us who have danced for twenty, thirty, forty years have a need to verbalize what we have done and what we are trying to do so that it remains clear and is not just something cloudy; something that you know you have experienced, but you don't know what it is.

*Neville:* One of the things that could go wrong, and this was not in what she taught but in what some people perceived, was that at times, people could end up in knots on the floor trying to think about who they were and where they were and all of that. And when that would happen some student would say, "Well, what if I just want to move?" and she would say, "Move." She taught that this information is for when you don't know enough about what's happening. Whenever people would use the method in a way that immobilized them, and there were a few who did, she would say this method is a craft tool to be used only when needed.

*Keuter:* I think everybody gets something different from a teacher. Implicit in all of the work from technique, to composition, to working in the company was the possibility of using all of these things we talked about. Transference and the use of image and the use of action were a set of tools. In the technique exercises, we had a lovely thing called the peacock and another we called the spider. They entered our consciousness. She might say, "Spanish!" and we would hear this as a correction or as a suggestion. It would give us a kind of heroic sense. I could hook into that. Helen's specificity made us all able to take leaps we might not have made otherwise.

*Neville:* This brings up something that was very important to me. It was possible for me as a raw dancer—my total dancing experience was less than a year—to produce a reasonably good work. Using this method which Helen taught, I was able to do things which I could not yet do technically. I was able to come up with movement material which was my own, which was interesting to watch and without having had many years of technique. In my own formation as a choreographer, this very short period of working with her has cast a very long shadow. When I teach people who have no choreographic experience and very little dance experience, or movement experience, it is an amazing tool. The results are astonishing and are substantiated by people observing the class. I've found no other choreographic method which does anything near what this method has done.

*Mooney:* She was a lady with her priorities very straight and very clear, and they're ones I admire. To her, the passion and the power comes first and the polish comes later. I believe in that very strongly. I don't think that a beginning choreographer needs to know how to deal with six measures of eight or four entrances and exits and the other choreographic details about changing level, dynamics, using the space, etc., etc. They're hardly important at that point.

Perhaps when you are going to put a group work on stage and you have to manipulate sixty-four people on and off, it becomes important, but if you deal with the passion, if you deal from where you are, you will deal with what's coming from inside and that, of course, can be beautiful at any stage. There is no one that cannot potentially produce a piece that will just knock your socks off. You know, anybody can do that if they are helped and given the tools to bring out what is inside. I think that was clearest to her, that you started from what was inside. All those other things she would never deny were important but are things that come a little later in the process.

*Scott:* Actually the craft aspects come from the inner truth. The others with whom I had studied, Louis Horst and Doris Humphrey, were trying to fill a form. With Helen the form came from us, was organic to us and in us. And yet I can remember Anna Sokolow saying, "All I needed was Louis Horst's course," and that was absolutely right for her. Those two courses[3] were everything that she needed or wanted. Louis knew I had taken his class two or three times. He remembered nothing I did. He was absolutely right. It was totally nondescript and undistinguished. On the other hand, there was something about Helen's approach that really sparked my work.

*Nagrin:* It makes no sense to make dances unless you bring news. You bring something that a community needs, something from you: a vision, an insight, a question from where you are and what churns you up. Choreographers have worked from many points of view. Some have taken fairly conventional movement and been able to use it in a ways that are personal, thrilling, exciting and news. Then there are some people caught within a traditional dance vocabulary, be it ballet, modern, jazz, whatever. Though their insides may have something very personal to say, they use their given vocabulary in a way that clouds and doesn't illuminate their personal vision.

The specific image, which Helen put at the center of our work, can bring out a movement vocabulary that is personal, while the trap of being addicted to a generalized dance vocabulary is such that even though the artist may have specific, exciting, personal images, this generalized or traditional vocabulary cannot reveal the shape of the personal vision—and so there is a distressing complexity happening on stage in which one senses someone trying to articulate something specific but coming across are old, familiar and irrelevant moves. And then there are people who have been able to take conventional movement vocabulary and shake us by their passionate and inventive ways of rephrasing and restructuring that material.

*Elizabeth Keen:* The main thing that I remember clearly about her teaching was oddly enough not from the composition class, but from the technique class, and it wasn't so much the specific exercises as the use of the imagination along with the technique exercise. For example: to do a deep plié as if you were drowning, or to walk as if you wanted to get somewhere. She always used to say "Have a sense of go." I remember very clearly that it was never enough to just simply do the movement. It had to be imbued with an individual attitude. This has really stayed with me and proved very valuable now that I'm choreographing primarily for theatre and opera. Five years ago, while I still had my own dance company, I would have stressed movement invention as the important aspect of Helen's legacy. She had a deep interest in and offered a technique for bringing forth new movements, inventing new vocabulary. I used this in my concert work all the time. Now that I'm working so much with actors, creating dances for a dramatic context, I find Helen's approach invaluable, as a way to connect with the performer and to enrich a particular dance. A "pure" dance can be enhanced with a movement for its own sake; the actor always needs to know why.

*Nagrin:* Phoebe, you mentioned "the tea ceremony." Can you describe it?

*Neville:* The exercise was simply to serve tea—without props of course. It was aimed at sense memory awareness. What are you holding? What kind of weight does it have? How are you relating in space to somebody else? Each person resorted to their own experiential background. I remember one person was serving them in oriental cups, so she held them in a different way. [See Workbook 5 for sense memory exercises.]

*Nagrin:* And was it a literal pantomime exercise?

*Neville:* Yes.

*Nagrin:* Were you ever asked to carry it any further?

*Neville:* Not to the best of my recollection. Cliff?

*Keuter:* No, I don't think we took it further. The flaw in the tea ceremony for me was I had never drunk tea before, let alone served it.

*Neville:* It does connect with her major concern, which was when you're taking an action from a specific into the metaphor you really need to start with the correct sense memory. You really need to know what you're doing literally and correctly before you can take it further into any degree of abstraction.

*Nagrin:* For most teachers of the Stanislavski method acting and particularly for the master teacher, Sandy Meisner, sense memory as a discipline was very important, because it is primary to the magic "if." If I were to pick up a cup of tea what would my hands do? What would it feel like? What is the taste and sensation of swallowing hot tea? All of that adds up to the ability to take what isn't so and make it so; the imagined cup becomes as real as the empty space it occupies. Innumerable dance movements gain quality if they are grounded in a specific sense memory. If the ground in your imagination is rough and dangerous, every move will be transformed and informed by a vivid memory. Working with the specific and particularly with sense memory extends the possibility of movement variation infinitely. Working with abstract generalizations keeps one's variations within the limitations of a given and set vocabulary of movements.

I want to throw out something about which I'm really very curious—design, design and structure. During all the time of my work with Helen, I never received any direct input from her on this matter of design or structure, either when we worked on the Broadway shows or when she critiqued my solos. It is something which I, as a choreographer, rarely deal with consciously. Every now and then, I will, as in *Bop Man* from *Jazz: Three Ways*. There, the man dancing is focused on design and structure. That's his conscious and passionate interest. That interest might be a metaphor for something deeper and quite emotional but that's in the background.

I never think about design. I try to follow the necessity of what I'm doing and assume that the work will have design. I never propose to my students, "Let's work on design." What do all of you remember about working on design? Helen never talked to me about design.

*Mooney:* I don't remember doing anything at all in terms of design. That to me, always came out of the necessity of the action and the tension. I don't remember Helen discussing the use of shapes or giving an assignment that focused on design as such.

As noted earlier, the conference ran for a day and a half. What you have just read is a distilled extract and a precursor of what is to follow.

# 2  A Method of Teaching Choreography

## Time, Space and Dynamics

The only space that interests me
is the distance
between you and me.

The only time that interests me
is the little we have left
to make a decent gesture.

The only dynamic that interests me
is the tenderness of your embrace
and the memory of the fist
that broke my face.

I look to the time when
there will be sweet air
and room for all.

Then will I have the leisure
to arrange three soft lines
on a sheet of pebbly paper

and listen to them
sing to each other.

In the Introduction, I underlined the belief that objectivity is not the frame of mind of anyone writing on dance or anything else for that matter. Thus, I find it necessary to let anyone reading this book have some inkling of my influences, beliefs and biases. Knowing this, the book may be snapped shut and discarded. Or, there may be a hostile curiosity. Or, there may be the sigh, "At last, the book I have been seeking."

I was early and late charged, changed and educated by Martha Graham. From my twenty-three years of work with Helen Tamiris, I built much of my methods and theories. John Martin's early book, *Modern Dance*, gave me the words and constructs that supported what I felt about dance, making dance and art. Ben Shahn's *The Shape of Content* further clarified my thoughts on art.

I began to study dance in the spring of 1936, fascinated by the technique of Martha Graham. My first teacher was Ray Moses, who had been an early member of Graham's company. In May of that year, in one week, I was privileged to view a panorama of dance in America. At the 92nd Street YMHA, the then-principal venue of modern dance performances, the National Dance Congress presented six evenings of every current style of dance. I saved enough money to go to every performance. It was the fundamental of my dance education. Strangely enough, my most vivid memory was a moment in a dance by an obscure dancer named Harry Losee. He was bare-chested and quite hairy, which in itself was startling as a "costume." He had backed off against some flats upstage left and was facing diagonally towards down right, wild-eyed and tense. Standing there utterly still, he suddenly violently contracted and expanded his rib cage several times. That unexpected gesture shook me, made complete sense and, unbeknownst to me, slammed down dozens of the walls marking out what was acceptable as a dance movement and what was not. It showed me that a solo dancer could create a world, even a complex world.

Three dancers acted like a constellation of wonders for me: Leonide Massine, Avon Long and Hans Zullig. José Limon doing his solo *Chaconne* and Carmelita Maracci strutting about a clothes tree and spinning on a piano stool mesmerized me. Bill T. Jones, succeeding or failing, is a groundbreaker. The two masters of our time, Cunningham and Balanchine, have elicited awe from me but rarely passion. If ballet was what Anthony Tudor exemplified, I would have tried so very hard to do it all in ballet.

Many arts and artists capture me, some more than others: early Chinese poetry and ceramics, archaic Greek sculpture, El Greco, Goya, Van Gogh, Daumier, Paul Klee, José Clemente Orozco and though I don't know why, Robert Rauschenberg.

My music shelf is thoroughly unbalanced: many recordings of medieval and Renaissance music, Bach, Mozart and Beethoven. The romantics are hardly visible. Among the moderns, I am partial to Copland's *Piano Variations*, Béla Bartók, Luciano Berio, Frederic Rzewski's *Coming Together* and many other contemporary composers but few that get to me as these do.

And then there is jazz, lots of jazz. Early and late there is so much that shakes my bones. There is John Lee Hooker to Sidney Bechet to Miles Davis to Cecil Taylor and so many in between. What is it about the rough voice and the steel guitar of a deep south blues that can tangle my emotions so? It's not my country and it's not my time, no more than Armenian music which also snared me in its sinuous lines and drew me into my first attempts at dance.

Perhaps my first rule has been not to ask too many questions when the blood goes from warm to hot. What do our adolescent philosophers urge each other? "Go with the flow." The admonishment may be familiar, but it is not banal. Every time I devised a good idea, I produced a less than successful dance. Every time a dance came at me, demanding to be done, I lost the knowledge of time working on it. Not for a moment do I denigrate intellectual processes, but for what we do as dancers, if any idea is not something floating on and being carried along by feeling, by emotion, look out. Try canoeing in a shallow river bottom.

At no point does this book attempt or even hope to be comprehensive on this matter of choreography. It presents a way. It does not for a moment dismiss the artistic validity of other artists, their work or their philosophy. I may find them unattractive, uninteresting, boring or even repellant but what difference does that make? I believe I am right with a passion—just as they do. With equal passion I am certain I may be wholly or partly wrong in what I say in this book. A student in one of my American Dance Festival choreography classes said, "The name of this course should be 'Uncertainty II.' It is precisely for this reason that students either gravitate towards what I teach or turn away from it.

The curse and the glory of being human revolves around this business of uncertainty. If you, sitting where you are as you read this, were to hear a distinctly unfamiliar sound, you would put away the book and try to identify what you heard. That impulse is the source of all science and philosophy. Unfamiliar sounds are the least of it. On every side, we are confronted with unsolved and unknown forces from that unfamiliar sound to the mystery of the space past death. Not many can live with the certainty that we can be sure of nothing. The solution? They believe. They search out something as irrevocably true. Too bad, for dance is a galaxy of unknowns and mysteries.

Too many enter dance through a Tunnel of Banality and emerge into a School of Vanity. The entrance into the dance world contains a conspiracy to eliminate all uncertainties. The studio has a mirror all along one wall. We face it through much of the class. We learn to look good. We learn to command attention. Many teachers speak with unquestioned authority, with an unembarrassed flow of hyperbole. Many of those for enough to dance at an early age get entangled in an apprenticeship garbed in sequi taffeta. Maturing in front of a mirror, some take the mirror with them wherever they *It takes time to unload that stuff and not everyone does.*

Very early, I began to spend long hours working alone in the studio. Sometimes there was a mirror, sometimes not; it didn't matter, I quickly learned not to use the mirror even when I was working on technique. When choreographing, at rare intervals, I might have felt uncertain about a passage and I would turn to the mirror to observe what I had done.

One of the shocks of my dance life was in 1967 when my then entire active repertoire was filmed in Idyllwild, California. Viewing it, I was regarding whole sections of my solos that I had *never seen.* Needless to say, I slammed into a deep depression. Those first views of ourselves are indeed difficult experiences.

Why did I avoid the mirror? Perhaps I didn't like what I saw. I always felt that I lacked a really elegant line. I never thought I was tall enough. Whenever I read a review of my work that spoke positively about my technique, I was incredulous. I was primarily aware of my technical insecurities. I never "see" myself as I move. I am aware of the feel of a movement, of the sense that I am living out the inner action of the moment, the testing of that mysterious consciousness and the rightness of the phrase, none of which I see in my mind's eye. It is all about *doing* something, not about *looking* like something.

I improvise a great deal, sometimes for the joy of it and sometimes to choreograph, since that is how I find new movement. If I happen to catch myself improvising in the mirror, I instantly become self-conscious and fear I am *trying to look good,* an effort that has nothing to do with improvising for the fun of it or the creation of choreography. I am certain that there are some splendid dances that have been created by, with and for the mirror. It isn't my way.

The ideal I hold up for myself in my own work and in what I have taught others can be summed up swiftly: find your dance, don't make it. It is there, in you and in the world around you. You do not have to make up anything. You do not have to pretend. Despite the costumes, the lights, the makeup and the entire baggage of theatrical make-believe, the core of your dance can be whatever it is that is alive on the other side of make-believe.

When Arthur Penn, a film director, begins work on a film, he exhorts himself, "Tap into what you don't want to say, tap into that secret place despite the agony, despite the personal pain . . ."4 If you find what's there, in "that secret place," you don't have to make-believe. All you need is the passion to travel to where it is. Once you look at it, you have to be able to pick it up and say to the world, "Ah, look what I found!" Could be what you find needs a pooper scooper and sometimes you find a rose, something that is painfully exquisite, but you have kept it hidden all this time.

In an interview for *Dance Magazine* in June of 1976, John Gruen asked me how I go about creating my dances. My answer was circumspect and yet it covered some of the ground.

Well, I read books. I look at people. I listen to music. In my dances I'm often dealing with certain moments in life where an individual has to cope with something alone—to face up to something, or do something that entails personal responsibility. In a certain context, you could say that the spine of my work is what is happening between people. That's what I deal with. Sometimes, it may have a political context . . . I don't believe that any aesthetic gesture is not also a social or political gesture.

A conception may be years in the making. Where an idea starts matters not. It may come from a piece of music, something you read, a dream, an improvisation, a conversation, a film, a dream or even from the air, from nowhere. *Write it down, immediately.* Just because you did get an idea is not enough to go to work on it. Before you begin to put out the kind of energy that a dance demands, the idea wants testing; does the thought of it quicken you? Does it make you breath a little faster? Supposing you did not work on it? Ideally, the idea should force itself upon you, *not the other way around.*

On principle, I never reveal the insides of my dances. I will do it here to make visible the approach I used in the making of one of my dances, *Indeterminate Figure* (1957): Out of a dozen hints, I began to sense the emergence of a dance. This was the early fifties. My first tape recorder was a Pentron, primitive and inexpensive. It didn't even have a cutoff of sound when put into fast forward or rewind. In these two modes, I had to turn the volume down or it would tear the ears off my head, but what I did hear intrigued me—as it did a whole generation of musicians who were getting their first taste of taped sound. Very quickly, I picked up on the outrageousness of playing a seven and a half inch per second recording at half speed or vice versa or even manipulating tempos in between by hand. In editing, jockeying back and forth, the reels produced sounds I had never heard. A new toy. What to do with it?

I was on the stage of the Kaufmann Theatre in the 92nd Street YMHA warming up for a concert. On the turntable backstage, I found a studio recording that John Cage had done for Jean Erdmann. I let it spin as I did my warmup. It was a perfect sound effect for the end of the world. Suddenly, from nowhere, there was a vision of a fop—a self-centered man grooming his hair while those terrifying sounds envelop him *and he doesn't hear them.* A year or two later, I decided to do a solo concert. I had enough material for half a concert. The fop was still floating in my head combing his hair. Sounds! The fluidity and weird possibilities I noted in that cheap little tape recorder and the fop whose self-focus excluded the world began to mix as one vision.

Talking about an emerging idea presents a paradox. It contains the substantial hazard of sucking out the energy behind the concept. Talking about it can become a proxy for doing it. And yet there is a kind of talking that can galvanize and clarify the work ahead. I needed a composer. I knew a percussionist named Herb Harris who had worked with me on Broadway and in Fiji when I did the choreography for the Burt Lancaster film, *His Majesty O'Keefe.* "Meet you for dinner in that Chinese restaurant across the street from the bus terminal." Over tea and fortune cookies, I tried to assemble my jumbled ideas to get Herb excited enough so that he would want to compose the music and assemble the sounds for the dance. As I talked, with no effort or planning, the entire idea assembled itself. The organization of *Indeterminate Figure* was so clearly assembled on a bit of notepaper in that Chinese restaurant that I kept it with me for the duration of the work on the dance as a guide. Herb made positive noises about the piece but for reasons I no longer recall, declined to work on it. Ultimately, I came in contact with Robert Starer, a teacher of composition at Juilliard who had already written one dance score for Martha Graham. In working with Robert, I shared the most personal details that entered into the dance, not one of which I would ever discuss with anyone: an intimate or a professional writer on dance.

Next, I went to Robert Blake, my sound engineer in Carnegie Hall. I told him about a man who gets many fantasies but is constantly distracted by trivial sounds even though he can't hear the obvious one that will destroy him and all the others. I laid out the rough outline, listing all the sounds and pieces of music that would enter into the piece. "What will it cost me if you made a tape like this for me?" "A thousand, no, better make it two thousand." Seeing my destroyed expression, "Look. Let me show you something." He placed a reel of tape on his studio Ampex, threaded it, ran it a short way, stopped and drew a length of the tape out and forced it into a shallow depression in a block of aluminum. With a razor, he made a diagonal cut by following a groove across the tape block, separated the edges and then brought them together again. Of course they fit exactly. From a dispenser he tore off a bit less than an inch of white adhesive tape, delicately and exactly laid it down in the groove over the cut and joined them. "There it is—splicing. Easy as that. Do it yourself and you save yourself two thousand." I went out and bought a better tape recorder, a Dejur-Grundig, not professional equipment but good. Ultimately, there were at least several hundred different pieces of music, silences and sounds spliced together to make thirteen and a half minutes of dance.

ᔕ

Every teacher faces a daunting linguistic challenge when the time comes to summarize succinctly and in writing the precious load of information that is to be delivered in the four months of a semester or the six weeks of a workshop. The order must allow for an intellectual encapsulation and also a hustle to attract the interest of students.

Two of my attempts:

"This class presents a way of creating a flow of dance movements and structures based on the use of specific metaphoric images and actions transposed into dance. The goal is not to make movements but to discover them. The method owes much to the thought of Constantin Stanislavski and Helen Tamiris."
And,

"This semester's work will examine an approach to choreography wherein all elements of dance—space, time, dynamics, structure, style, motions, etc.—become metaphors for the specific images of poetically juxtaposed events."

Wherever there is extended time for the class or workshop, I add required reading:

The Art of Scientific Investigation by W. I. B. Beveridge.[5] This is the best book on the creative method I have ever encountered. The focus is science—biology, but the problems of the searching are startlingly close.
And,

"Duende," an essay by Federico Garcia Lorca.[6] This essay should be read by every artist at least once a year. It posits a profound challenge.

To give students sufficient space to dig into their choreographic assignments, the initial time of class work is focused upon improvisation problems that illuminate the approach to choreography that I teach. At no time is there the demand that this way be used in their own choreography. It is presented as a method for them to try or reject. What they produce is judged within their own premises. The bare conceptual outline of the work:

THE SIX QUESTIONS:
1. Who? or What?
2. is doing what?
   action analysis:
      a. the spine
      b. the beats
      c. the subtext
3. to whom? or to what?
4. where/when?
5. to what end?
6. engaging what obstacle?

This approach is explicated in the next chapter.
What does emerge from all of these questions is a someone or a something of distinctive and individual qualities. In the course of developing this way of working the idea

of an "X" is introduced. Why use "X" to designate the character or the thing? "X" is the private creation and possession of the performer. The student choreographer creates/finds an "X" that gives what is needed to feed the imagination. We, the viewers, students and teacher, can only deal with the dance we see. In my dictionary it says "X" is: a.) math, a symbol for an unknown number. b.) an algebraic variable. c.) any unknown or unnamed factor, thing or person. Thus, the use of "X" gives the sense that regardless of how much one "knows" about "X" there is much more which is not yet known and may never be known.

～

Professor Tony Kramer is a dancer, choreographer and teacher at Stanford University. He took several classes and workshops with me and came to Arizona to learn *Strange Hero*. While he was here he cornered me for an interview which follows. It comes across as a good cross-section of my thinking and teaching:

Interview, August 29 1989, Tempe, AZ

*Tony:* Is communication the essential element in art for you?

*Daniel:* I wouldn't put it that way. I start out with an intense focus on some part of my existence that engages me, baffles me and demands attention from me. When the work is completed, it is given over to audiences with the hope of drawing their sensitivities to certain ways of thinking and places to look. Communication has didactic overtones. I'm giving out questions, not communiqués.

*T:* Does an audience help you?

*D:* Oh yes! The attention of an audience gives me strength. When I'm working on the material in the studio there is no awareness or thought given to anticipated audiences. My attention is to the center of the whirlwind that wraps around the enigma at the heart of my dance. It could be a piece of music, a relationship, a certain kind of person. I think about it. I walk around it. I dance about it. I become it. In time, I show what little I have found.

*T:* Is the fact that when you dance you become a person of primary importance?

*D:* That's the way I work.

*T:* And you don't worry whether somebody else wants to do curves and straight lines?

*D:* It worries me that there are artists who are barely interested in human beings, but that worry reflects my values, not theirs.

*T:* You can become the people or the things that you see. Do you have a method to do that or does each thing have its own way of becoming?

*D:* I don't consciously pursue the paradigms which I set out for my students. Once I get into the studio, I avoid methods, schemes and structures. I urge my students to do the same. The methods and structures are there only for the times when we slam into obstacles. The fact is, the way to do it is a function of what you want to do, when you want to do it, to what end and so forth. It's really a function of Tuesday.

*T:* And what happens on Thursday?

*D:* Let's wait until Thursday. I had an early basic training in the Stanislavski technique of acting and have a facility of slipping into someone else's skin whether I'm telling jokes or describing someone I saw on the street. It's a game I love to play. I could go over to your side of the table and become you.

*T:* OK, do it.

*D:* Oh no. You would hate me. Tell me anyone who accepts their own portrait. In any event, that is what I do for a living and I love doing it. I am always amazed by those people who in the course of studying with me begin to exhibit fear that they might lose their precious individuality if they were to find themselves in someone else's skin.

*T:* But isn't that the whole point?

*D:* Not *the* whole point, but it is *my* whole point. They get frightened. They think they're in danger of not being able to get back to who they are! This technique for becoming someone was formalized when I began the Workgroup. Though the dancers that joined the company were eager to engage in this way of working, there were uneven levels of experience in this art of becoming "X," the someone in the role to be danced. I started them with the exercises Circles and Each Alone. Before the Workgroup I never worked that schematically. I'd get a clue to someone and work my way in; probably not unlike the way moles dig, blindly.

*T:* I can relate to that feeling about making a dance.

*D:* I wonder, am I just a little bit different when I "come back" from an impersonation? There are times when I get a feel about someone and all I have to do is a quarter turn and I'm "X." If I saw my student work that quickly, I'd say "No, no, no!" because if they do it too quickly at their stage of the game they are more likely to go into cliché. Do I slip into clichés? Probably, but I do keep building a library of people seen and sensed.

*T:* And then you put this into your library of observations.

*D:* It's not that conscious. It's all just there, and when the time comes to work on a dance, some human rises up as the metaphor for what I am thinking and want to say. I don't ruffle through the reference cards of my "library" and pick out, "Oh, this one will be perfect . . ." I do specific people, some I have known and some just appear in my imagination and they possess all the specifics of a "real" person. Three of them have been women.

*T:* Are there certain things that always come up when you teach a choreography class?

*D:* Every class is inhabited by different people and I feel my way from one need to another. In not enough of my classes have I given assignments in observation. When I do, I give them a weekend. I say "In the course of these three days, four days, you'll see many things. Someone along the way is going to quicken you, upset you, delight you, whatever. Become that person."

An artist is a person who goes out there and forages in the corners of our lives and comes back with something that hadn't been seen, noticed or considered. Human geography is as valid a part of life as any other geography. I just think a lot of impoverished art rises out of concealed cases of indifference.

*T:* Daniel, you have worked in isolation most of your life. How else did you make all those solo dances?

*D:* I meant isolation from human concerns. When I go to into the studio to work it never occurs to me that I'm there alone.

*T:* Walter Sorrell quotes Mary Wigman as saying that the solo dance is the most condensed form of the danced messages.

*D:* The soloist has an enormous burden. He.she can't let the string go slack for a moment. But if there are half a dozen gorgeous young creatures garbed in skin tight shiny leotards and tights, revealing every gracious detail of their young bodies and if the choreography slips a bit, a beautiful pair of buttocks can fill out an empty time nicely.

*T:* In your choreography, you have many moments of standing still.

*D:* Standing still is doing something. That cat is still and being very active.

*T:* Yes, but I was wondering about a quiet moment in a dance.

*D:* To be valid, it should contain a furious, thrashing about.

*T:* You have said that for a soloist there is no special need to be concerned about amplifying small gestures or minimal movements.

*D:* You do what you do. You don't make it big. You don't make it small. You don't say that because I'm a soloist I have to dance differently. If you have to lift one end of a piano, you have to exert great force and if you have lift a salt shaker you don't. It's as simple as that.

*T:* You said you're one of the few people that doesn't use any of the movement vocabulary of your technique for your own choreography.

*D:* I stopped going to class very early and developed a way of working out by myself. It tends to be quite simple, unadorned and doesn't attempt complex dance phrases. I work on specifics: feet, back, legs, turns, my placement, my alignment, balance, my elevation and, then, when I start to dance, I never use that material unless I am doing something about doing dance technique or I'm trying to use it as a metaphor for being a dancer. The vocabulary of technique does not appear in my choreography. The sources of dance vocabulary are potentially infinite and only one reservoir out of that infinite variety is a particular dance technique. I am at best a fair teacher of technique. I am not a great technical dancer. I don't teach my students any movements out of my choreography. The few times I've tried it have been utterly hopeless ventures. If I try to give them what I actually do, physically and rhythmically, it looks dreadful. My rhythms tend to be idiosyncratic, either syncopated or a bit ahead or behind the beat. It takes hours for them to learn. If I simplify them so they can learn it more easily, I get upset because I see my stuff ironed out with the corners blurred and all is transformed into generic modern dance. Thus, I very soon gave up teaching any phrases out of my repertoire.

*T:* Do you ever look at the books on choreography?

*D:* I glare at them.

*T:* Do you find them helpful to you?

*D:* I can't read them. There may be great value hidden there and I may be depriving myself of nuggets of gold and wisdom. I don't seem to be able to get very far into them.

*T:* There's none you recommend?

*D:* How could I? I've only glanced at some.

*T:* My impression of them is that they *do* have nuggets of gold in them *and* that they are corny. They come from a point of view that has adopted the idea of composition from musical forms.

D: Corny? I don't know but I do agree that most are very strongly influenced by the teaching of music composition.

T: Do you ever use musical forms a la Louis Horst? Do you ever choose such a form as a way of developing a dance?

D: In making my own dances?

T: Yes.

D: I never deliberately take a musical form. In *Bop Man*, a solo to Thelonius Monk's *Blue Hawk*, I do what I call "an augmentation." It begins with a brief phrase which is repeated, adding another brief phrase and still another, until I have an extended sequence. Then, I took each of the phrases and developed them individually. Is there a musical form like this? I don't know. I was trying to think in the formal way that was true of the bop musician in the dance. When I've done group choreography I don't think I've ever deliberately said, "Oh, I'm going to do a canon" or "Oh, I'm going to do a fugue."

T: So many choreographers have used those forms.

D: I have danced to, with and for music. In *A Gratitude*, I used Armenian music because I love it so and because it was the first sound that intoxicated me with dance. In that dance, I made love to what I was hearing.

T: I want to ask you about improvisation. I've seen your *Jazz: Three Ways*. It looks like improvisation. You made it using improvisation. It's intricately interwoven in the creation of your dance.

D: So what's the question? You just gave the answer.

T: You don't make a big division. I sense that certain dancers do find a split between improvisation and choreography. I imagine that if they were to improvise to choreograph their choreography would look a lot different. Balanchine's work doesn't look as if he improvised any of it. For you, improvisation appears to be the main tool in creating movement for your dances.

D: I try not to make up movement. I try to find it. I find it out of what happens. Let us say that "X" is entering upon a scene. I know there is danger, so the longest way possible from upstage right to downstage left creates the tension of someone entering an area that is fraught. The slow progress becomes a close-up from a long shot.

All that I just said is nonsense. I never rationalized any of this when I did the choreography. I felt my way from offstage from where the man is entering a space. It was the place, who was in it, what they meant to me and what I had to do that created the long diagonal entrance of *Strange Hero*. What I just said was a rational explanation of what was found irrationally.

*T:* I've taken choreography classes from a number of people and I've never come across anything resembling your way of working. Do you think it's more suited to doing solos and do you think it's applicable to all?

*D:* Tamiris, working this way, choreographed for groups all the time. It's a liberating mindset for those who are open to it. There are a significant number of young choreographers around the country who are prolific, productive, doing good work and who spent concentrated time studying with Tamiris and myself. Some who studied with us made no connection at all. It's a big world.

*T:* It all makes sense to me. "Who is doing what to whom?" Do you believe there are principles that should be taught about choreography?

*D:* There is no recipe for art. I shudder at the word "principles." It calls up imperatives, rigidities and hard rules. I have dozens of ground rules, theories, warnings and ideals, many of which contradict each other and I expect to see them contradicted and cast down in time. For now, they have served me and quite a few who have studied with me. One of my favorites is by the author of *The Shape of Content*.

*T:* Ben Shahn.

*D:* Thank you. Shahn says that there is nothing that is not grist for the mill of the artist, just so long as there is a passionate connection. Nobody can say what is appropriate material for an artist.[7] I find this a particularly useful observation for young artists who have a serious problem respecting what they know best and what really touches them. The weight of tradition sets up standards and choices which make their strongest and most immediate concerns appear trivial to them. My "rule," "principle," "suggestion," "advice" for them is that if the idea doesn't quicken them, disturb them and stick to them unrelentingly, it's not worth doing. Well, in this interview, did I answer anything?

*T:* I can't tell.

*D:* Perhaps this story will give you your answer. I was touring England. This was after a concert at a girls' physical education college. The young women and some of their boyfriends came to a little repast. There was a little talk about England and America and then the questions started. After about twenty-five minutes had gone by, one young man raised his hand to catch my attention and I nodded. He said in his lovely, precise and clipped speech, "Mr. Nagrin, we have been listening to you for the past half hour and I have yet to hear you give a direct answer to anything." I inquired his name. He said it was Henry. "Henry, what would you think of me if I had given direct answers?" A very, long pause, then Henry said, "Thank you."

*T:* A smart young man! And thank you!

⌐∽

What interests me the most is what happens between people: who is doing what to whom? What transpires between people draws my attention, rather than the speculations on the space in which a movement takes place, the time in which the movement takes place, or the force with which a movement takes place. As a prime focus, those to me are uninteresting unless they cast light upon a specific human interaction.

⌐∽

Just as Tony Kramer in the course of his interview brought out a cross-section of how I think and work, another student, Julie Hall, a talented choreographer, took some perceptive notes, which she let me read and which I have, with her permission copied. They cover some aspects of my work and teaching in a more objective manner than I can summon.

Composition class with Daniel Nagrin always began with an improvisation session. He had us find a particular space in the room which seemed to pull us there. We would begin in our found space. Nagrin would then tell the class to shut our eyes to help us get in touch with our inner selves. Next he would have us find our "inner pulse." (See Internal Rhythm in Workbook 2.) He explained that this was different from our pulse rate or heart beat. Each of us has a unique inner rhythm which changes each day, perhaps each hour or minute. In order to find this inner pulse, one must probe deeply in one's consciousness, filtering out extraneous thought to discover this quiet place inside ourselves. It is important to note that this process takes time. One does not *try* to find their inner pulse, nor does one place any judgement on the thought processes that occur during this cleansing of the mind. As in the philosophy of the Taoists, the idea is not to *do* anything, but let it happen. This process cannot be forced, and Nagrin stressed that above all else we were not to force it or make it up. Some participants were unable to find their inner pulse which Nagrin accepted without question of judgement. He never pressured us which would have been contrary to the point. The response was varied. Some broke into tears, some wanted to scream, some were totally confused at first. Through more explanation and repetition of the process it became somewhat easier. Once our inner pulse was found this was the energy we worked with that day; the point being that this energy was *true* to us, individually. This, I understood, was the source of the inner motivation, the "found movement" which Tamiris and Nagrin explored.

The significance of Nagrin's working method of finding the inner pulse first: I found this process gave me a real sense of courage and freedom which I had never felt before while creating. I dared to try new ideas and ways of moving because I knew the impetus was coming from a place inside myself. It was not an easy method, for often I did not like what I discovered. Nagrin emphasized that we should not judge what we found but use it in the work.

Our first assignment in composition class dealt with clearing the mind. The image that kept recurring in our minds we were to expand on and use in a dance. Nagrin felt that a recurring image must have personal significance and hence it would be coming from a true place. This reflects his idea that an artist must go where his passion takes him. Over and over again he stressed the importance of working from an image which he called "X". This would help us avoid stringing movement together without an idea or motivation behind it

The next assignment was to choose to make a dance about "something that quickens you." The point here was to find something that was immediate and personal to us. Next, we were to take the word "celebrate" and decide what particular significance the word had to us personally. We were to act it out literally through pantomime and then metaphorically. We performed both in whatever order we chose. This particular exercise was demonstrated by Nagrin in his lecture-demonstration in the Playhouse Theatre. He began with the most abstract movement and through five different movement studies arrived at the literal movements of sewing.

The following quotes and paraphrases are taken from a three week composition class with Daniel Nagrin. They include critiques of students' compositions and studies as well as general comments about aesthetics and art:

- What you are looking for is somewhere in your peripheral vision.

- Is that the way it (the image) is or are you trying to make it interesting?

- Could it be that you're not crazy enough to follow through on what you have started?

- Any work of art is highly suspect unless it contains a significant hunk of the unexpected.

- Your dance is not as good as the idea. You're dragging the idea down by your own stylistic limitations.

- Don't let go of the image. Get wet with it.
- The metaphor should sink you deeper into it.
- An intelligence in full command becomes predictable.
- What is the color of the observation?
- Follow to the edge of the cliff.
- Don't tell the class the image you're using. We can all go to our own danger.
- Facing directly front is one of the most delicate things you can do.
- The best thing you can do for an audience is ignore them.
- If you follow through and love the image, the virtuosity will be there and not for the sake of virtuosity.
- Don't be satisfied with the first solution. Find ten others before you decide to use that first one.
- Change is where the excitement lives: the art of turning the corner.
- Humor is an envelope for tragedy.
- On some level when you do a dance you need innocence.
- Even chaos has patterns.
- The artist's task is to go where the passion leads.
- Your metaphor is too close to the real thing.
- A dangerous idea will bring your body to a dangerous place.
- Is it being done to you or are you doing it?
- Get drunk on it.
- Be conscious of everything. Make conscious decisions.

[Fascinating what people draw from a teacher. I don't believe I ever said that last statement because I am so inclined to accept choices that accept me. I may have said that ultimately you are responsible for all that you do on that stage, thus pointing the finger at artists who allow emotion to dominate their process from beginning to end.]

- You draw the ground rules of a work from its beginning. A major mistake of young choreographers is that they don't keep and build upon the strength of the beginning or the frame for the dance as the piece progresses. They walk away from what they started. They don't follow through.
- The most wonderful substance in the world is water because no matter what

vessel it is poured into, it remains unchanged as it assumes that shape completely. We must work to do this with our imaginations.

- Being stuck in one style is death for an artist. Just when you get comfortable kick yourself into some new area.

[I hope I did not say the last sentence. Deliberately forsaking one style for a different one for the sake of variety smacks of a pervasive cerebral manipulation of one's work.]

Another student, Kerry Kreiman, collected these from classes at the American Dance Festival:

- Above all avoid perfection. To demand perfection is to demand defeat.

- Filter your movement out of the necessity of the piece, rather than from a collection of a your brilliant bits.

- Nothing is quite itself; everything also is something else.

- When you see something very beautiful, you won't quite know what it is.

- Traversing the tightrope of art requires a balance between infinite care and reckless abandon.

- When being correct is in the forefront of your mind, it means you don't trust your own intuition and choices.

And from Jean Elvin's class notes:

- Is it possible that you can shake hands all your life and that your hand will always maintain the identical configuration for all or will the shape of your hand change with the clasp of each new hand? Are you paying attention to the moment or are you ignoring it?

- Art and love are so similar. They both provoke our passion, our curiosity, so much of our attention and yet resist our understanding.

- Never confess to a poverty of expression. You're not impoverished. You are a sun in the middle of your universe, your multiple body parts and their devious histories, your generation, your friends and foes. You are infinitely wealthy.

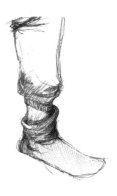

# 3 Choreography and the Specific Image
## FUNDAMENTALS OF ONE APPROACH TO CHOREOGRAPHY

It cannot be stated too often that the approach to the work of choreography presented in this chapter and elucidated through the rest of this book is to be used only when necessary. When would that be? When you sense that there is a gap in the flow of your choreography. When you stop believing in what you are doing. When you hit a wall and nothing is happening despite the hours in the studio. When is it not necessary? When the flow of creative work is sustained by an inner conviction. It is rare that the entire aborning life of any creative work proceeds on such a halcyon path. It is more probable that almost every artist at some point in the creative process rears back in shock with the realization that what they are doing is worthless and ripe for the trash bin. It takes only a slight shift of perspective to make a work appear hopeless. The capacity to live through that nightmare is required of every artist.

In the course of working, it would be debilitating to consult regularly with the outline to be given in this chapter as if it were a map for locating the end of the rainbow. A carpenter has a shop full of tools and uses just a few for what he.she needs for each task. Analysis, per se, is a procedure that is a threat to the creative process. Like surgery, it should be done only when necessary. Like surgery, if it goes on for too long a time, the patient's life, (the work of art), is threatened. However, upon analysis, *every* dance work can be examined in the light of The Six Questions:

THE SIX QUESTIONS:
1. Who? or What?
2. is doing what?
   action analysis:
       a. the spine
       b. the beats
       c. the subtext
3. to whom? or to what?
4. where/when?
5. to what end?
6. engaging what obstacle?


# 1. "Who? or What? . . ."


Someone or something is doing the dance. If the role to be choreographed is a literary character, say Romeo in the fifteenth century, a set of parameters and paradigms appear that should guide the choreographer. If the dancer is to embody a thematic line in a contrapuntal piece of music, again there are particulars present to shape the movement. The character of the music is the specific within which the choreographer operates. This does not for a moment mean that the dancer would mimic every beat, rise and fall of the music, though some choreographers do choose that course. Counterpoint and consonance each have their place as sensitive responses to music. There is a wide range of possibilities in this relationship to music. One can ask "Who or what is alive in the music?" Turning to Balanchine, in choreographing the *Melancholic* section for Hindemith's *Four Temperaments*, did he have a specific individual in mind or was he dealing with the general idea of melancholy? My guess is that either he or his performer had a specific individual in mind, known or imagined, but would never say so.

And what if there is to be no music and no sound score of any kind? It can be assumed that the imaginative envelope that is calling the choreographer into the studio is not a blank. The most abstract conception has a taste, a shaped space, an ambient sound and even an odor. The painter Robert Ryman has spent over twenty years producing white paintings. *Every one of them is different and has a specific character and direction.*

If an identity is established, a choreographic line and style is implied. How does the choreographer make a link between the identity and the moves that shape the choreography? There are as many ways as there are choreographers. Some design the result in their heads, some carve it out alone in the studio before facing the dancers. Some search among the dancers for the qualities they seek. In the Workbook, there are many improvisations that can help the choreographer create a persona with the potentials and limitations which will define the identity of *who or what is in the dance*:

**WORKBOOK EXERCISES FOR WHO OR WHAT**

Inner Rhythms
Evolving Repetition[s]
True Repetition[s]
Dedicate Your Motion[s]
Circles[s]
Backdoor[s]
*The Hub Meditation[s]
*A Duet
Each Alone[s]
The Duet as a Structure
Before, After and On[s]
Seeing Through the Eyes of Another
*Who or What Is Alive in the Music?[s]
Inside the Outside[s]

The three exercises that are starred, "*", bear most directly on the creation and locating the "who" or the "what" that will live in your dance. The assumption here is that if an identity is found, movement that flows from it will bear the specific imprint of that vision, no matter how dramatic or how abstract.

A note for individuals who may wish to work alone at what is in the Workbook: not only is it possible, but I personally spent my career doing just that. Every structure that can be profitably pursued by one person working alone will be followed by a superscript "[s]". Thus Faces needs two to come alive and has no superscript, while Riff Cactus[s] is a solo activity and is marked with a superscript "[s]".

## 2. "...is doing what?"

*action analysis:*

*a. the spine*

*b. the beats*

*c. the subtext*

The choreographer has an infinite number of options to delimit the action(s) of each dancer. "To dance" is only one of ten thousand and more actions from which to choose. By "action" is meant the inner life that drives what we see on the stage. Inevitably, the counter thought imposes itself, "True dance has motion at its center. Imposing 'intent,' 'motivation,' and all the trappings of literal theatre intrudes emotionalism and literalism that do not belong on a dance stage." This is an argument which has been hammered out over and over again for the last forty years and though it still serves the needs of a significant number of contemporary choreographers *it no longer will do for many of the new generation that believe they have the right and even the obligation to use their considerable craft, talent and imagination to confront in dance the issues that haunt their dreams, confuse their days and delight their lives.* They are no longer intimidated by those who would hold dance to some ideal of purity when so much of what they are living through is neither homogenous nor pure.

Backing off and looking at the entire concern and reason for this book, the word "action" becomes central. It refers to the *verb* that drives the dance and the dancer. The dictionary lists "ing" as a suffix meaning "action." I turn to my computer and exploiting its search function I type in "*ing" where "*" means every word in the language that ends in "ing." I press Enter and the screen reveals twenty-six words, all beginning with "a" and ending in "ing," all verbs:

| | | |
|---|---|---|
| abalienating[8] | abducting | abnegating |
| abandoning | abetting | abolishing |
| abashing | abhorring | abominating |
| abasing | abiding | aborning |
| abating | abjudging | aborting |
| abbreviating | abjudicating | abounding |
| abdicating | abjuring | abrading |
| abducing | ablating | abridging |

At the bottom of the screen there is the line, "Press any key to continue." I do and there are fifteen screens following in alphabetical order with *verbs* beginning with "a" and ending with "ing," the last of which is "awakening." In my many years of observing student —and professional—choreography, how many times have I witnessed a dance of awakening?

Just to belabor the point, I type "z*ing" to the search function, press Enter and see at the bottom of the screen "zoning," the very last of the "ings" in the dictionary.

It staggers the imagination to consider how many words there are through the whole dictionary that end in "ing," words that *are verbs and loaded with action!* Somewhere between "abalienating" and "zoning" is the gorgeous and exhilarating verb, "dancing"! Don't even try to count the number of exquisite works that are dances about dancing. "To dance" for the sheer mystery, joy and ecstasy of dancing is there on a par *with any other reason for dancing*. It's not a better reason and it's not a poorer reason, it's simply there for the doing by whomsoever for which it is a passionate necessity. It is equally possible to analyze a dance about dancing with The Six Questions. In every such dance there is a "Who or what is doing what to whom, when, to what end and engaging what obstacle?" There is not a single abstract dance that does not contain an answer to each of those questions. Finding the fleetest motions for the body to carve soaring arcs of space engages the dancer's space and the dancer's body in a duet filled with dynamic tension if that is the vision and taste of the choreographer.

The question I put forth to you, the reader, is how many dances may be driven by one of the many verbs other than "dancing"? More, did you ever see a dance whose prime action was encompassed by one or more of the verbs brought up by my computer? Any one of the following: "abdicating, abominating, abandoning, abhorring, aborting," could easily be the core action of a piece of choreography. Is it so difficult to imagine a dance work in which someone abdicates power or responsibility? Is it so difficult to imagine the richness of motion that could flow from such an action? All it needs is a context, a passionate connection, and the choreographic work can flow. The movements created for that action have an impetus that should express the voice and the vision of the choreographer.

Purists and formalists will immediately cry out in horror, "Literalism"! Yes, choreography is just like golf in that there is no way of doing either of them without encountering hazards, traps and bunkers and being literal is one enormous hazard. Can one imbue a dancer's movements with the actions of "abdicating" or "zoning" without being literal? Of course. If the reader wishes, this is as good a moment as any to put a marker in this page and go forward to read Chapter 6, The Play of Metaphor. If what is put forth there makes sense then continue with this chapter. *If not, put the book away altogether.*

Workbook exercises in the list below probe the use of an action in the creation of dance movement. They are listed in order of complexity, each preparing the way for the next one.

WORKBOOK
EXERCISES
FOR USING
AN ACTION

**Dedicate Your Motion**[s]
**Circles**[s]
**Hub Meditation**[s]
**Gesture Permutations**[s]
**Gesture Rondo**[s]
**Cliché Rondo**[s]
**Each Alone**[s]

**The Duet as a Structure**
**Who or What Is Alive in the Music?**[s]
**Inside the Outside**[s]

Every one of these improvisations calls upon the dancer to initiate movement from an inner action. In all this work, the choreographer and the dancers are always digging into the material with the aim of discovering *the* movement metaphor that poeticizes the action or the verb. Perhaps emphasizing "the" presses an unfair burden on the search for the "best" metaphor. Different artists will find different metaphors for the same task and the same artist might, on Thursday, find a metaphor utterly different than one on Tuesday. Differences pour out of individuality and the confluences of the moment. Approaching the creation of dance movement along this path, the possibilities for a fresh and personal vocabulary of dance are staggering. Every gesture is modified by the particular and specific "who or what?," by the "doing what?" and by the sensitivity and life of each individual choreographer.

To offer a list of suggestions for choreography would be the height of presumption and yet in the attempt to make vivid what is stated generally, we can take a leap back into a radically different time. In an awesome book by Joseph Needham, *Science and Civilization in China*, there is this:

> THE FIVE ELEMENT THEORY
> *Water*: soaking, dripping, descending, dissolving (saltiness)
> *Fire*: heating, burning, ascending (bitterness)
> *Wood*: accepting form by submitting to cutting, carving instruments (sourness)
> *Metal*: accepting form by molding when in the liquid state and the capacity of changing this form by remelting and remolding (acridity)
> *Earth*: producing edible vegetation (sweetness)

In early Chinese philosophy and science, nature was characterized by these five elements:

> . . .the conception of the elements was not so much one of a series of five sorts of fundamental matter . . . as of five sorts of fundamental processes. Chinese thought here characteristically avoided substance and clung to relation.[9]

The wonderful provocations of ancient Chinese thought suggest the idea of a suite charged by all the ". . . ings" of THE FIVE ELEMENTS, but not by "soaking, dripping, descending or dissolving" in general. No. Instead, become one of those magnificent Danish ice statues caught by the sun in an early spring morning. There is no end of verbs for the making of dances. What wealth!

*action analysis:*

> *a. the spine*
>
> *b. the beats*
>
> *c. the subtext*

These are terms that are commonplace within the acting profession and there is no reason why this should not be true for dance. They are conceptually valuable tools to penetrate the meaning and methods of other choreographers and equally so for clarifying whatever choreographic work is at hand. They apply most directly to what enters into making vital performances and thus are critical for the realization of the entire choreography.

### A. THE SPINE:

This is the overarching intent that defines the major thrust of a dance and each of the characters. Iago is out to destroy the pride and equanimity of Othello. There is not a single moment for the entire ballet that that impulse leaves Iago. Or, there is the celebration of the serenity of Tchaikovsky's *Serenade in C*.

| WORKBOOK EXERCISES FOR THE SPINE | |
|---|---|
| | Circles[s] |
| | Hub Meditation[s] |
| | The Duet as a Structure |
| | Inside the Outside[s] |
| | Your Familiar[s] |
| | Possessed by a Mannerism[s] |
| | Why Do You Dance?[s] |

### B. THE BEATS:

These are the changes that occur on the way to realizing the spine. Iago affects loyalty and concern for Othello as a part of his strategy. The long, even lines of *Serenade* begin to sparkle and turn into a flurry of leaps and turns.

| WORKBOOK EXERCISES FOR BEATS, BITS OR UNITS | |
|---|---|
| | Evolving Repetition[s] |
| | Riff Cactus[s] |
| | Gesture Permutations[s] |
| | Gesture Rondo[s] |
| | Before, After, and On[s] |
| | The Duet as a Structure |

Prison[s]
Poems[s]
Why Do You Dance?[s]
Inside the Outside[s]
Props Fantasy[s]
Body Contact

In the course of a dance, or even in the course of a dance phrase, the source of the movement impulse can change.

### C. THE SUBTEXT:

What is on the surface differs from what is hidden from sight or even the conscious awareness of the character. Iago conceals, even from himself, his awe of Othello and always feels diminished by his presence and authority. A dancer in *Serenade* who feels but holds in check a resistance to the unison, discipline and submergence to the group activity will exude an electricity in whatever she does.

WORKBOOK  
EXERCISES  
FOR THE  
SUBTEXT

Evolving Repetition[s]
Riff Cactus[s]
Gesture Permutations[s]
Gesture Rondo[s]
Before, After and On[s]
The Duet as a Structure
Prison[s]
Poems[s]
Why Do you Dance?[s]
Inside the Outside[s]
Props Fantasy[s]
Body Contact

Being conscious of and using the concepts behind these terms will bring a texture and eventfulness to choreography. They have each been examined and explicated in great detail in the previous book in this series, *The Six Questions: Acting Technique for Dancers*.[10]

# 3. "...to whom? or to what?"

At one time, when I taught this material, it was presented under the rubric *The Syntax of the Performing State*, because in its barest expression we are dealing with "Who is doing what to whom?" a question with a subject, a predicate *and an object*. The core of the philosophy of choreography given here is stated in the title of the book, *Choreography and the Specific Image*. Without an object, the specific dissolves in a soup of generalities. It is altogether possible for a dance artist to have in mind a specific "who or what?" and a specific action (". . . is doing what?"), *and not have an object*. Not having an object means the dancers are set loose on a stage without a focus. Without a focus, even abstract and formal works are floating in formlessness. To have an object means "the who or what" has a specific and particular focus. It is this structural triad of subject, predicate and object that I believe can support strong choreography. It won't guarantee good choreography. Nothing can do that. It will give good movement, a daring conception and a coherence that will be compelling to view.

As an integral part of the improvisation structure called The Duet as a Structure, a sentence is uttered that provides the framework for the imagination of the partners in the improvisation. In every one, there is a "whom" implied that becomes a focus for the work. Here are some examples:

- Someone/something is leaving. You are the one leaving or the one being left.

- Someone/something is lost and must be found.

- Someone/something is curved and impacting with someone/something that is angular.

- Someone/something exists in a chaotic fashion in proximity with someone/something that is precise, ordered and controlled.

- Someone/something is protecting and keeping someone/something safe and warm. Are you the protector or the protected?

- Someone/something needs support. Someone/something needs to be supporting.

- Someone gains dignity by helping another find her.his dignity.

- Someone whose dignity depends on another losing her.his dignity.

In choreography classes, I often presented the following two as the earliest assignments:

- There is something/someone of which you are in awe. Become that someone/something.

- There is something/someone which fills you with fear and loathing. Become that something/someone.

These were to be solos. Have I ever given them to beginners? I did teach a few such classes at State University of New York at Brockport and some lively stuff came forth. Why give such grim tasks? I like to think that it is to make it clear from the start that as a teacher, I am only interested in seeing work that centers on what is really important to them. This is not one whit different from what I look for in mature artists. There are a sufficient number of these who churn out well-crafted art designed to attract a wide audience and containing little that is of real import to the producers of such art. Some people believe that this is a good way to "do the art business." Some do not have the confidence to deal with what concerns them profoundly. Some even think that what is turning them inside out and upside down could not possibly be of interest to others *or is not proper material for art.* My hope is that these two assignments will open a door to what really matters to the young dancers as the individuals they are, not merely as hustlers in art as a commodity.

WORKBOOK
EXERCISES
FOR CONCEN-
TRATION ON
THE TO
WHOM OR
THE TO WHAT

*Listing all here would be a redundancy. There is no end to the verbs, the "whos," the "whats" or the "whoms." The options before a choreographer are infinite, which can be frightening. All that is needed is to narrow the field down to what it is that engages the passion of the artist.*

# 4. ". . . where and when,"

Every metaphor gains depth and vividness when the artist uncovers its physical context. Every dance motion gains an immediacy when the choreographer brings into play the air, the times, the texture of the ground, the hot or the cold and the very odors that are its envelope. How does one do this? Simple. Give the imagination free play.

WORKBOOK
EXERCISES
FOR CONCEN-
TRATING ON
THE WHERE
AND THE
WHEN

Blind Journey[s]
Goldfish Bowl
Prison[s]
Poems[s]

As I review this small list of exercises, I become aware that this is an aspect of the work to which I have paid scant attention in my teaching. I think it deserves more. It merits creative time in classes and workshops where the concentration is emphatically on "the where and the when."

# 5. ". . . to what end?"

A friend, a teacher of dance, came from New York to live and work in Arizona. I greeted her with the usual question, "So, what's happening in the New York dance world?" She replied, "They dance and they dance *and nothing happens!*" An exaggeration, I presume, but still what she said could very well describe the work of many. When the forces in a dance are trying to make something happen, there is a most desirable dynamic at work. The forward movement of the choreography is sustained and the performances of the dancers are compelling. The prior work of "The who or what is doing what to whom" implies "to what end?" Does it have to be spelled out literally? This, like every part of this syntactical analysis of choreography, is nothing but a tool to be brought into play only when there is a need for clarification. Few choreographies, even the best, have an unimpeded flow of successful realization from beginning to end. Most often, there are bumps along the way. Suddenly becoming crystal clear about what all of that motion has been working towards can break a log-jam in the creative flow.

WORKBOOK
EXERCISES
FOCUSED ON       *Every one of them.*
MAKING
SOMETHING
HAPPEN

# 6. ". . . engaging what obstacle?"

Assuming that all the components that have gone before—the "who," the "doing," the "to whom," the "context," the "goal"—are present consciously or intuitively in the mind of the choreographer, nothing in the dance will come to life without the electrifying unity created by the obstacle. There may be an intent, a direction, a dedication to some action and some purpose and yet, without a force set up against all of that, there will be no dance, no theatre and no justification for the work. Call it ambivalence, conflict, contention, controversy, dissension, friction, strife, clash, contrast, confrontation, contest, struggle, tussle, opposition or contradiction; these are what create a life in the dance and in every form of art. Whether this life is tragic or hilariously comic, lyric dance or grunge, an obstacle that creates ambivalence or contradiction must be present.

In the teaching of choreography that I have observed, this factor of the obstacle, the conflict, is rarely mentioned as a requisite. Its absence may be felt too infrequently.

Surprisingly, the best acting teachers often ignore it. For the choreographer, its presence needs to exist not only between forces but *within* the character of each dance role.

Few things in nature can absorb our attention so fully as the sight of a rocky shore confronting an ocean. The long fluid swells of the sea are blocked and shocked by the imperturbable chaos of ancient stone. An axe is an elegant shape but we know nothing about it unless we have a piece of wood to chop. We do not know a human being unless he is declaring his love for an enemy of his family. There is no revelation without a conflict. Any number of times I have seen on stage some young people doing something lovely but it doesn't impact on anything else. There's no white water. It's just a stream that slides downhill. This is not a matter of making something interesting. Without a passage through, with, up, against, around, defeated, victorious, something, somehow, there is no revelation.

The most hilarious comedies are about falling down, literally or metaphorically. If there were no troubles we would not need art; instead we would be satisfied with diversion and decoration. People come to the theatre because they have too little or too much. Some come because they ache. Some bed down with one they don't understand. Some have children who don't like them, who can't stand the sight of them. Some have jobs they don't like. Some spend their lives trying to get something or somewhere and end up shafted. Some have holes in their hearts. Some are bleeding. Some don't know how to hack it. To complicate matters, good things happen and that can be equally unnerving. Good things scare the hell out of them. How many of us fear to congratulate ourselves when there is good fortune? We knock on wood to hold off the jealous gods. Success is a dizzying pinnacle demanding a superhuman balance.

People come to the theatre because they are in trouble and need to know more about it. Some of these come to serious and unusual events like dance concerts. What a wonder and a solace it is for them to see others achieve soaring elevation and beauty of line. These are lovely metaphors. It appears that it is possible to be beautiful. It is possible to flow through the air. It is possible to look perfect. That's exciting. That helps people. But there's more to it. The contradiction inherent in virtuosity and exquisite line is the pervasive threat of failure. There is no virtuosity without risk. Risk means danger and danger is the electricity of the theatre. I have been the unfortunate witness of university dance programs that fail for any number of reasons in developing student physical virtuosity. Concert after concert without one leap that sucks the breath out of the body.

Beyond physical risk there is emotional risk. It is precisely here that modern dance made its profoundest contribution. For most of its history, dance in Western culture was an entertainment with little of the weight of the other arts. Dance, from Isadora Duncan to Martha Graham, Doris Humphrey, Charles Weidman, Helen Tamiris and Hanya Holm, fearlessly engaged with tragic and epic themes. It is through conflict that we define tragedy or comedy. Significantly, there is a contemporary generation that is once again gradually turning to themes fraught with conflict.

More thoughts on this matter of the obstacle:

- The obstacle cannot be invented. It needs to be discovered within the nature and matter of the concept.

- For every action there is a reason *not to do it.*

- When you see someone, you are also looking at a history and the shadow of a future.

- Everything and everyone is a mess of contradictions. An ideal of purity will dilute the energy of a work of art.

- If I'm a decent man, I'm concealing a son-of-a-bitch. If I'm a destructive brute, I'm terrified of being seen as soft and giving.

- A "this" without a "that" and there is no dance. Men and women get together and have babies. That's a "this," a "that" and "another this!"

- On stage, anything that does not contain its own opposite is a bore. A fall contains a compelling excitement when it is resisted. The dream enclosed in the most beautiful leap is a sustained stillness.

- You have no dance unless you have something/someone to push or lean against.

- There is a danger in a blade of grass.

- I carry within me my death, my victories and next week.

- Dance is where two or more rivers meet.

It matters not what the medium is—ballet, modern, commercial dance, flamenco—nor does it matter whether the substance of the dance is abstract or dramatic; the dancers you place on the stage and move about have specific characters and are engaged in specific actions. It may be that the dancers *are dancers* and they are moving to glorify *moving*. If that is the case, the choreographer's choice of vocabulary and flow of motion must support that vision. If the choreographer presents a scenario loaded with human relations and emotions but gives the dancers motions that are actually about glorifying motion as such, we have a self-defeating contradiction. Such a stage will not be filled with the evocative mystery of the choreographer's poem but rather a collage of mud. It will be a mismatching of the conception with a dance vocabulary lifted from a traditional technique.

There is not a word of the last few pages that is not contradicted and resisted by a significant portion of the audience, perhaps even the majority. They come to the theatre, and to all art, for entertainment and diversion *only*. They are hostile to anything that lives off the reasoning and beliefs just stated. That audience schism is one that challenges every artist in every field of art. For whom will you dance? You owe it to yourself and your audience to be clear about that choice.

∽

I can think of no better summation of this chapter than a recapitulation:

THE SIX QUESTIONS:
1. Who? or What?
2. is doing what?
    action analysis:
        a. the spine
        b. the beats
        c. the subtext
3. to whom? or to what?
4. where/when?
5. to what end?
6. engaging what obstacle?

# 4 Improvisation

## AS A TOOL FOR CHOREOGRAPHY

Improvisation: the gold mine, the library, the holiday, the forbidden country, the testing ground, the training ground, the meeting ground, the basement, the attic, the house of horrors, the buried treasure, the land beyond the horizon, a time to footle, a time to slip into the music, to do battle with the music, a time to be surprised with what you contain, a time . . .

You finish the list—if it can ever be finished. Before the crucial act of pinning down the moves that will be the dance comes the skirmishing, the feints, the experiments, the getting into the feel of what is to come, the digging into what is hidden in your bones, in your blood, in your terrors, in your ecstasies, in your dreams, in your journal!

Whenever there is a group poised to study choreography, I lay out several possible projects, allowing an interval to prepare what they will show. In that time of waiting for the students to complete their first studies which could be one, two or three weeks, there is improvisation. Only occasionally are short choreographic problems given in class to be worked upon and reviewed then and there. Most of the time is spent on carefully graduated improvisation structures. There is a method to all of this: finding freedom in motion, learning to crystallize the action of the specific image and finding sources of movement for the choreography.

Improvisation structures are described in the Workbook. They are grouped in an order in which each one prepares the way for the next one. Towards the end, there is a selection under the title of More which are in no particular order. They are there for the choosing. In fact, all the improvisation exercises, games and structures are presented as raw material, to be used as is, in any sequence, altered or ignored. I believe that any group, class or workshop that puts in two to four weeks of intensive exploration in improvisation will emerge enriched with masses of material, armed with ways of finding fertile dance ideas and the courage to plunge into the hazards of choreography.

The suggested ground rules for improvisation have one positive:

- Pour all of one's energies and mind into the moment and the action of the specific image.

plus several negatives:

- No working to the mirror.
- No working to look good.
- No working to be beautiful.
- No working to be interesting.
- No working to be creative.
- No comparing self to others.

Unless your improvisation is about one or more of these.

It should be evident that I regard improvisation as a vital tool. In my own way of working, it is the first physical step in constructing a dance. Almost always, there is an initial mental process of reflection, conjecture and imagination that draws me to the idea. When I arrive in the studio, I do not come with any visualized sequences of dance. I find all of that in the space. First, there is the warmup to ready the instrument. Sometimes I finish the warmup with a free-flowing improvisation to music that is quite irrelevant to what I have in mind. I am, as it were, circling the idea. This weird process conforms to my usual practice of first going left, if what I really want to do is go right. Going away before going at it gives me a distance that takes the edge off the tension of this outrageous attempt to *create a dance*. In my mind's eye, it is related to the easy, lengthy stretch-back of a pitcher's arm before unleashing the full power of the arm. Thus, for me, "getting to it" is a drawn out process.

If I am using music for the dance, I make every effort to have the score done before the business of choreographing. Before anything is the question, where am I when the dance starts? On stage? Off stage? In the light? In the dark? Before the music begins? After? Simultaneously? Every dance creates its own beginning. There is not a single rule available to help make any of these decisions. In due time, I know where I will be and what I am doing when the dance starts and when the lights and music declare their presence. Coming to this set of choices is a process of many false starts. It may take the entire first session—or twenty minutes.

Once the way is clear to move ahead, I probe further into the action of the dance *by improvising!* Just as finding the beginning is a simple matter of persisting with many attempts *until there is that uncanny moment when it feels right,* I continue to improvise until I find a sequence, a position, a stillness or a tempest of moves *that feel right.* How do you know when it feels right? It's almost as clear as when a picture that has been hanging crookedly is set straight. If it is not clear, then I have more and more work to do until that subtle sense establishes itself and I am ready to move on.

I go back to the beginning which is set and enter into what I have just found *and then continue on into the unknown, the unplanned and the unexpected until I wander into what feels right.* Immediately, there is the task to do what it is that feels right often enough so that it will be *remembered* not only for this rehearsal, but for the next one.

This is almost like the builders of highways who roll their trucks over the part that has already been built right up to the part that is yet to be finished by adding gravel, cement and/or asphalt. They, of course, know what each step of the way will be, and we only know it after trying this, that and the other way until we know it is right and can go on to the next as yet unknown segment. I am sure that there are a few choreographers out there for whom this sequence is familiar and many who exercise a radically different process. Here, there is no correct way, only what works for you.

Until now this consideration of improvisation has referred to its value in gaining freedom in motion, a wider range of movement possibilities, getting in touch with inner resources and releasing the creative impulses. The dancer may have an experience and/or an insight that lights up something new and exciting. The immediate wish is to somehow retain what happened for the future. The dancer senses, "What just happened is beautiful or terrifying." In any case, the dancer knows that he.she will want to return to it. But how? Improvisation is by its very nature ephemeral. A swift answer is videotaping improvisations. Lacking sufficient experience in this way of working, I'll refrain from commenting on it.

Recapturing the exact movements in an extended sequence intended primarily for an improvisation exercise is a near-impossible task. I can imagine that there are a few near-geniuses who have this ability. Still, there is this from Oliver Sacks, the author of *The Man Who Thought His Wife Was a Hat.*

> It is recorded of Mozart, whose musical memory was one of the most accurate ever known, that if he was asked (after some astonishing improvisation) to "play it again" he never would, never *could,* play it precisely again, but would always come up with some new variation. Mozart, in this sense, may have been a failure as a recording machine, but this is how it is, and how it should be, with a healthy living brain.[11]

What can be grasped, retained and *returned to* is the state of mind that led to that exquisite time. Any dancer aware of having found something important must quickly find the moment to pin down *from where it sprang* and not so much *where it went.* I learned this during a rather painful experience. I had an idea for a dance and what remained was to find a good score. I brought a number of recordings to the studio. None seemed right until I came across the second movement of a piano sonata by Roger Sessions. I already had a rough concept of how the dance would evolve. Moving tentatively about with the Sessions seemed to bring me close to the idea. Tamiris was due to pick me up at the studio but she arrived earlier than our agreed time. I was excited about the music and I wanted her opinion. Starting the music, I found myself walking through what I conceived might be the beginning. Without planning, and certainly without choreography, I found myself dancing—full out! Going with it, I began a leaping run in a circle. Only later did I realize that in addition to the air work, there were phrases when I had been running in that circle in a deep plié and once or twice I was down on my knees—still running. Uncannily, I continued into a quiet section, another burst of energy and then a finish that dovetailed with the end of the music—a score which I barely knew.

There was no question. The Sessions sonata was the choice, but in the ensuing weeks I realized that between the soft lyricism of the music and the inordinate rhythmic complexity of the score, I would have to look further, even though I was certain that I had much of the movement nailed. I went to work without a score. The beginning flowed just as it did in when I improvised for Tamiris but when I got to the exuberant running, leaping circle, I couldn't get near what I remembered. Technically, I could not figure out how I had been running in a circle at that wild pace in a deep plié and *at times on my knees*. I must have tried to recapture that original circle for a month before I capitulated and did a circle that *evoked* what had happened.

In time, I came to realize that almost all that we do—choreographically—is an attempt to recapture what has been lost—what was. That could be one of the many useful definitions of art. Having had an overwhelming experience in an improvisation that cannot be remembered in its details and specificity, there is the challenge to remember what it felt like, to remember where it came from and to follow through with the action that drove it. There is a certain perfectionism which treats the inability to recapture the details of an improvisation as a total disaster. Better to treat the ache and the loss as a core, a center and a stimulus for further creative work. The loss and the pain of the loss becomes the grain of sand around which a new pearl can grow. It will never be the same but it can be a work of art about what was lost. Of course, now we do have videotape. But that, too, will bring new problems.

# 5 "Rules" for Choreography

## IN NO PARTICULAR ORDER

> "There are no rules."
>
> *Daniel Nagrin*

This chapter is not being broadcast from Mt. Sinai. It is, rather, a grab bag of hints, tricks and tips that have been accumulated from years on Broadway, in films, the concert stage and teaching. Some I heard, some were dinned into me and some I figured out after falling on my face. As the years roll by, subsequent to this book being published and read by thousands and taught to many, I have a hope for the future: that one by one what is said here will be revised, contradicted and/or proved dead wrong.

## Problem #1

When the curtain rises and the lights come up on your dance, your audience is waiting to be engaged and drawn into your work. Your first task is to snare them into the action. Until they know specifically who or what is at the center of your work, there will be a distance. The sooner that space collapses the better. If your beginning is a blur of activity, your audience will not know who or what is making that blur.

### The Rule

Within the first half minute of a dance be sure to have your key dancers be still long enough to let the audience know who is dancing.

# Problem #2

For most people in the audience, when the house lights are dimmed to begin a perform-ance, almost everything they have read in the program, title and notes, is deleted from their minds. A few have come late, had no time to read the program and haven't the slight-est idea of what to expect. A few desperately peer at their program in the dark or even light matches. A rare and select group remember everything they read in the program. Most have blank anticipation.

## The Rule

Never let the perception of your choreography depend upon a title or a program note. Assume your audience knows nothing of what you are going to do until they *see* the dance. Rely *only* upon your actual choreography, music, setting and costumes to convey critical information.

# Problem #3

A title reveals its worth only *after* the dance has been seen. A good title will evoke the memory of the dance because it and what was danced are wrapped about each other. Also, it might help the critics say something intelligent later on.

## The Rule

Esoteric titles with an independent life and poetry apart from the feel and smell of the choreography serve little but the vanity of the choreographer.

# Problem #4

Every method has its own hazards. Choreography that uses the specific image and specific actions is no exception. Among the dangers of working with the specific image are those moments when the choreography calls for an extended focus on something that creates in the performer an overwhelming act of passive witnessing. The internal life of the per-former can be tumultuous at such times but the audience will become more and more alienated because there is nothing they can hang on to except the obvious, a dancer look-ing at something.

Any phrase that involves the act of looking/seeing something *not visible to the audience is fraught.* Looking without reflecting, physically, what is being seen is dead time on a dance stage. The choreographer may give the dancer an image of overwhelming vividness and specificity but sustain that act of looking for more than a bit and the audience slips into the fatal mode of *looking at a dancer who is looking.* What the imagination of the dancer sees may be astonishing. What we see slips into a generalization about the act of looking. The body in the act of looking can become a thing of beauty but if that looking becomes a prolonged passive witnessing, the viewer is not getting sufficient material to identify with what the dancer is experiencing.

## *The Rule*

If what you as the dancer see is searing your insides, be buffeted, swept, lifted into the air, spun about, embraced by it: *become what you are seeing.* A column of water in a fluted green glass vase loses not a bit of its integrity as water. The dancers body can be a fluid vase into which a dark blue sky has been poured or its opposite, the sky slipping into the vase. *Seeing the body seeing* should inflame our vision with a view that transcends the dancer. One of Martha Graham's great, early solos was *Frontier.* It was a *looking* dance and whatever she saw transformed her and we saw what we believed she was seeing.

# Problem #5

This one is difficult to express neatly but it points to a failing that happens too often. Quoting from one of my class tapes, "Your dance is all around the church but never enters, never breaks down the door or even knocks. The dancer is always at a distance." So many young dancers will dance about and around what is the deepest concern of the dance but never come in contact with that something, nor become that something, nor let a metaphor for that something to appear or be felt. I find myself quoting Anna Sokolow in her composition classes, "More! More!" "There is more to what you have begun. Your dance is only a beginning. What about that which really touches you?"

## *The Rule*

The one person from whom you dare not keep secrets is yourself. With a powerful poetic metaphor, no one need know that exactly what is there on the stage. That is your secret. Alive in a metaphor, it becomes the possession of both you and the audience, but if your secret never leaves the wings, what do you have left to share?

# Problem #6

A more serious error that can overtake those dealing with the specific image is slipping into a sequential and logical progression of ideas, metaphors, inner text or narration. Modern choreographers have few metaphors that they share with their audience. To a lesser degree this is true of some contemporary ballet choreographers. Part of the challenge is the creation of new personal and imaginative metaphors for each new dance, modern or ballet. Let there be a sustained string of movement metaphors that are connected logically, either as a narrative or a conceptual structure and the audience is staring at a sign language which is excluding them. A Hindu *kathakali* dancer tells stories but his.her audience knows the intent and meaning of every gesture—*of every sign.*

An example to make the above specific: A graduate student presents a powerful beginning, seated, rocking from side to side, hands on each ankle, gradually lifting one leg and then the other, opening the legs in a way that is at once pained and erotic, followed by some rolling and twisting on the ground, coming erect to a section speared by elbows that seem to stab the self. Then there is a walking theme, a back roll repeated several times, a reaching half rise to the feet, a lashing of the face by the hands, covering the face and finally going back to the opening position, rocking on the floor, hands on the ankles. My response to the student:

> There is nothing that is not compelling and interesting in this dance but our initial interest becomes vitiated by the continual introduction of new material. After a while, we are getting the signal that there is a story behind all of this, *but we do not know what the story is.* We can't even begin to guess because we are given signals and signs that are private *and known only by the choreographer and never developed by the choreographer.*

> Close your eyes. In your life, there is an event—an incident to which your mind returns many times. Look at it once again. (After a while:) What are you seeing, the beginning? the middle? or the end? Her answer: "Something in the middle." Return to it . . . Now what are you seeing? "Something in the middle." The same? "Yes." Return to the incident again . . . Now what are you seeing? "The beginning."

> That, by the way, is how Martha Graham constructed her dances and *that is how your mind constructs its memories.* Your mind makes poetry as it remembers. The choreographic procedure you used crushes the poetry and lines up the event or any matter that concerns you in a *logical, linear, sequential order.* It takes very little time for us, the audience, to sense this and we sit there wondering what is happening *instead of knowing what is happening in our own terms*, which would be the result of our poetic reconstruction of what we are seeing.

A similar consideration applies to more abstract material. The story is told that when Peter Martins was working at his first piece of choreography, Balanchine dropped by on the very first day of rehearsal. Martins had choreographed less than two minutes. Balanchine nodded and as he left said, "No more new material. You have all that you need."

If, in the process of creating a dance, a choreographer finds it inundated with movement motifs, is that the time to ask, "Is this multiplicity a sign of arriving at quick, easy and evasive answers? Have I dug deeply enough to find the key theme for my dance—a theme that rises out of the heart of what I am creating?"

*The Rule*

It is better to squeeze all you can out of a little than to create a panorama of constantly new dance phrases. The constant addition of new movement material often gives the impression of a secret narration. Better to exhaust the richness, the juice and the possibilities of a phrase before adding another and another. The same phrase repeated exactly in a different context can have a different meaning. The same phrase bent just a bit becomes a new phrase. The most amazing example of this is *Last Look* by Paul Taylor. It has only one eight bar (eight counts each) phrase through its entire length. I have been told that it is done at changing tempos, levels and intentions. The repetition is not at all apparent and in addition, the work is terrifying.

An irresistible diversion: My custom in writing these books has always been to ask colleagues whom I respect to review them before submitting them to the publisher. I was honored when Paul Taylor consented to read the manuscript. With a touch of his sly humor, he wrote in the margin next to the passage above:

This is true. The 25 minute dance was done in a 2 week rehearsal period (2 hrs. a day, 5 day week). Cast of 9, all learning the same 8 bar phrase, thus saving time when making variations of it: practical way to work when having limited rehearsal time.

To bring this matter home, a class assignment could be helpful:

To a short piece of music with no prohibitive rhythmic complexity, give a specific choreographic problem: two are on a journey. One is hot to go on, the other is reluctant. Each dancer should find three movement metaphors for the need of her.his character. Jointly make a dance for this situation with no new movement invention. Only variations and developments of the three movement phrases are permitted.

# Problem #7

At Arizona State University, there is a black box experimental theatre open twice a year to any and all who have a piece they wish to show. There is no jury. At one of these, a tall, slender man circled the audience. He was blowing a horn to the taped, intermittent accompaniment of sea gulls crying. It set up an atmosphere of loneliness and despair, but he went on and on with an unrelenting lack of development or change of any kind. After almost ten minutes of this, it added up to a rude imposition. Just as an audience rebellion seemed imminent, there was powerful explosion and the lights went out.

He had committed one of the most subtle errors in art. He was doing something evocative *in limbo*. He lacked a frame. Had the piece begun with the explosion, then the circling of the audience, the lonely sound of the horn and the sea gulls' cries would all have lived in a *frame*, a context *within which our imagination could live*.

Another dancer presented a study that called forth the following:

> There is something about Kelly's initial position, her profile, the rigidity, the symmetry—and immediately ritual, ceremony, religion, some kind of trying to get in tune, all come to mind. In those first twenty, thirty seconds of looking at her in that position it is possible to see bird decorations done on native American pottery. I don't *know* what the dance is about, but I am not lost. My imagination has found a place to work. An arena has been established. I am engaged in the dance. It is extremely difficult to say just how it has been done, but there it is.

The artist can only deal with but one part of the universe. Forcing our imagination to ramble anywhere and everywhere is self-defeating. The task of the artist is to get everyone to point the telescope of their imagination to one part of the mysterious everywhere. Establishing a frame locates the dance and has nothing to do with explaining it or spelling out its meaning. At the heart of every work of art is a mystery. The frame tells the audience in what arena the mystery lives. This problem of a work without a frame is not uncommon. It occurs quite readily among artists who consider themselves avant garde, highly sophisticated and fear above all being considered simplistic or literal.

## The Rule

*Establish the frame in which the dance will live within the first thirty to sixty seconds of a dance work.* Sometimes, all that is needed is a hat with a feather or a cigarette. Merce Cunningham's work defies easy explanations and yet on one level audiences almost immediately know *where to look and where to wonder*. Curtain up on one of his pieces reveals three lithe figures in stippled unitards, a woman and two men, standing still and close to each other. They are looking straight out front. There is music and, as if electrified, they go into action, dancing full out and paying no attention to each other. Not for one second does anyone in the audience imagine that this is a ménage à trois. No time is wasted. The audience knows exactly where to look and wonder.

Since writing this I have stumbled across a possibly more helpful way of understanding this problem. Over a morning coffee, at the kitchen counter, I found myself staring at a calendar photograph of a young cat, who was staring at me. It was the upper half of January. "It's only a cat. What is so mesmerizing about this photo? What is this amazing power of photographs?" Out of that flowed the next thought, "A good photograph is the neatest, simplest metaphor for art. With the precision of its imminent presence, it implies a past and reverberates with a future." This is certainly true of the best dance photography. It sends echoes back and forth to where the dance came from and to where it is going.

Consider the beginning of *any* dance work—or *any work of art*. It is not and cannot be the actual beginning. All of us and everything we know—and don't know—has a history, unless you go back to, "In the beginning God created . . . ," or the Big Bang. Choose your jumping off point. *After either one of those events, everything else has an antecedent.* Nothing you can create in any art form is without a history or an absolute beginning. The opening sounds of music call up a period, a culture and the history of music that made those sounds possible and available to the composer.

In light of this concept, can we rewrite the rule stated above?: *Within the first thirty to sixty seconds of a dance work indicate—imply—establish the history and the antecedents of the dance figures we see before us.* Implicit in this rule is the assumption that the dance will then function within the arena—the frame—the history—that was marked out by that first thirty to sixty seconds.

Teachers of choreography, make an experiment: gather the videotapes of half-a-dozen or more classic dance works. Run each tape for forty-five seconds. Have your students write out all that they know and assume from what they have seen. Ideally, most of the dances should be unfamiliar to the students. Have them, one by one, read out what was written. In subsequent sessions, run each of the tapes in its entirety, discussing 1) how close or divergent were the original impressions of the class as a whole and 2) how on the mark were the assumptions about the work to come.

To tie it up: Every artist has the responsibility to determine what his.her audience *must* know with a certainty and what must remain ambiguous. The frame supplies the certainty, the ambiguity feeds the imagination. The work of art contains both in a tension that commands attention.

## Problem #8

Much excitement: One of the brightest of the graduate students is doing her master's thesis based on Dostoevsky's *Crime and Punishment*! Talk about ambition. It turns out to be a dazzler. The dance sequences, the costuming, the groupings, the performances, the lighting are all engrossing. There are a few problems: Raskolnikov's murder of the old woman is witnessed by the entire community. The old woman, a pawnbroker in the novel named Alyona, is danced by a wildly athletic young woman. Two women, characters never appearing in the novel, are seen with capes decorated with a skull and bones and appear to be bestowing a (Satanic?) benediction on each individual, one after the other. The crowd berates Raskolnikov but then he joins them. Sonya, the victimized prostitute, appearing like a pure angel, takes the body of Alyona off stage in the beginning and returns with it at the end. The work ends with all facing upstage praying while Raskolnikov turns to look at and point to the body.

I say, "Christy, except for the murder of Alyona this has nothing to do with *Crime and Punishment*." Christy, "But this is a deconstruction of *Crime and Punishment*." I have one response to her defense and here, I will put it forward as a "rule".

### The Rule

Beware of fashion. Beware of buzzwords, they can mess up your mind and kill your work.

## Problem #9

If an idea for a dance comes to you, discuss it with no one—not even your bed-mate. Talking about what you have yet to do will dilute the necessity and passion to do it. Talking at any time before the work has been premiered could easily invite theft; ideas are precious commodities and there are people who steal. You must talk about your idea with your collaborators, designers, dancers, composer, etc. in order to draw them into the world you are creating. As you do this you must swear them to secrecy.

What follows is a personal predilection and I suspect that there are not many in the dance or the other arts who take this position: After the work is done, there will be an influx of people who will desperately ask you, "What it is about? What are you saying? What does it mean? *Tell no one anything*. You will get most of your flak from publicists and interviewers. You should have but one answer. "Look at the work and draw what you will from it."

*The Rule*

*Don't discuss your ideas with anyone except your collaborators, not even after the work is completed, is being performed and in your repertoire. Just dance and shut up.* To this injunction, Paul Taylor added his own thought, "Amen, however, interviewers need help. Tell them the dance is about 25 minutes."

In 1993, I was asked by Carla Maxwell, the artistic director of the José Limon Dance Company to set *Spanish Dance, Strange Hero* and *Indeterminate Figure* on several of the company members for their season at the Joyce Theatre. She also asked for material about the dances for publicity. I wrote to her:

> May 23, 1993
> Dear Carla,
> I have serious difficulty talking about my dances. It feels wrong. It feels like a betrayal—as if I do not trust them to speak for themselves. Further, the more I talk about them the more completely I intrude upon the insights and the imagination of any audience that receives my verbal information ahead of seeing the dances as would be the case with publicity.
> Who but I am the authority on what my dances are about? But no, that is not the case. A work of art—if it is a work of art—is an object that gains its weight and meaning in the space between the artist and the audience. Its meaning is a variable shaped by the makers and the viewers. Let the artist spell it out before it is experienced and the audience is cheated out of their own personal response. A work of art fires the artist and each subsequent one who comes in contact with it in a different way.
> I hope you can make use of the enclosed publicity materials. Bend the stuff as you will, using the names of the critics or not or even paraphrasing. I am sending them because they hint at what the dances are about without going into specifics. I am aware that there is the perennial problem of publicity and the press. People *like* to know ahead of time, because they do not trust themselves and because they have the false assumption that *there is one correct meaning to each dance.* Unfortunately, there are enough critics out there who foster this illusion, because they want their readers to turn to them to *learn the truth.*
> If this is not enough, complain and let me know.
> Love,
> Daniel

Further, every dancer in the Limon Company who learned the solos was asked to sign a contract agreeing never to divulge to any one any of the internal images and meanings of the dances which I might have communicated to them or any they might have arrived at out of their own imagination.

Actually, there was a tradition in modern dance that made it acceptable for choreographers to explain the intent and/or meaning of their work. In the early days, this explanation appeared in press interviews, in press releases and in more or less subtle forms in the program notes. I speculate that it goes back to the time when there were few knowledgeable dance critics and a very small audience. It was not unusual for publications to assign a music or theatre critic and even, at times, sports writers to review dance events. The information given out by the pioneer choreographers may not have been directed to the audience so much as to the people who would be writing about the dance and communicating to the public-at-large.

Gradually, the program notes became more terse, but the press interviews and the press releases often continued the tradition. In time, less information and no explanations were forthcoming, but then an ironic twist occurred. A hallmark of "avant garde" and postmodern dance has been the amazing verbosity spilling all over the program explaining the process of their most abstruse pieces.

Personally, I believe in doing my work and not interfering with the work of the audience. It is their task, or joy, to enter into what they see, experience and if possible, to draw a relation to their own lives. Does it require a sophistication? Some dances do more than others. If a viewer becomes fascinated by dance, in time a mode and sheer skill of looking at dance will evolve. If there is a love of dance, the means to perceive it in its many forms will be found *without it being spelled out by the choreographer.*

# Problem #10

The early part of every dance work establishes a style, a set of rules, a way. It is a dangerous and tricky ploy to switch away from what has been established. Stepping away into the field of music: if a composer were to open with a dissonant score in the serial mode and then, in a middle section, turn to a romantic, harmonic treatment, listeners would feel betrayed and confused. Similarly, if a choreographer were to mount a dance full of dramatic overtones and interactions, but part way through insert an irrelevant, upbeat section full of high physical virtuosity danced straight out to the audience, the result would be bewilderment and resistance.

## The Rule

Juggling styles within a particular work is dangerous and yet it is conceivable that it can work, *if change is built in to what has gone before.* In my own work, *The Peloponnesian War,* switching styles *was the style*. The dance was about war and the irrationality of war and thus the constant unsettling of the rules reflected the experience and the madness of war.

This rule is not meant to discount changes and surprises. They not only give a work excitement but reflect the truth of our lives. The task of the artist is to discover surprises that are organic to what has come before. As we are startled, we think, "Why yes, of course, that is the way it is!"

# Problem #11

It is hazardous for the choreographer to change one meaning for another for a dance character, a prop, a costume, a set or a movement metaphor. Switching identities for a soloist is a slippery ploy unless changes are signaled with props, costume changes or the idea of character changes are presented early in the piece. This is equally true in a group piece when the choreographer wants a dancer to switch roles.

## The Rule

All changes of character or meanings attached to metaphors must be *seen* taking place on stage and never merely in the mind of the choreographer or the performer.

# Problem #12

And now what may appear to be contradictory to much of what has just been said in favor of simplicity: the dynamic that drives vibrant dance is ambivalence. A dancer in a choreography class at the American Dance Festival knelt a little off the center of the space. She sat on her shins and instep with an elegant poise for a time of great concentration, and then slowly crumpled to the floor on her left side. She lay there for a bit and then eased herself back up to the original seated position and then repeated the action several times, with no variation. She maintained this ritual for quite a time, finally paused to rise, indicating that she had finished. What she had done was impressive and yet empty. I can imagine some teachers and some critics might have accepted the piece as a valid work. The class was uncharacteristically silent. Finally, I spoke up:

So far, so good, but where is "that"? Every dance needs a "this" *and* a "that." There is no art form that I know of that is not subject to this rule. Call it "opposition," "conflict," "this and that," "ambivalence," "contradiction," whatever. This is but half a dance, a fall. The matter of being erect, of having to return to the erect posture was not examined. Becoming erect again was too casual and pedestrian to qualify as a "that." If the recovery were dealt with in depth, the dance would have had a "this and a that." Every now and then a phrase will become embedded in our language. "Pigeons in the grass, alas, alas" became the sign-post of Gertrude Stein's work. On examination, it is a classic case of a "this and a that." "Pigeons in the grass," is the equivalent of a "this," but it is not just hanging there. The "alas, alas" introduces a mysterious perspective with infinite possibilities.

## The Rule

Every dance needs a "this" and a "that."

# Problem #13

A graduate student in the MFA program at Arizona State University presents his solo in a choreography class. He has a strong beginning, rushing in running backwards in a full stage circle at a high speed. Arriving down stage right he does another phrase of backing up at a slower tempo while throwing his hands out from side to side in an even, symmetrical fashion, reaching up stage left. The rest of the dance is a similar string of long repetitive phrases, sometimes walking, sometimes thrashing in place or rolling on the ground or more running forward or back. At this writing, I can't recall how he finished except that he did it with the air of one who had done a solid piece of work.

Suspecting that what we had been looking at was not choreography, I asked him to do the first two moves, the entrance and the diagonal backup, not once, but three times. Each time it was different and each time he used the music differently. Even then he did not realize what he had done. Or rather what he had not done. He was *sketching* a dance, not choreographing a dance. I myself have done this business of sketching a dance when presenting the idea and the possible structure to a composer as a suggested framework for her.his music. Sketching is a form of structured improvisation that *indicates* intended choreography.

## The Rule

Choreography is generally a controlled sequence of moves that can be repeated physically and musically. Improvisation is sequence of unpredictable moves that are discovered in the course of performance. Choreography may include passages that are improvised and usually occur within set time periods. Sketching is a loose indication of what a choreography might be. It is the art form of impatient dancers who are not willing to risk genuine improvisation in performance or rear back from the hard work and tedium choreography demands—in addition to the inspiration that gives it life.

# Problem #14

If it's about the sun, could you show us the moon which gives off no light but rather reflects the light of the sun? The moon can be a metaphor for the sun.

## *The Rule*

Find the metaphor that illuminates the object. A powerful metaphor will evoke a whole constellation of objects in the audience, all of which will hover around your object.

# Problem #15

When you attempt a work of art, it helps to be ready to see, smell, be jostled by, surprised by the most unexpected things which exist in you. It's matter of peeling away the layers of years and days, the layers of concepts of what is nice, what is acceptable, what might work, what might be beautiful; all of that to find out what is there under the layers. Much of the time we don't know what's there because there's a slip cover over it, a slip cover of expectations, preconceptions, propriety and good taste. You might remove the slip cover and surprise, it's not a couch. It's your grandmother, the one you disliked, the one who raised your hackles, who upset you. Most of the time we have attractive slip covers over what is neither permissible nor acceptable.

## *The Rule*

Plan on the unexpected. Allow the unattractive. In the creative process don't permit "good taste" and "good manners" to screen out what is there. Almost all innovations in art were greeted with disgust and horror by the establishment. For years, Martha Graham's dirty feet and "grotesque" movement received more attention and jokes than the insights she brought to the stage.

# Problem #16

The moment I settled into my first Broadway show with a steady salary, I enrolled in an acting class taught by Sanford Meisner. He was one of the three master teachers in New York, at the time. My first session, I sat far in the back, awed by the number of established professional actors present. The first scene was quite credible and lively. One of the students was a well-known Broadway actor. The scene finished, and Sandy said, "Norman, we all know you can act. When are you going to become an artist? It is not enough to be truthful. At some time in your career you have to bring your insight, your terror, your love of the character." Dennis the Menace makes a subtle contribution to this problem: "Joey, you must always tell the truth . . . even if you have to make it up!"

At the Summer Graduate Program of Wesleyan University, a student took a rare risk. Her piece was a tantrum. We were recording those classes. What follows was my critique:

> An accurate, well observed performance of infantile rage is not enough. It appeared quite genuine but all we saw was a literal performance. To me, what you did was opaque. I could not see inside, through, beyond, or around the anger. You never found the context that would make your enactment translucent, or a grill work, or a calm containing that violence, or a wounded snake. In short, this is not a dance. Giving us it, itself, is necessary but only the beginning.

## The Rule

The artist gathers the material of her.his concern and then shapes it to give us an *angle of vision that illuminates the whole.* She.he gives us a *lookout point* which can make us breathe faster, laugh, weep and see afresh.

# Problem #17

Tamiris told us all early, "There is one thing that no audience will accept from a performer: self-pity. What you do may arouse pity in the audience but if your action is self-pity you will probably alienate any who view you."

## The Rule

The characters of your choreography may be overwhelmed by pain, disaster or failure. There are a thousand ways of dealing with these, but in the theatre, avoid any thematic material that reeks of self-pity.

# Problem #18

In some art forms, a bare gesture can evoke a world. Vermeer's paintings are miniature compared with most masterpieces. Emily Dickinson rarely took more than a page to write a poem. Anton Webern wrote *Four Pieces, Opus 7* for violin and piano that lasted four minutes and twelve seconds. The Japanese have an art form built on this kind of brevity, the haiku, a bit of poetry never more or less than seventeen syllables. In my own experience, I have never seen a "haiku" dance succeed. Doris Humphrey was quoted as saying that, "All dances are too long." She has a point, but turning the other way, they cannot be too short.

## The Rule

A brief dance statement with little or no development probably is a mistake. Why is this so? I cannot say and I can't wait to be proved wrong.

# Problem #19

Whenever I showed Tamiris a new work which I had choreographed, she always would pick away at any phrase of movement which she recognized from my previous choreography. It was only when I began to work alone that I rethought the validity of using material from earlier dances. I came to believe that an old phrase in a new context becomes a new phrase. And yet, I think every choreographer should be aware of "recycling" dance material. There is a dangerous temptation involved here. If something delivered beautifully in one dance, "Why not . . .?"

Every teacher, coach or friend who is observing and/or critiquing a new dance should point out familiar phrases, not as a "No, no," but as a fact that must be noted by the choreographer and a question answered; if the phrase was appropriate in another context, organic to the place where it originated, *is it appropriate to its new place?* Another reasonable question, in as much as it *is* a new context, is there a better way of expressing what is needed at that point?

## The Rule

Ask those you trust to see your new dances, and among other things, ask whether are there apparent repetitions from your previous choreographies. Always question recycled dance material. Does the new context make the "old" "new"?

# Problem #20

A perennial problem in choreography is the matter of time. One of the most common faults of young dancers is the speed with which they will shift gears in a dance. For example, starting in an involved and tortured complexity, a dancer very quickly becomes erect, clear and free. This kind of an abrupt change induces a loss of credibility. At the outset, we believe the figure is experiencing a great difficulty, but getting out of it so easily discounts what we have just been seeing. Or, taking the same sequence of events, the dancer may delay rising to the point that the viewers are flooded with an impatience of waiting. There is no easy, schematic answer to this problem of time.

My first professional job was in a summer theatre where we did four performances a week. Every week we put on a new musical revue, a variety night, a Sunday afternoon concert and a new play. The first play was *Winterset* and I was cast as the second policeman. The hero is confronting the gangster and telling the police that there is a dead body in the next room. The police sergeant orders me to go and look. As I entered the door to step offstage to go and "look," I was horrified, for in the rush of the first week, we had never rehearsed this scene. I realized that every second I was offstage looking, *nothing* was happening on stage. How long a time was I to spend offstage "looking"? Simple. I looked all through offstage right for a body, found nothing at all, came back on stage and said as much. The summer season lasted three months and the rest of the cast never let off mimicking me looking, looking for a dead body.

There is an envelope of awareness that contains all that we do in the theatre. It is a consciousness unlike any other. In my own way of working and as I have been teaching, if one has a specific task within the context of a specific image whatever we do/dance will take as long as it takes to do what we are doing. Would this be the same time span as it would be in "life"? I doubt it. Would it be faster or slower? No firm answer is possible. It could go either way. What can be trusted is the world created by the magic "if." That world has its laws and its clocks. That imaginary land of metaphors in which we choose to live and dance has a reality as substantial as the floor upon which we slide, turn, leap and fall. But it is substantial only if The Six Questions have been answered, deliberatively or intuitively.

## The Rule

If you are living in the world you have created, take as long as it takes to do what you do. No more, no less and do it fully. Don't shorten it to be "theatrical." Don't lengthen it to be "profound." If you live your time, we will believe you.

# Problem #21

Stillness possesses the entire dynamic of the most violent action if there is an internal life going on that demands stillness.

## The Rule

Do not fear stillness in your choreography. When it contains an action, the stage will not be static.

# Problem #22

There is a trap when the choreography includes characters and/or forces for which the choreographer has contempt and hostility. If the character is seen solely from the shell, the result will be melodramatic and not believable. It behooves the choreographer and the performers to reach into the inside of what is abhorred *and find the place of innocence*. Those we conceive as contemptible are sustained by self-approval.

## The Rule

On your stage, whatever figure you consider to be ignoble must act from a profound inner justification. This will demand of you an understanding and even a compassion for what you hate.

# Problem #23: The Final Rule

Approach each new choreographic challenge with *no rules at all*. You will always be beginning. Assume nothing and be ever ready to jettison every one of your principles, style or methods. *This includes every rule noted above.*

# 6  The Play of Metaphor

*The play of metaphor is the play of poetry is the play of dance.*

The premise of this book: nothing is itself only. Everything resonates with something other than itself. Our speech, our clothing, our food, our dwellings, our motions and above all, our actions are what they are and also more than they are. In our speech, the use of metaphor and simile is most obvious, whether it is Shakespeare's "this is the winter of our discontent," or Jimi Hendrix calling out "Stone free, like a breeze." Dance, too, is drenched in metaphors. But, there are those who make much of a dance that is pure motion, devoid of metaphors and free of the burden of meaning. It is time to pause to pin down this word, "metaphor," not only to be clear as to how and why we are using it but to point out that a significant segment of the dance profession abhors and avoids its use.

> *metaphor:* a transferring from one word the sense of another . . . a figure of speech in which one thing is likened to another, different thing by being spoken of as if it were that other, ". . . all the world's a stage." *Webster's Unabridged Dictionary*

> ". . . our vocabulary is largely built on metaphors; we use them, though perhaps not consciously, whenever we speak or write." *Fowler's Modern English Usage*

> The Lord is my shepherd
> My cup runneth over
> A heart of stone
> Thy word is a lamp unto my feet
> The long arm of the law
> A stiff upper lip

There is no end to them. They weave in and out of every expression *and every thought and every human movement.* What gesture is not a metaphor? A handshake offers the hand that could be bearing a weapon. Hands clasped in prayer are a symbol of subjection—

hands voluntarily tied together. Bowing diminishes one in size. Shaking a finger is waving a stick or a club. Thrusting arms overhead, "Look at me! I won!" Posture is a metaphor for who we think we are or who we think we have the right to be. What is the flamenco dancer saying with lifted chest, arched back and head high?

Consider the lexicon of "pure dance movements." The attitude that was so shrewdly stolen from Giovanni da Bologna's *Mercury* by Carlo Blasis is the perfect metaphor for being airborne while standing or turning on the ground. Mercury was the flying messenger of the gods. The line of the lifted back leg spiraling up to the curved upper arm is so powerful it eliminates from our consciousness the supporting leg and not only Mercury but the dancer, too, is in flight.

The arabesque presents and thrusts forward the warmest, the most sensitive and vulnerable parts of the body with everything else left streaming behind. It can be a metaphor for flight or for offering oneself to another or for exposing one's vulnerability to others. The reader and I are quite aware that there is a whole school of dancers who flatly deny all of this. To them, the paramount significance of an arabesque is itself. To them, loading it down with meanings and metaphors drags it down into sentimentality or sets it up as a mysterious sign which the bedeviled audience is required to decipher instead of simply exhilarating at what they are witnessing. To me, to Tamiris who schooled me in my beginning, the sheer elegance and physicality of an arabesque is one of ten thousand ways of seeing and experiencing it, not the only way.

In essence, they, and all they represent, have declared dance, as metaphor, dead. They ask, what is there to see, to experience, to interpret or to analyze except the movement and the shapes they fall into?

In a left-handed way this whole matter came up in a discussion with a man who was in the Workgroup:

*Charles Hayward:* One of the most wonderful things we were constantly able to do in the Workgroup was how we designed ways to again regain and retain the child.

*Daniel:* What you are saying casts an interesting light on large portions of the modernist and post-modernist movement. These people lost the ability to play, to make believe like children. They were terrified of make-believe. They tried to do what they thought was "real."

The mainstream of modern art, through all of the "schools"—abstract, non-objective, formalist, avant garde, post-modern—flowed away from the game of pretending, representing, having meaning, from playing. Most of the results are humorless and rarely do they even approach the tragic. I agree that it is always interesting to see someone walking or running and to many of us it is equally interesting and important whether they are trying to get away from something or go someplace.

In Chapter 5, I referred to a dance by Merce Cunningham, in which the curtain is raised on two men and a woman in leotards and tights. They stand in alert, lifted positions, and in a moment they lash into a fury of brilliant unrelated moves in all directions. I stated earlier that no one is going to speculate that this is really a ménage à trois. The reason no one will misinterpret the intent is that the ballet-based moves, interspersed with a rare contraction and arbitrary arm motions, immediately present the *metaphor of people dancing.* "They," including Mr. Cunningham and his partner, John Cage, might shudder at my phrase, "... the metaphor of people dancing ..." but does it not denote a sign, a statement, a conviction, a flag as it were, a view of life, a philosophy, that of all the possible ways of dancing and using dance, this is the way chosen? All they are presenting is a set of given motions executed by highly skilled dancers. Is not this choice—prepared with much labor and care and presented to the public—a metaphor for a profoundly held belief?

Seen in another light, dance that is alive always has a shimmer of the ineffable that distinguishes it from dance that is lifeless. We know that we are looking at an unsuccessful dance when the things that fill our consciousness are the dancers, their efforts, their costumes, the music, the lights, the stage, the person sitting in front of us, the theatre and whatever else can be perceived at that moment. A dance becomes alive when we are "hooked," caught up, drawn in, forget the bad seating and join the dancers in their dance. We are not experiencing merely their motion any more than a true performer merely experiences the act of moving about. So, what is this "ineffable"? It is something more than a leg raised, more than a motion. "More" is another name for poetry and the bones of poetry are metaphors.

Every action, in or out of art, can be seen as a metaphor for something else. Metaphors are what we do for a living. In improvisation, we are never literally rough with each other. It is unthinkable to actually eroticize another in the course of our work. And yet, we can do *anything* in dance as long as we are doing a metaphor for it: murder, rape, the tenderest of gestures or just plain hotshot dancing. We impoverish the depth of our artistic life if we avoid dealing with any and all these impulses poetically.

There are startling moments when the metaphor and "it" coincide. A handshake, an embrace, a thrust fist are all literal gestures which have been used in dance time and again with powerful effect, but only when they are spare islands in a sea of evocative signs and metaphors. At other times, they are banal, sentimental, trite and worst of all, lacking in poetic vision. The fear should not be of gesture, of meaning, of an inner life, of representation, but of slovenly and opportunistic attempts to be entertaining, to use "accessible" as a cover-up for lightweight and the single-minded determination to be "successful." All of these vulgarize and abdicate the dangerous and difficult task of being an artist. The purists who shun meaning fail in the search for the holy grail of purity in that whatever they do is drenched in and expressive of a specific and precise attitude towards life and art and that, if anything, is dance crammed with meaning.

The purists assumed that the choreographers whose works were weighted with meaning were also purists of a kind. They charged that behind every move of Graham's or Tamiris's or Humphrey's choreography was a *word* that had to be understood and known, otherwise the impact of the dance would be lost. With close examination of Graham's, Tamiris's, or Humphry's dances, it will be seen that whole stretches of their gestures and phrases can be felt and experienced only as unnameable. Words fail us continually, and still we communicate with each other. Knowing this made the modern dance possible. A human in motion creates eddies and swirls as colorful as a rainbow. No motion is without a feeling, without an emotion. A few can be clearly articulated verbally. Most, at best, yield words that fall far short of what it is we really mean.

It is hard to think of any gesture in daily life that is not metaphoric. Confused, the hand goes to the head. Does that help? No, but the head is where the answer might be found. The news of Yitzhak Rabin's death brought hands to cover the face and eyes of many. Did it block out the unacceptable? No, but it was an attempt. Many vital adolescents walk with an upward jounce. That "spring" in their step sings of a superfluity of energy. Driving an automobile in a thick fog, almost everyone juts their head forward, "peering through the fog." Bringing the eyes forward three or four inches affords absolutely no visual advantage. It is simply a metaphor for seeing more. Observe yourself and others and make a collection of movement metaphors in daily behavior. We are all pouring continuous streams of signals and messages out of our bodies. Sculptors use wood, clay or marble. Dancers use motions.

A graduate student brings in a study for the problem: Something/someone goes on forever. She starts in the center of the space and runs in an expanding spiral, reaches the limit of the space and stops. "Did you have a specific image?" "Yes, time." "Time is too much of an abstraction for dance. Find a specific for time."

The next week she presents a study again and again she takes her place in the center of the dance area, facing forward in a right diagonal *and proceeds to not move at all.* This is a rather conservative and conventional student and here she is doing "nothing" forever. I laugh at myself. First you challenge your students and now you are being challenged. But wait! Has she changed her position? It's hard to tell. She is still facing the right corner of the room, but is it my fatigue that moved her a bit? *A few minutes later it becomes clear that she is revolving in place, turning clockwise. But I never saw her move.* She is as she was in the beginning, utterly still. How is this done? Completely engrossed in this dynamic stillness I wait for the moment when she will be in profile. Four, perhaps five minutes later, she has turned what would be an eighth of a circle and arrives at (from the angle of my position) an absolute profile. That arrival has an impact as if a symphony orchestra struck a major chord, tutti. Incredulously, we watch her standing absolutely still *and* continuing to revolve in place, until an aeon later, she arrives to facing the left corner of the room and says, "Close your eyes." We do, for quite a long time, until we hear, "Open your eyes," and she is back at her starting position facing the right corner of the room and not moving, at least not moving visibly until she reaches the profile position of facing the right side of the room. "Close your eyes," and after a short bit we were told to open them in a tone of voice that told us the "dance" was over.

The class was divided. Some were in an indignant fury. Others were exhilarated by the excitement of witnessing this daring and mysterious construct and gave her a standing ovation. I was overwhelmed. She did that dance for us three more times. Once, it lasted twenty-four and one-half minutes. At the end of term showing of class work for the rest of the dance students and faculty, she took twenty-seven and one-half minutes. No one ever could figure out or duplicate the feat of being utterly still and revolving in place. Years later, when she gave me a copy of her notes from that class which I used for this book, I learned that her secret title for the dance was *Sundial*. Of course, that interval when we were told to close our eyes was night and we opened our eyes to witness the beginning of a new day. None of us were privy to this secret name that would "explain" the dance and thus each of us, including those who hated the dance, were sucked into the mystery of her moving stillness and in some part of out mind we made something of it. We found for ourselves a specific image and odds are that no two viewers had the same image, but they were probably all about time.

This ambivalence is a characteristic of metaphors. Occasionally, to underline this quality, I would go through the following "routine" for a class:

Do any of you smoke? You have a cigarette with you? For shame! All right, give me one. There was a time when I was a heavy smoker and I often asked myself why I smoked so much even though I wanted to quit. My mind would go back to the first cigarette I ever smoked. Morley Alexander was the only one of us in those depression days that had a job. He worked for a tailor, had a bit of change and would treat us. Does smoking a cigarette give off a sign to my insides that now I can afford to buy my own cigarettes? On the other hand, some of those first cigarettes I stole from my mother's purse. What does that mean? Am I trying to make a connection with my mother? Smoking was always a sign of sophistication and maturity. Does it make me feel adult and so very soigné? On the other hand, Freud says slender objects are phallic symbols. I'm sticking a cigarette in my mouth and what does that mean? Doctors say it kills us. Is this the expression of a death wish?

Through this entire speculation, I am dealing with a prop, a literal thing and a literal act. Am I ever simply smoking a cigarette or am I *really* doing a substitute for something else? A metaphor, but which metaphor? It is the protean nature of metaphors that defines the shifting, mysterious quality inherent in all the arts.

↩

One metaphor of early Gothic art was the mystical and unknowable nature of material existence and the diminishment of the individual. The revolution of the Renaissance pierced this veil by elevating the observed fact to a central focus of artists and scientists. Dissections of corpses yielded knowledge of what the body was, not what it was assumed to be. From the question, "What did the eye actually see?" came the laws of perspective. Thus, *the observed fact became the metaphor for a new world view.* Every epoch of art has metaphors such as these that are the spine of their style and aesthetic.

↩

### The Mad Scene

From *Selected Poems* 1946–1985 by James Merrill. Copyright © 1992 by James Merrill. Reprinted by permission of Alfred A. Knopf, a Division of Random House, Inc.

Again last night I dreamed the dream called Laundry.
In it, the sheets and towels of a life we were going to share,
The milk-stiff bibs, the shroud, each rag to be ever
Trampled or soiled, bled on or groped for blindly,
Came swooning out of an enormous willow hamper
Onto moon-marbly boards. We had just met. I watched
From outer darkness. I had dressed myself in clothes
Of a new fiber that never stains or wrinkles, never
Wears thin. The opera house sparkled with tiers
And tiers of eyes, like mine enlarged by belladonna,
Trained inward. There I saw the cloud-clot, gust by gust,
Form, and the lightning bite, and the roan mane unloosen.
Fingers were running in panic over the flute's nine gates.
Why did I flinch? I loved you. And in the downpour laughed
To have us wrung white, gnarled together, one
Topmost mordent of wisteria,
As the lean tree burst into grief.

*James Merrill*

One can sense, standing back in the shadows of Mr. Merrill's mind, a scene and a cast of characters that were as material and "real" as the book you now have before you and the action you pursue of reading it. He could have talked and/or written of it exactly as it was but that would not be a poem. Treasure and hold close whatever it is that inflames you and demands to be danced, but don't bring it out in the air for us to stare at. Find the metaphor that illuminates your "it" or the color of the light that pours out of it. Decipher its shadow on the wall, its reflection in the water, its transfiguration in a dream or the echo of its laughter. And even these might be too close to the "real" thing to resonate the complexity of its overtones. The strategy of this ambivalence and uncertainty is simple. The human passion to *know* will galvanize your audience to know in terms of their own lives what you are doing as you dance. The pedestrian term for this is "audience involvement." Spell it out literally, accurately, as it is and it will be seen as *your* problem by a cold and distant audience. Tamiris's phrase for a too literal expression was "too close to the bone." Involved, your audience will be dancing on stage with you. All who watch will fashion their own poem.

     ↬

An idea as such is not dance material. A specific image for an idea that makes you weep, or laugh, or wonder is seed for a dance.

     ↬

We are shown a solo in which the dancer gives himself what appears to be an injection of a drug. His next move is a conventional pirouette which is followed by a sequence wherein the dancer seems tossed about by a maelstrom. I question the impetus of the pirouette for what became a passive section. I claim that a classical pirouette is the action of one who is in control. The move is initiated by the arms and that generally connotes control. "The pirouette does not look passive. It looked like something you chose to do. You were on top of it and not lost in a storm." I give the example of a lemon peel being stirred in a cocktail glass. Both the peel and the stirrer are moving at the same speed but their actions are diametrically opposite. One is active, the other is passive.

The choreographer defends himself saying that the whole appearance of losing control was a pretense. "Do you mean that this man's actions are, in fact, deliberate? If you let us get a glimpse behind *that* facade, the dance would be chilling."

     ↬

Choreographing movement is easy, but developing it, plumbing its depths, revealing its dark side and its light side, locating it within a larger concept are just the beginning of the tasks that can create a vital choreographic work. Any dancer can walk into a studio and pour out reams of movement, remember them, rehearse them and have a dance. Some do just that. Others start with no more than a "feeling" and go from there. Is this choreography? Certainly it is. Can it be "good" choreography? I'll beg off answering that one. It's one more way and in this big world there's room for many ways.

～

In a Seattle workshop, a student positions herself to show a choreographic study. She takes the classic beginning of young dancers—the fetal position, with this difference; her head is away from us and her bottom is toward us. The solo lasts at least five minutes. She never leaves her place on the floor or changes her body axis. There are rolls to the left and to the right, sometimes with the legs extended in a split and sometimes doubled to the chest. The dance finished, she sits up and is ready for critiques. The student observers are strangely silent. After a time, I heave a sigh and hesitantly ask her whether she realized what she had shown us. Puzzled, my question only confused her. Finally, I had to ask her, "Didn't you have any idea that you made your bottom the subject of your dance?" Perhaps I was unkind. Her eyes only widened and she said nothing. I went on, "If the body is your instrument, you cannot afford to be an innocent about its powers, its connotations and *its metaphors*. In fact, it is wiser to think of it as a collection of instruments like an orchestra. The flute brings to the music what a cello does not have. Your head as a focus in a phrase gives it a tone and metaphor radically different than your bottom. You left us no choice but to consider the motions and changes of your bottom and to wonder what was the metaphor that you intended. "Oh! I didn't mean anything like that!" This was an innocent and that is the kind of innocence that no choreographer can afford. A foot is not a chest and it has its own particular reverberation and its own metaphors. They are not static or precisely spelled out. They vary with the dance, the choreography and the culture in which they are seen. Early in the nineteenth century, a woman's foot was a sex object. In the long run, you have to be culturally sophisticated and know there is a difference between your front and your back.

～

The terror that a dance will not be understood can lead to translating its internal life into unmistakable, billboard demonstrations. Teachers of acting have the perfect term for this. "You are illustrating!" is their most crushing criticism. Not trusting the fact that having done something and even felt something in a genuine way is enough to be understood, the choreographer spells out its intent and meaning without making the slightest demand upon the imagination and intelligence of an audience.

It is possible to do something, think something, feel something and not be understood by some people. Could be they're insensitive. Could be they don't want to understand. Could be the dance itself is muddied. If the need is to be seen and understood by everybody, then give up and compose a billboard. Translate your dance so that everybody will understand it and by that token, whatever complexities, paradoxes of feeling, contradictions and insights were in the work will be undercut. The dance will at best express a banality. The alternative? Accept the fact that some people are not going to get the point.

There is a solo in my repertoire called *Path*. In it, I carry a twelve foot two-by-four beam of wood in a repeated phrase of eight steps that, for a long interval, do not seem to cover any ground at all. In time, it becomes clear that I am advancing slowly from upstage right to downstage left, that I will probably not change the phrase at all and that it will take a very long time to arrive downstage left. There is no audible music—only the sound of my feet sliding on the floor.

Do you know how many different ideas people have of what I'm doing in *Path* when I carry that board? I had a specific image and I doubt whether one person in fifty understood or knew precisely what was in my mind. Bob Dunn, one of our seminal teachers of choreography, was the closest any human being has ever been to what was in my mind. But I am not trying to communicate something as precise as a telephone number. I'm not talking about something that can be quantified, specified and laid out in a clean sentence because that's not the function of art. The function of art is to stir up a soup around a certain mystery that engages you and you fervently feel should engage others.

I was once seeing a woman who was an artist. Not being an enthusiast of non-objective art, I was upset by her work. Her drawings were nearly invisible, slender lines and little squiggles with barely perceptible bits of colored pencil dash marks. A couple of lines looked like hairs dropped on the page. And that was it. Shortly after I got to know her and her work, I went off on a concert tour, an automobile tour. As I was driving, I suddenly became aware of a hyper-consciousness of everything that was slender and linear. The telephone and power lines were almost singing out to me. There was nothing deliberate about this. Lucky it wasn't autumn for I would have been overwhelmingly distracted with a sky full of twigs and branches. Her work did something to my eyes. I never will know what was in her head. She could have told me and that would destroy the poem. Of course, I never asked her.

～

In a graduate choreography session, a perceptive student picked up on the ambivalence of a choreographic study that betrayed an uncertainty on the part of the choreographer:

*Student:* I couldn't tell whether there was something pulling you or if you were just stepping forward.

*Dancer:* There is a shift in my line of focus and force.

*Daniel:* It changes?

*Dancer:* Right. That could be something that I have to deal with and make a statement one way or the other.

*Daniel:* I think your response was open-minded and good and I think your critic is knocking on the right door. I'm going to throw out an almost-rule. Write it in very faint ink or better still in pencil. If you do something that is almost literal, perhaps it is better to be very clear about what you are doing.

↜

The question is, how much information do you want to give? If the nature of the work is such that there is some one thing the audience *must* know, don't waste time—let them know right away—do it in a way that would be clear to all. A dangerous generalization, but possibly useful: The only time we use pantomime or any literal gesture is when the choreography depends upon the communication of a specific piece of information.

↜

There are two deaths on the dance stage: one is a dance composed primarily of literal gestures. The substance of the other is a multiple string of personal metaphors connected by linear logic. The literal dance makes it easy for the audience to know what is going on and waves the banner of "communicating," being accessible and entertainment. What it lacks is the magic of art—mystery. Its only salvation lies in the insertion of spectacle and virtuosic dance. Its opposite, a multiple string of metaphors, rings a death knell as the audience asks, "What is it all about?" With that question, a cold moat will fill the space between the viewer and the struggling dancers. In each case, the role of the audience is cancelled. Either one of these approaches defeats the creative capacities of the viewers. Perhaps the ultimate challenge for every artist is giving something to the audience that challenges them to be creative in their perceptions and imagination.

But what if the artist needs to express that for which there is as yet no symbol in the shared culture? I don't believe there is such a "that." Every "unfamiliar" gesture churned out by Graham, Tamiris, Humphrey, Holm and Weidman was culled out of the blood and bone of their times. They lived in the same world as their audience but saw what few would see. By their dances, new dimensions were added to the consciousness of those who came to see them dance.

There is another way: taking a cue from potters as they work a chunk of raw clay prior to throwing a pot. They slam the clay, cut it in two, fold it back again, knead it, roll it this way and that, forcing its inside out and back in again and in the process are already feeling and sensing what will finally emerge on the wheel. They call this process "wedging." If you "wedge" a movement metaphor choreographically, all who witness this process will be drawn into the work going on and with every variation and repetition will glean more and more meaning and connection with the dance. And then of course, along will come a choreographer who will disprove every word said here and I can't wait to see *that* work.

⌒

### Bulerias

My sorrow is great.
My fatigue is great.
I'll take them to the grave with me
And say nothing to anyone.

Sallow, with rings under her eyes?
Don't ask her what's wrong.
She is truly in love.

I am brown and poor.
Even browner is cinnamon
And the nobles eat it.[12]

These are the lyrics of a song from a show of flamenco music and dance that toured the world, including New York City. *Flamenco Puro* was its name and in the program were printed the words to about a dozen of the songs. Consider the meaning of the poem above. Can you conceivably *know* what the poet was saying? I can't, but I have no choice but to *try* to know—for myself—what is meant. I make strange and fantastic connections as I am thrust upon an unfamiliar landscape which has been made vividly alive for me. The silent man (or is it a woman?) fills a grave to its limit. A woman has been weeping for a long time. A hungry someone watches the lavish table of the rich. I have already built a world inhabited by the specifics of this poem and the vision gives me a tightness in my heart. My scenario? It is vague and prismatically changes its colors and shapes, but I will not tell you what it is. It is a private creation that has come alive in the space between the artist and me. I don't spend time wondering what the artist is saying. I wander among the words and all that they evoke in the vast forest of my mind and my memories and suddenly I blunder into a clearing and *I think I know what the poem means*—for me. Our work is like that of the poet's, not like the short story writer's. In poetry, each thought is like a falling star, slashing out of the dark and vanishing only to be followed by another one in a different part of the sky. We glance desperately from one to another, hoping, needing to find a link and surprisingly, finding that link in ourselves.

⌒

Some of the most unselfconscious people create art that is etched in the minds of many. Their work is unsigned and none of us ever know who was responsible. So many times when I have found myself leaning against the railing of a lookout point high in the mountains with my eyes hungry to forever retain what I am seeing, my mind goes to that engineer designer tramping through those hills *planning the roadway* and choosing scenic turnouts where we can stop and look. Driving, one catches glimpses of where one is and senses something of the land, but getting out of the car at one of those designated lookout points can be, on occasion, an epiphany wherein the land lies exposed and naked in a beauty that draws involuntary banalities in the place of poems we cannot compose quickly enough. That vantage point was *chosen* by someone whom I, for one, dub an artist.

Artists in every field tramp through the hills, along the streams and through the canyons of that part of their life experience that rouses them to a fierce concentration. They get to know more about that area of their concern than anyone, but knowing is not enough. Telling us about it is not enough. What they know and what they have experienced has to be positioned in such a way that we can *see* as we have never seen before. Wherever you go in northwestern New Mexico, you see northwestern New Mexico, or rather you see *parts* of New Mexico. But a great lookout point gives you the illusion that you are seeing all of New Mexico or that you are looking into the very heart of that place and you are breathing faster. A good work of art lets us see. I always have thought that we weep when we really see.

Flaubert was known for his fanatical search for "*le seul mot juste,*" "the unique right word" for each expression. Could it be that half of successful choreography is the choice of *la seule métaphore juste* that will rouse the creative energy of the audience around, near and about what is at the heart of the artist's statement?

꙳

The materials of this next section may prove objectionable to some readers. The reader's discretion is advised.

꙳

How to find *le seule métaphore juste*? If you aspire to be as fanatical and precise as Flaubert, expect to work *very* slowly. If you grasp at the first one that occurs to you, don't expect too much. Choosing the metaphors that drive your work deserves substantial and careful meditation. What follows is a devious story that finally comes to the point. In the early fifties, Harold Hecht and Burt Lancaster invited me to come to Fiji to direct the dances for *His Majesty O'Keefe*, starring Lancaster. After three months, I completed my work on the film and I was on my way home. Waiting with my luggage on the veranda for the taxi to carry me to the airport, I saw Harold Hecht (the co-producer) hurrying up the steps with an awesome object in his hands, a Fiji war club. With little ceremony he thrust it at me, wishing me good luck and a safe trip. This was no tourist trinket. It was a magnificently carved club with a little brass plate reading, "TO DANIEL NAGRIN, GRATEFULLY, HAROLD HECHT, *HIS MAJESTY O'KEEFE*."

Along with the club, I had been handed a problem. There was no way that I could stuff it into my bags; to make a separate parcel would take time I did not have and then there was overseas excess baggage charge. I had no choice but to use it as a walking stick. Boarding the plane in Nandi, I was startled by the attention I received from the stewardess. All through the flight she was not far from my elbow asking whether I wanted this or that. I am not an imposing presence and generally do not attract attention in public—and this was the same flight that took me to Fiji and possibly the same stewardess.

Arriving at the magnificent Hotel Fairmont in San Francisco for an overnight layover, I was again surprised at the aggression of the chief doorman who hustled the bellman out of the way and personally took charge of my luggage. As I approached the desk, the clerk, seeing me coming, excused himself from a conversation with someone and greeted me in a way that no hotel desk clerk had ever done.

Years later, I installed the club on the mantel piece in the front of my studio. On occasion, friends I had not seen in months would drop by. More than once, I would open the door, the friend would start to say, "Daniel! How . . ." look over my shoulder, ask, "What is that?" and rather rudely walk past me to get a better look at the club, finally turning to me, "And how are you, Daniel?"

A few years later, I had to move the club for a studio performance and noticed that the brass plate was hanging by a single nail. I found a hammer and a tiny nail and set the club in my lap, *upside down,* to nail the plate back. My repair work was interrupted by my awareness of what I was looking at. The classic pattern of a Fiji war club was a straight shaft ending in a curve with a knobbed tip. At the crest of the curve was a short forked shaft. Holding the club upside down, it was startlingly apparent that I was looking at the carving of an awesome phallus with all the specific details: the knobbed head, the thick vein running underneath and the short curved shaft had been carved as a testicle. It was quite realistic but I had never seen it upside down and thus I had never seen what had been carved so carefully, *and neither had any of those people on the airplane, in the hotel lobby nor my friends visiting me in my studio.*

What is the point of this digression? Or is it a digression? The carver had chosen a specific image which is a very unsubtle metaphor for male power, but he turned it *upside down.* He gave it a flip. Anyone observing this club, felt its power and sensed that *something was going on.* It had gained a life which it did not have right side up. Not only was it apparently a skilled carving but it was interesting in a way that all of us could feel and none of us could articulate. I will not venture to guess what impact it had for Fijians who lived and died with those clubs in their hands.

The point of this story is double. When the metaphor is a specific image the work has life. And when the literal is flipped, our imagination is fired up. How do you flip? We do it all the time. In our speech, in our gestures, in our posture, in our actions we are forever expressing ourselves, saying one thing to mean another thing. In choreography, a flip can go into another century, to a different part of the body, to an animal, the list is endless.

An archeologist who had been in one of my beginner classes asked me to do a bit of choreography for the Museum of Natural History in New York City. She wanted a dance around a model of an Aztec temple. How or why I got a classically trained dancer to do it finds no place in my memory. I gave him the task of creeping into the mind of one of the priests who performed human sacrifice as a daily ritual. Then I asked him to go through the most thorough evisceration of a human heart with the conviction that this was a holy action—in slow motion. Then I asked him to do it as realistically as possible in terms of tempo and physical details. Then we set the motions to a percussion score which I had chosen. Then I said, your elbows are your hands. Do all that you did using your elbows. With no training in modern dance, this man possessing a perfect, classic, fifth position become a free-wheeling horrifying figure that seemed to step out of those harsh relief figures carved on the Aztec temples.

⌇

And now to wrap it all up with a quote from the author of *The Heidi Chronicles*, Wendy Wasserstein:

> I was once on a plane coming home from East Hampton. I was looking at a woman who looked just like Georgette Mosbacher to me. She was in a suit and her nails were done and she was sitting there with her baby and this giant ring and I was looking at her and I thought, God, our lives are so different. This woman is like a UFO to me. I have no idea what it's like to be her. . . . At the end of the plane ride she came up to me and said, "Are you Wendy Wasserstein?" I said, "Yeah." She said: "I love your work. You write about me. How did you know?"[13]

# 7 Modern Dance Choreography— Ballet Choreography

Could it be that the greatest difference between modern dance choreography and ballet choreography is that the moderns expend mountains of energy teaching and talking about choreography while the ballet people just do it? Witness this book by one from the modern fold. Has anyone since Noverre written anything about the craft of ballet choreography?

A possible explanation: by and large, ballet choreographers experience, in their bodies and in their rehearsals, the work of many different choreographers before engaging in the craft themselves. Modern dance companies are mostly homogenized, i.e., most tend to perform the repertoire of one choreographer. Thus, the dancers usually work with but a few choreographers. Another explanation is how very early modern dance found a home in the colleges and universities of America. This is not true of its development in Europe. In the academic environment, the doing of dance needed the making of dances. Ballet dancers everywhere have an international repertoire of dances available for learning and performing. The performance of modern dance classics in academe is not a frequent practice. (Too bad!) That modern dance has not only survived but grown consistently in academe is astonishing when one considers that the repertoire displayed to the university and the public at large is, in the main, by students and dance faculty. Compare this with university music departments which have world literature at their disposal—from Monteverdi to Stravinsky. The theatre department has Sophocles, Shakespeare and Miller to play with. Ballet has Petipa, Fokine, Balanchine.

This observation is not meant to demean the accomplishments of modern dance in colleges and universities, but rather to note what can only be described as their massive achievement: a repertoire created by students and faculty that commands a public—not as large as the other performing arts but it is there. In fact, there are few major American universities that do not have major dance departments. Their presence is based on the teaching of choreography, or composition, as it is more frequently called. Students, undergraduate and graduate, fill the stages with their newly acquired craft. Talented faculty stage complete evenings of stimulating and often innovating dance. Bitterly, it must be noted that not one of the Ivy League universities in America has a fully accredited and established dance department.

Wherever ballet has been incorporated into the collegiate atmosphere, it bolsters much of its program with classic works from the traditional repertoire in addition to some work by resident faculty and students. I have had the good fortune to witness at American College Dance Festivals some brilliant works by students from schools that focus on ballet.

Is choreography essentially a different matter for ballet and for modern dance? Perhaps the best place to begin to examine the question is the classroom. There is the premise that inherent in every dance technique is a philosophy. The postures we assume, the actions we take and the tasks we undertake are declarations of who and what we wish to be, where we wish to position ourselves in the world, what we can give and wish to take.

Walk into a ballet class and observe the stature and the motions. They are not much different than what Rameau, the eighteenth century composer and choreographer described as the correct way to hold the body:

> The head must be held erect without any suggestion of stiffness, the shoulders pressed well back, for this expands the chest and affords more grace to the body. The arms should hang at the sides, the hands be neither quite open nor quite closed, the waist steady, the legs straight and feet turned outward.[14]

Rameau then goes on to describe the five "absolute" positions of the feet:

> What is termed a position is nothing more than a separation or bringing together of the feet according to a fixed distance, while the body is maintained upright and in equilibrium without any appearance of constraint, whether one walks, dances or comes to a stop.[15]

This was written in the time of Louis XIV. In today's ballet classes, the same ideals prevail though the turnout is now a 180-degree straight line, the shoulders are asked to hang a bit forward rather than pinched back and the technical complexities are exponentially complicated.

Class music? Chopin reigns. There are class accompanists who improvise in a contemporary manner but they constitute a limited number. The rhythmic structure is quite obvious and the romantic melodies sweep the dancers to the "correct" downbeat. Certainly, sophisticated ballet choreographers and teachers will have none of this. They are attuned to modern composers and do not shy away from rhythmic complexity either in the music they use or in the dance phrases they teach and/or create. They stand in opposition to their early environment and training.

The modern dance class cannot be easily categorized, since by its very nature, everyone's teaching is a variant on someone else's teaching. The range of technical goals and styles taught under the rubric of "modern dance" is staggering. The "traditional" or "classic" period of modern dance had a heroic intensity, a sensual zest in the use of body weight, a constant exploration of the expressive range and power of the torso, a hyper-consciousness of the dynamic of all transitions and no fear of the grotesque, the awkward or the "unlovely." What was out there in the world, elegant or crude and gauche was not to be excluded in the studio. Today, the spectrum of modern dance technique runs from this description to classes that to the unsophisticated eye would best be described as ballet classes.

John Martin made one distinction that I believe still holds for many in dance today. For the traditional ballet dancer, the aim of motion was to arrive at an ideal position. For the modern dancer, the attention was/is on the act of reaching the position. One of the reasons that Nenette Charisse always attracted a large following of modern dancers to her ballet classes is that she *thought and spoke* like a modern dancer. Her images were all about getting there.

A consistent goal in all ballet classes is virtuosity of linear perfection, elevation, turns and toe work. Ballet men jump higher than most modern men. Compared with their beats, turns, *á terre et en l'air*, the modern men would appear to be more limited. Ballet women with their toe work, bourées and extravagant extensions similarly have a battery of moves beyond the ken of most modern women.

The matter of technique classes is introduced here because what they create is what comes into the rehearsal studios of the choreographers. There is no way that a painter's palette will not have a profound effect on his.her work. Oil paint gets significantly different results than acrylic. A choreographer facing a company of professionally trained ballet dancers cannot but be aware of the tremendous technical resources at his.her disposal. The temptation to exploit this prowess is rarely resisted, even when it might be gratuitous.

The modern choreographer might be dealing with dancers who are breathtakingly beautiful movers but are often hemmed in by the technical limitations that are endemic to most modern dancers. The tribe, as a whole, comes to dance later than professional ballet dancers. Some of our best modern dancers first find dance in the universities at the age of seventeen or eighteen while at that same age, their colleagues from the other side of the road are on the verge of becoming professionals. Be that as it may, these very limitations have charged the imaginations of modern choreographers to the extent that modern dance along with jazz are the two most original American contributions to world culture. Obviously, there are exceptions, but generally, the modern dancer is intellectually more cultivated than the ballet dancer.

Among the younger modern choreographers, there is a new virtuosity to be found. Contact improvisation created by Steve Paxton and Nancy Stark Smith has spread through the country like a brush fire. Many classes and workshops, a national publication and performances have made contact a lingua franca in the modern dance community. It was inevitable that it would enter the choreography. By now it often reaches the level of virtuosity and the inventiveness begins to rival the best efforts of ballet choreographers pushing the pas de deux to new levels. Just as the pas de deux is too often incorporated into ballet choreography inorganically, prolonged sequences of stunning contact moves are stuffed into many modern works with no relation to what transpires before or after.

At the same time, it must be noted that the lines between the two forms have been crossed and recrossed with greater intensity and frequency as the years go by. I doubt whether there is a well-trained, professional modern dancer who has not had several years of intensive ballet training. Though most university dance departments emphasize the teaching of modern dance technique, all include some classes in ballet technique. Do university dance departments that emphasize the teaching of ballet require some study of modern technique? I do not know.

To repeat the question: Is choreography essentially a different matter for ballet and for modern dance? There is no question that facing a company of ballet dancers is a radically different matter than facing a modern company. The tradition that binds the dancers is different in both cases. A common technique, spectacle, entertainment and virtuosity are the hallmarks of the traditional ballet repertoire. Probing seriousness and a constant search for new ways and new forms are what shape the modern dancers. Of course, there are many exceptions to both of these characterizations but in the main they describe the difference. Even to rebel against a tradition is to be affected by that tradition.

One element skews the ballet enough so that the fantasy that one day the two will merge or that one will be swallowed up by the other can only be called just that—a fantasy. Gender. The relations between men and women in ballet are almost always snared in the nineteenth century and the arrival of the twenty-first century will probably not change that. Men are defined as supporters, carriers and ingenious benders of the bodies of lithe women, and women are the passive clay or the delighted princesses of the pas de deux. Just as in theatre there is the obligatory scene, the pas de deux is all but a requirement for ballets. Here and there are a few changes, but the bulk of an evening at the ballet conform to this relation of the sexes. If the women are ever strong, they are bad, as in Jerome Robbins's

*Cage*, Roland Petit's *Le Jeunne Homme et La Mort* or the harlot in Balanchine's *The Prodigal Son*. Ah, la femme fatale!

Modern dance, originally so much the creation of strong women, has dealt with relations between the sexes in multiple ways that more truly reflect the complex relations found in contemporary society. Thus, between gender consciousness and virtuosity, the differences in choreography are pronounced.

There is more. Except for a few short-lived chamber ballet companies, the classic repertoire demands large companies, lavish costuming and sets. When the budget is enormous, whatever keeps the box-office busy is sacred. Money! Crowd pleasers *must* be in the repertoire. There are modern dance choreographers who are really in show business and presenting what could best be described as vaudeville. Not only are they successful but they are in the minority. The spine of the field is composed of stubborn choreographers who would bare their teeth at the suggestion that they create a "sure fire attraction." Their personal expression is their raison d'être and if the public accepts it, they are in raptures and if not, they are down but not out to discard what they have wrought.

~

The story goes that when Sam Goldwyn was reviewing the budget for "The Goldwyn Follies," he muttered in wonderment, "Choreography, George Balanchine, $10,000. Balanchine? Who is this man? Have him come to my office." When Balanchine arrived, Goldwyn asked, "Mr. Balanchine, what is this choreography?"

"It's really quite simple, Mr. Goldwyn." Balanchine picked up a tray full of pencils, "Let us say this is a line of eight girls and this ruler is another group of eight girls. The first line enters from up here and circles around to the other side of the stage. Then the second

group enters from the opposite side and circles around in the same way. Then they change sides and pause. Now, let this inkwell be the male soloist and this little vase of flowers, the female lead. They too enter from opposite sides, circle the stage and meet center stage. That is choreography!" Goldwyn, studied his desk for a bit, looked up at Balanchine and said, "I like it!"

Pressed to speak of the art of dance Martha Graham always dragged in the heart. Perhaps, in deference to his wit, brevity and genius, we should let Balanchine and his commentator have the last words.

# 8 Choreography for the Solo Dancer, Choreography for a Group

## THE PROBLEMS AND DIFFERENCES

Earlier in Chapter 5, Rules for Choreography, there appeared this "rule": "Every dance needs a 'this' and a 'that.'" Call it a conflict, a tension, an opposition, a contradiction, a seduction, whatever, unless an ambivalence of some sort is setup at the very beginning of the dance and unless it is developed throughout, the work will not be alive. It should not be too difficult to succeed in doing this when choreographing for a group, but how is it done for a solo dancer? More to the point, how can it not be done? What individual has ever crossed this great divide without experiencing inner conflicts with enveloping forces? Choreographically, it is quite common for the soloist to create an awareness of someone or something other than the visible dancer. Even the most vulgar, pelvis-snapping routine is focused dead on the "big spender" who must be won over. It is unfortunately quite possible to create a solo dance that is monochromatic, one that does not in some way bring vitality to the "that." Without the other, without the contradiction, there will be an emptiness.

This weakness is all too common in the work of students. A classic example is a solo in which the figure is experiencing a strong emotion: a great distress, a sweeping ecstasy or an unleashed fury. The dance phrases are rich and personal, the use of the music is sensitive and the sheer dancing is exciting. Despite the fine quality of the work, the questions that must be put are, "Where is the other?" "Where is the contradiction?" "Where did all of this frenzy come from?" "Where is it going?" "Doesn't it ever get exhausted?" "Does it change into its opposite?"

There is an inherent fragility in solo work. It is under great pressure to be "interesting" through every moment of its time. Its forward progression must constantly evolve, whether we are looking at a quiet, lyrical statement or a turbulent ferocity. The burden of this movement is shared equally by the choreographer and the performer. A tear in the fabric of attention, either due to choreography or performance, can easily derail the solo work. Both aspects of a solo demand a rigorous discipline: the structure must be solid and the inner life of the performance sustained throughout. An audience will always forgive a technical mishap if the performer has enough time left to recover. It will drift too far away if the choreography sags, even for a bit.

A choreography for a group can commit a multitude of "sins" and still be "successful." Dull moments can be lightened by unwarranted virtuoso displays, exploitation of voluptuous bodies, scenic effects, the latest technical devices of video, film and sound and the old standby, unison.

Unison is a choreographic device favored by many. It would be silly to apply any blanket generalization to its worth except for one: unison motion on the stage is a powerful metaphor, but of what? What are the conditions when humans move in unison? The answer is obvious: military personnel, dancers and of course, the Rockettes. Every individual in these groups has been told what to do, i.e., they are subject to the authority of another. They may smile, cheer and put forth vivacious energy but they are under orders.

But what of a standing ovation for a performance? A congregation kneeling at stated intervals in a service? A crowd's response to a ninth inning home run? Aren't they individually motivated? Every one of these and more like them are subject to the phenomenon of chaos. There is *no* unison in these conditions. Odds are every one did not go with the crowd. No two responded in exactly the same way. One choreographer, to my knowledge, recognized this—Anna Sokolow. In some of her pieces, everyone on the stage goes through the same sequence of motions but no two are alike in intensity, timing, spacings and facings.

Lovers sometimes move in sweet unison, as in walking, but rarely otherwise. Almost all acts of loving are complementary, not identical. Thus, when choreographers give dancers prolonged dancing in unison as a metaphor for love, they impose a test of credibility. Communities that have a traditional dance expect unison but usually there is allowance for an individual's style and attitude in the given moves. Hence, being precisely together is not an issue or even desirable. The individual joins in with the traditional, joyously or not, and that opens the door to an individual performance within a unison dance. For many, unison can be an ecstasy. Witness the madly intense involvement of the high school movement teams with their tough-guy moves, sprinkled with bits of hip-hop, accented with pumping, fisted gestures.

Unison is a seductive tool for choreographers. Audiences tend to love and even *admire* it. Why? They know it is not easy for a mass of people to do the same thing cleanly and accurately. They appreciate this form of virtuosity. The foundation of Radio City Music Hall rests upon the precisely calibrated high kicking of a large group of women disguised as the same person duplicated thirty-six times.

Add the fact that it is a choreographic labor-saving device to give one sequence of moves to all the dancers rather than designing differently for each dancer. We must further assume that unison dance is not a spontaneous activity, but rather a recurrence or a ritual; that all the moves have been repeated and rehearsed prior to the time we observe them. Finally, unison is too potent a metaphor to be resorted to without careful thought as to its validity and *necessity*.

⌒

In choreographing for a group of dancers, one of the central challenges is the ability to control the focal attention of the audience. If the audience does not know where to look, the key points of the work will be diffused or lost. Great choreographers and stage directors can fill a stage with masses of people and yet there is never any doubt for the viewers as to where to look. This is one problem that solo choreography does not have. With one person on the stage there is no choice.

Tamiris would reduce to stillness the dancers who were not to be the focus of a particular section when she felt that this was an action that had to be perceived by the audience. This is not an unusual device but some part of my mind always had trouble with that and especially when I was one of those who had to be stilled. I was on stage. How was I supposed to bring what is essentially a choreographer's problem to life when who and what I was didn't know there was such a thing as a choreography? It is a convenient solution to the matter of focus and yet it never fails to bother me, whether I was caught there in stillness or observing it as audience. I dare not dismiss this as unacceptable. Too many wonderful works use this device.

There are other obvious ways of catching the eye: with light, either by heightening the intensity or using the traditional spotlight; costuming with brighter colors; staging on a higher level than the other dancers; reducing the range of motion of the dancers who are to be background and giving the entire group unison activity that differs from that of the soloist(s). Using a symmetrically balanced stage and placing the key dancers center is an obvious solution but the very banality of symmetry gives the eye the liberty to roam.

A good director is an invisible follow spot. I am recalling a moment in *Paint Your Wagon*. The scene is the bar room, abuzz with action, brightly costumed women, colorful men in large hats and boots all talking, flirting and moving about. That is, all but two shabby men far over on stage right seated at a table engaged in hand wrestling. They are neither moving much nor talking. They are quite still since they are evenly matched and there is no predicting who will win the match. Voluptuous, prowling ladies notwithstanding, it mattered little what went on the rest of the stage. Until one or the other won, the eyes of the audience were glued to that far off corner of the stage.

I'll attempt a dangerous generalization: The more people that are dancing on stage, the more effective is the use of simpler steps. And in unison, there can be a prolonged repetition of a simple phrase that is highly impressive. Ask a solo dancer to repeat the same phrase the same number of times and the stage would die. The complexities allowed and even expected of a solo dancer would in most cases mess up a stage full of dancers.

The short story and the novel. The solo dance and the group dance. There is a resonance here. Every detail is of major importance for both the short story and the solo dance. The novel can sprawl, dawdle, pick up speed and dawdle. Group choreography can parallel a form like this and still work.

# 9  Abstract Dance versus What?

Is there anything more vulnerable than the defining of any art form? That is as it should be. Art, like science, is about what we don't know, only more so. Who dares define "abstract art"? A friend, a painter named Arthur Getz, once told me of the time he encountered Philip Guston, an acquaintance and also a painter. It was the time dominated by the abstract expressionists and Guston was a well-known figure among that group. Guston asked Getz, "So, what are you up to these days?" Arthur said he answered, a little defensively, "I'm doing realistic work." Guston replied, "So am I."

Whichever and whatever, let us risk a definition. Abstract art has for its subject and prime focus, the materials of the art concerned. Painting about paint is abstract art, *even if there are specific and figurative objects on the canvas plane.* Choreography primarily concerned with the configurations and energies in space and time is abstract dance *even if there is the semblance of characters involved in some sort of scenario.* This definition can be spun out to refer to all the other arts.

I have a resistance to what I have just defined as abstract art when it is applied to painting. I can be literally intoxicated by an abstract textile design, a mosaic floor pattern, some ceramics, but the same pattern within a framed canvas calls up a negative reaction. Consider it my problem.

For the major portion of this century, many of the leading theoreticians and critics of art have hailed the liberation of art from the "burden" of representation and extolled the purity of abstraction. Granted, there are many who do not follow this lead and actually argue and create in defiance of this credo of art about art. Still, the fact is that in our journals, press and universities, the formalists who sanctify abstraction have maintained a subtle and pervasive influence. It is also true that this influence is diminishing. Teaching in the modern dance, particularly in the universities is still dominated by theories that bolster abstraction. This little essay is here to help those choreographers who have been led to believe that abstract art exists on a more lofty plane despite their predilection to make art about something other than itself.

Consider the law of necessity that governs a cracked window pane. If you take, say, an automobile window that's been struck by a rock, the direction of the cracks is random only to a limited extent. The specific nature of glass cracking produces a breathtaking design. One of the most exciting things about Chinese potters is their discovery of the beauty of the glaze cracking in the furnace. There was a whole school of ceramists who produced crackled surface porcelains which are ravishingly beautiful. Is there any more consistent and formally elegant beauty than the chaos of clouds?

Take a lecturer and an audience. One talks and the others listen. One faces all the others. The necessities of the roles being played creates a design, not chaos. I recently sent a postcard which is breathtaking in its simplicity and beauty. It is a ski slope, with possibly two to three hundred skiers on the crest of a snowy slope, about to engage in a marathon. They are all standing there waiting for the starting signal. From all over the world these racers came to this spot on this day to be ready for a starting signal and there on that white slope is an exquisite design of many tiny dash marks, all ready to slip down the slopes. Haphazard? Random? Undesigned? Miró or Klee would have been proud to have created a pattern as exquisite. When I do my own work, if I am working out of the necessities of who is doing what, where, and when; a choreographic design emerges without any conscious structural choices on my part.

When the first draft of *The Six Questions: Acting Technique for Dance Performance* was completed, I sent it out for feedback to half-a-dozen dance artists whom I respected. One of them, commenting on a passage referring to the need for specific images in the creative process, wrote in the margin, "Isn't the audience capable of asking these six questions? The audience at large seems more equipped to read 'Character and motivation' than 'pure' qualities of form. If the dance is the vessel, the 'form,' then the spectator fills it." Now this is really a deft argument justifying abstraction. It is an ironic note that this was Bill T. Jones speaking, a brilliant man who is so passionately committed to an art caught up in humans thrashing about to find their locus and their dignity. And still, when confronted with an unabashed defense of the consciousness of content preceding preoccupation with form, he resisted it. This absolute ideal of purity still maintains a subtle influence.

If his argument is pursued, all the artist has to do is to create a "pure" form and let the audience fill it out as they will. Both Cunningham and Nikolai relied on this for the unsophisticated elements of their audience and on their sophisticated critics to appreciate the abstract qualities. Everybody's happy and no one is responsible for saying anything. I am indeed grateful that Bill T., in spite of this comment, has been responsible for the daring, provocative and stunning expressions that distinguish his works and contradict his remark.

One of my better students at Arizona State University, in preparing her written document in defense of her Master of Fine Arts thesis choreography wrote what, for her, was a very clear path through the contradictions of form and content:

> To begin, I discover a thought, an idea which creates a content, a very basic content (an outline). I then separate the evident fundamentals that spark emotion and the ones that stick out the most from the material that surrounds them. This opens new perspectives. This beginning process only refers to the piece choreographically, not the performance quality; that comes later.
>
> Form now dominates as content is put on the back burner (being kept in mind). Form sets the order and materializes the movement.
>
> Once form has taken shape, I then refer back to content to combine the idea and movement into a performance quality: a character, a feeling, an emotion, the expression.
>
> My choreographic process requires both form and content which feed off of each other in rotation. I think that they are separate in the process, yet together in the final product. Content, however, remains the constant throughout even though its importance is set aside while form plays its role to construct.

Cynthia Dufault, April 15, 1992

Actually, the work she produced was quite strong, and yet I must fault her logic, while pointing out that it is *all too common*. Get a good idea and then create an attractive shell that is generated out of external necessities. That done, stuff the internal life into the magnificent form of great dancing. Her last paragraph is a miracle of contradictions and wanting to have it both ways: " . . .form and content . . . feed off each other . . . (but) they are separate in process . . .Content . . . remains the constant throughout . . . (but) is set aside while form plays its role . . ."

This is the price of a generation that was trained to produce abstract, formalistic dance and yet desperately needs to speak to the ridiculous madness, the confusion and the pain that weaves through our times. Recently, one of the brighter stars of the younger contemporary choreographers confused a New York critic. He had produced a work of enormous complexity that failed utterly, according to the critic. A few weeks later, the identical work was presented in another venue but some sort of disaster had befallen the sets and costumes. Nonetheless, *it was performed in practice clothes*. The reviewer was astonished at how fine the choreography appeared in this bare version. How I wish I had seen both performances. At this distance, reading between the lines, I am assuming that the choreographer took the approach of Ms. Dufault. He had an idea that required such and such set of costumes and sets and then carved out some magnificent dancing that grew out of its own separate logic. He placed a fascinating hat on top of a fascinating dance. Together, they created a disaster.

One day, before a small group of talented graduate students of dance, I put on a little show. "Choreography is a snap! Watch!" The studio had a performing area which at the time was lit. I walked into the heat of the light, stood very still for a bit and then from the feeling of the moment—and the awareness of their eyes, I began to move—to dance. With no effort at all, movement poured out for about three or four minutes until I stopped. "Of course, the problem here would be to remember the moves, but then I could have rigged a video camera and I would have it. There's really nothing to it." I did not have an idea in my head other than letting one movement follow another on the impulses of the moment. Did that dance have content or was it an abstract dance? We are playing with imponderables. Nothing here can deliver a firm answer, only more questions.

A talented student deserted the graduate program in dance at Arizona State University for another program that was spear-headed by a teacher who had evolved a concept of human existence and dance creation based on a few basic emotions. I hated losing this man from our program and tried to get him to reconsider:

> April 22, 1986
> Dear Chris,
>
> The irony of all your theorizing is that the strongest dance that has come from you is built from specifics and very often from barely metamorphosed literal gestures and signs. It matters not that in the conceiving of the movement your image may not have been clear, precise or even conscious. When the heat rolled you followed it. Clarity and definition can come later or even never if it works and flows. Though the danger is that if you never pause to back up and clarify, when the not improbable moment comes that what flowed hot is caught in a frozen stalemate, you will be left with no resources to breath life back into the movement, phrase or dance.
>
> Chris, the trouble with the generic, with the general, with the so-called three basic emotions is that to realize them is a probable path to the conventional, the cliché and to previously learned dance movement. While to realize a specific image, a specific act, a specific persona, a specific locus, a specific context through metaphoric leaps that illuminate your vision for you and for us, is to arrive at unexpected movement and a truly personal dance vocabulary. Each new dance can contain innovative movement *without even making the effort to be different or inventive.*
>
> From what I have seen of your work to date, this is what appears to me be the case with you, particularly in your solos. William James, the psychologist, says exactly what Stanislavski says. The action produces the emotion. Stanislavski says, never work for

or from the emotion; only work from the specific action and the emotion will follow. Who you are; what you are doing; to whom and in what context are the questions to be answered by the performer and/or the choreographer with the additional task to work from the place of the illuminating metaphor.

But you've heard all of this and you don't believe it. I say it because perhaps you will hear it one day. I think at this point in your life you need more answers than questions. So be it. Where I work from, indeterminacy and uncertainty prevail and answers are few.

He returned the next semester.

Now, to attempt to tie up a slippery mass of terms and contradictions. Throughout this discussion, there was no problem in using the word "abstraction." The hesitations occurred when seeking an equally suitable term for its opposite. "Realistic"? No. "Expressionistic"? No. "Humanistic"? No, for each of these covers too narrow a field. "Naturalistic"? This comes a little closer to covering much of the ground of the first three terms, but it is one rarely used in the discussion of art, for it would appear to be limited to "nature" and all of the ambiguities covered by that word. Rather than attempt the task of finding a single word, one could speak of "art with content," but that gets us into more trouble. Dare one say that there is no content in *any* of the works of Merce Cunningham, Lucinda Childs, George Balanchine or Trisha Brown, *no matter how "abstract" they appear?*

Early in Chapter 3, Choreography and the Specific Image: The Fundamentals of One Approach to Choreography, the following appears:

Upon analysis, *every* dance work can be examined in the light of The Six Questions:

THE SIX QUESTIONS:

1. Who? or What?
2. is doing what?
    action analysis:
        a. the spine
        b. the beats
        c. the subtext
3. to whom? or to what?
4. where/when?
5. to what end?
6. engaging what obstacle?

Though the terminology of The Six Questions is taken from the theatre and is most obviously and vividly applied to dramatic forms, *there is no reason that it cannot be applied to abstract dance.* If we are looking at X number of movements linked by the chance throws of the I Ching sticks, *that is what we are looking at.* That is its content. The dancers are doing something to the space, each other and themselves at a place and time, with their own clear reasons within the tensions of an independent sound score and an audience of enthusiasts, doubters and haters. Most probably, Mr. Cunningham never consciously formulated what he was doing in terms of The Six Questions but I believe they are alive in the folds of the work. Seen in this fashion, one cannot say that an abstract work does not have content. In its own fashion and focus it is as realistic as Philip Guston quipped and it is a meaningful expression for Mr. Cunningham. "Naturalistic"? If it is grasses and trees that we mean, we are caught in a confined corner of our existence. What can be excluded from "nature"? Parking lots? Humans create them, but they also create gardens and dances. The definitions and compartments of meaning begin to dissolve upon close examination and what we are left with is our prejudices and preferences. At the beginning of this chapter I offered my "definition" of abstract art and declared my bias and this is all it is. A bias. Did we need this discussion? Most definitely, for the reason that I believe that what is offered in this book can be used by anyone who is or will be making dances and should not be too easily dismissed as a way that must be confined to one particular style of dance. When there is trouble and when there is a block, The Six Questions can clarify and set up the priorities to move the work forward.

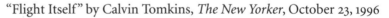

Although his work inspired several generations of abstract artists, Brancusi denied that he had ever tried to make a pure or abstract form. He once said, "Those who speak of abstraction when contemplating my sculpture are completely off the track and prove that they have understood nothing. For what my work is aiming at is, above all, realism; I pursue the inner, hidden reality, the very essence of objects in their own intrinsic fundamental nature; this is my deep preoccupation."

"Flight Itself" by Calvin Tomkins, *The New Yorker*, October 23, 1996

# 10 Music

There are as many ways of using music, sound and silence as there are choreographers. What follows are a set of personal observations, reflections and principles that have guided my work and my teaching. If any appear to be useful, fine and if not, fine.

In Chapter 4, Improvisation, reference is made to the aborted attempt to use the music of Roger Sessions for *Dance in the Sun*. A few weeks of working with it ended in frustration. The constant and intricate metrical shifts were taking all of my mental energy and I realized that the dynamic structure taking shape in my mind had little relationship to Session's *Sonata*. Much as I was attracted to the astringent power of the music, I decided not to use it. I continued choreographing the dance without music, all the while ransacking the scores of contemporary composers. I even had a miraculous session with the late and exquisite concert pianist, William Masselos. At Nola Studios on Broadway, he played Copeland, Griffiths and Ives for me. Wonderful scores and a wonderful afternoon but nothing seemed right. In time, the dance was finished and only then did I find a composer, Ralph Gilbert.[16]

Presenting Ralph with a finished work obviously meant that he had to compose within the precise rhythmic framework of what I had created. That he did and brilliantly but I never found the freedom and flow that I experienced dancing the piece in silence. Why? Was it the initial experience of working with the Sessions score that subtly nudged me into uneven phrases that were ironed out by Gilbert's music? Or, was it that lovely as his music was, it might have had more fire if he had had the freedom to proceed with the idea for the dance on his own without trying to match a finished dance? It was a good score but I never again created a dance before I had the music.

A few years later I discovered a process that served both the composer and me. *Indeter-*

*minate Figure* was a complex collage of music and sounds. I created, bought and edited the sound effects. The five musical segments and the introduction were composed by Robert Starer. Before anything, I did a rough study for each section. When Starer would arrive at the studio, I would hand him my treasured Heuer stopwatch, get out on the floor and using the study as a core of an improvisation, I would dance what I felt was the length of time I needed. Starer would time what I did. I would never say, "This should be in a fast 4/4," or, "This should be a tango," because I thought it was possible that he might feel a tango underlying what I thought was a 4/4. I never suggested what the music should be, I only let him witness the improvisation and told him what was the inner action that drove the movement. Thus all he had from me was the approximate time of the section, what I was doing/feeling and the freedom of his own imagination. He received not a single musical request nor instruction from me. (A minor correction. When I improvise in silence, as I was for Starer, it is difficult for me to avoid making sounds: grunts, breath explosions, bits of scat expressions, etc. Did these influence him? I don't know.)

I would do no further work on what I showed him until he would return to play a piano version of his music. I never just listened to it. Rather, I improvised using the original study as its nucleus. I wanted my body in motion to hear the music, not my head, which I feared would be weighted with inevitable preconceptions of what I might think was right. If I felt this was the music, fine. If it just didn't interact with the texture and intention of that section, I would of course speak up, asking for more of this and less of that or something radically different. It was up to him to accept or argue for its validity. If we agreed that he needed to do more work that's what he did. If I felt he had brought what I could use, he would record it, leaving me to my job of choreographing.

Times were when the new music would present no problems. Other times, the tempo would be off, or the music too long, or the dynamics inadequate to the intensity of the moment. At the next meeting with Starer, I would voice my reaction to the music. We worked so well that there never were any serious disagreements. A skillful composer and a flexible person, he made adjustments. If at any time, he felt quite strongly that something had to remain just as he had written it, I would accede to his need. Part of my logic, regarding this deference to the composer is that his.her name will be attached to the music just as mine will be to the choreography. Ultimately, whatever is danced on that stage is my responsibility for good or for ill. I never felt I could deprive a composer of that particular right, that he.she could accept full responsibility for every note heard.

I have no idea how widespread this process is, but I think it has many virtues, principally, that though the composer is given some parameters regarding length, structure and the inner life of the work he.she has the freedom to bring all of that to life according to his.her own artistic vision. I'm sure that some composers have written wonderful music after being presented with a complete bar-for-bar scheme. My preference is for this more open-ended way.

For those who find this of interest and possible use, here is an outline of what we can call An Open-Ended Composer/Dancer Collaboration:

- The dancer makes a study for each intended section.
- The dancer relates to the composer the intention and internal life of each section while avoiding any musical suggestions.
- The dancer improvises for the composer the approximate length and quality of the section while the composer times from the dancer's cue of "Go" to the dancer calling out, "Cut."
- The composer writes his.her understanding of the music needed. The dancer waits upon the score.
- The composer plays the new section as the dancer improvises.
- The composer and dancer discuss how well the music works. If there are problems the composer deals with them until both dancer and composer agree.
- The dancer choreographs that section. If, in the course of this, problems arise, the dancer and the composer confer to arrive at a mutually acceptable musical solution.

Choosing music out of the vast library of world music that is available is no simple matter. For all of that wealth, there are pitfalls along the way. The first safeguard is an in-depth knowledge of this music literature. Find every opportunity to listen and take notes on everything that attracts you. It is the easiest of all the arts to absorb from the radio, concerts and the incredible variety of recorded material that is accessible. Not enough money to build an extensive personal library of recordings? Spend time in a music library. Discover what moves you and then buy.

Time. Too much of what we do struggles under the pressure of time. From students to professional choreographers, deadlines force quick decisions. The perfect score is not found? Either of two solutions: commence choreographing without a score or seize upon something that is almost right. In either case, the anticipation is that the "right" score will be found in time. This ploy contains a hazard which traps not only students of choreography but professionals. Sooner or later, people following this path find the "right" music. Whether the dance was finished without music or with the less than satisfactory score, a monumental problem lies ahead, for in either case, the odds of the found music "fitting" is slim and compromises are made all down the line. This leads to what I call Parallelism. The found score seems so "right" for the choreography—even though its metric structure and rhythmic flow are not "quite right" or its climaxes are out of phase with the dance. Still, they are satisfied to go ahead if the overall impact and atmosphere of the music is "right" for the dance. It does not seem to matter where in the music a phrase of movement falls, as long as it times out. The choreographer lets the music have its life and flow and the dance keeps to its course with landmarks along the way that tell the dancer that he.she is a bit ahead or a bit behind a clear musical mark and accordingly, there is a slow-down or a speed-up. Some dancers have become quite skillful with this technique and with sufficient rehearsal and a talent for timing, they have no problem performing in this manner with considerable authority.

This almost relationship of movement to music, the ignoring of the music pulse, the out-of-phase climaxes, all tend to drain the movements of their vitality and either make the music barely sensed wallpaper or the opposite, draw attention to the music as the separate entity it in fact is. It is a weak solution. It is a process that also happens when the choreographer chooses a piece of music whose rhythmic structure eludes the understanding of the choreographer and/or the dancers. This is the case with some contemporary music: thrilling to hear, fiendishly difficult to analyze and hobbling to many dancers. Here too, organic interaction with the particulars of the music is foregone in favor of Parallelism.

⌒

Music and dance, how close should they be, rhythmically and dynamically? There is no correct answer to this one. Every answer is a function of the taste and the philosophy of the artist. Until we get to Balanchine, much of ballet choreography followed the swells and ebbs of the music and mimicked its rhythms. Isadora Duncan spoke of music visualization which is essentially a similar approach. Denis-Shawn's movements hewed close to what was heard. Conversely, all of the modern dance founders, in their prideful assertion of the preeminence of movement, sought a dynamic relationship wherein going with the music and going against it were equal options that were continuously exploited. The composers that attracted them used odd rhythms, change of meter, discordant harmonies and untraditional instrumentation.

When the modern dancers did use traditional music, from Renaissance to Bach to romantic, it was, and for many, still is unthinkable to "mickey-mouse" the music. For those unfamiliar with the term, "to mickey-mouse" means every movement follows every dynamic, rhythmic and melodic shape of the music. The phrase comes from the film industry that learned very quickly that unless the dynamics of the music corresponded with the dynamics of the filmed motions there was a serious loss of vitality. The cartoons exploit that principle to the hilt and so did Fred Astaire. Modern dancers asserted another excitement by juxtaposing their movement rhythms against those of the music. A violent passage might occur during a quiet movement phrase. The rhythms of the dancers could counterpoint those of the music and when appropriate, music and dance would mesh in unison. In the rush for popularity, any number of contemporary choreographers are returning to the charm of music and dance, "doing it together." For them, a strong accent in the orchestra demands a strong accent on stage. Who is right? What is your taste? What is your necessity? I know what mine is, but that is irrelevant here.

~

What to do about scores of great excitement and dazzling complexity? They simultaneously attract and repel. Improvising to them is irresistible. Choreographing to them can be a nightmare. Coping with intricate rhythmic structures can distract from spontaneity. Though the choreographer might be highly skilled musically, it is rare that all the dancers share that ability. Throughout my early choreography, I avoided using music with difficult rhythmic complexity. In that time, I had to know precisely where every movement fell in the context of the score. This arose out of my fear that I was not really musical. Ironically, years later, when I began teaching my solos, I learned that rhythmically, they were considerably more complicated than what most dancers had experienced.

A change took place when I began to work alone in 1964. In the course of choreographing a suite of six dances, *Spring '65*, I fell in love with two pieces of music. One was the second movement of Charles Ives's *Piano Sonata No. 1* recorded by William Masselos. The other was a score I commissioned Cecil Taylor to write for me. Both are devilishly difficult. In the past, pressured to know the correspondence of each movement to each note, I usually resorted to counting. For much of the Ives and Taylor, counting what I heard would have become the central focus of the work: a certain way of destroying the dance. My improvisations to both were abundant fountains of dance phrases. At first, shifting from improvisation to repeatable moves seemed an impossible task but my emotional involvement with both scores held me to the work. Gradually, I found a method which has served me since. The simplest image for this is a boy taking a shortcut home across a stream littered with boulders. Leaping here and there, he crosses safely. Rarely does he step on the same sequence of stones. Never does he lose awareness of all that lies in his path. He never gets wet.

Dancing this way, I no longer would take myself to task if a move did not fall exactly upon a preset note. It sufficed that I knew where the note was, choosing to punctuate it or slipping a bit to the front or the back of it or leaping over it. In a sense, I was constantly interacting more intimately with the music than I ever did when counted precision prevailed. This method worked for me in my solos. It does not work choreographing for another or for a group when the precise coordination of several dancers is a necessity.

~

A side note on the music of Ludwig van Beethoven: Is it not remarkable that his music is rarely heard in the dance theatre? No, it is not remarkable. One of the most magnificent gifts I ever received was the complete set of Artur Schnabel's recordings of the thirty-two piano sonatas. I was just beginning to assemble my solo program. Here was one of the glories of Western music. Improvising to search out which I would use for a dance, I learned very quickly that there was no room for me in that music. Every time I launched into an improvisation, I found myself crowded out. It was as if Beethoven was not only creating music but to my ears and body, he was also dancing. I have witnessed a few attempts to use this music and viewed them as weakened for that very reason. He is the dancer and needs help from no one.

Sophie Maslow used part of the *Pastoral Symphony* for a massive group dance in Madison Square Garden. Being in it felt good. I have no idea how it came off to the audience. Years later, I used *Piano Sonata No. 13 in E Flat Major, Opus 27, No. 1,* in an evening long work called *Ruminations.* Complaining that I was so limited in time, touring and doing New York performances, I asked the forbearance of the audience if I took a little time out to choreograph a piece for the next season.

Actually, I was quite in love with this particular sonata. It had an elegant lyric line with wonderful contrasts and was not at all as long or as densely scored as the others. It was one of my most deeply involved stage experiences. I really got work done, *in performance!* By the end of the New York run, I had choreographed about seven or eight minutes of a twelve minute piece. The next season, I did go into the studio with the firm anticipation that finally, I would choreograph a Beethoven work. I couldn't move one bar further than what had been accomplished on stage the year before. So much for Beethoven. I look forward to being proved wrong.

~

I have always been in awe of dancers and choreographers who have had a solid musical training. I imagine they do not have to resort to my ingenuities. Among them are those who insist that they never count. More power to them. A few of these flaunt their skill in such a way that the "counters" are made to feel seriously lacking. When I have taught either technique or my choreography, I will ask the dancer(s), "How do you grasp the music best, by counting or by not counting? Either way is fine and neither way will ensure that you are a wonderful dancer."

~

Silence is a potent presence when the choreographer is continuously alive to the rhythmic life within his.her choreography. To create movement after movement without an awareness of a musical flow that unites the work is to ignore the musical flow that is inherent in life. If you are doing choreographic work without music, you might gain strength if you create an internal score and/or rhythm. There is in the Workbook a section called The Rhythm Series that can help one delve deeply into this matter. (See Workbook 2.)

↩

No discussion of music and dance is complete without referring to the audacity of Merce Cunningham. As is common knowledge, his scores are commissioned independently of the dance. His choreography is conceived and created without reference to them. I would assume that many times there are counts which help the dancers coordinate their movements when they are supposed to be coordinated. The dancers never hear the score until dress rehearsal. Some portion of every audience finds this intolerable, particularly since most of his music collaborators not only shun any hint of melody but fearlessly exploit the full range of electronic sounds, pretty or not. Cunningham says his dance and their music coexist as do most things in life. Who shall gainsay him? For most of his audience, (and for myself), it works in the context of his aesthetic and philosophy. I am not aware of any or many choreographers who have adopted this as their way.

↩

A while back, I saw a three hour film of American Ballet theatre, practicing, traveling and performing. One segment showed Kenneth MacMillan directing four women in a unison activity. His criticisms were detailed and specific. He ran them through a short phrase at least half-a-dozen times, giving corrections each time. For all of that precise care, he never said a word to the one woman who was consistently behind the beat. All her moves were correct and late.

In the *New York Times* of July 20, 1995, Edward Rothstein reviewed the work of a twelve-year-old pianist, Helen Huang:

> The playing in the concerto was evidence of properly learned lessons . . . Ms. Huang knew how to breathe with Mozart's explicitly marked phrases, but she did not attend to the other layers of breath in this music, to the ways in which small phrases are nested within larger ones, or the ways in which ordinary scales and arpeggios create *suspense and anticipation.* In the final movement, the rhythms should have danced with relaxed freedom, in the second movement, there was too little sense of melodic tension. [Emphasis added.]

Again in the *New York Times*, Anthony Tommasini wrote in the July 16, 1995 issue a review of the pianist Alan Feinberg, a classically trained pianist whose CD, *Fascinatin' Rhythm*, focused on classical composers writing jazz-inspired music and some pianistically superb jazz compositions.

Mr. Feinberg's rendition of (Fats) Waller's "Ain't Misbehavin'" . . . is graceful and impressive for the clarity and control of inner voices. Yet it don't mean a thing if it ain't got that swing, as another song goes, and it sounds too practiced. Mr. Feinberg plays Duke Ellington's soulful "Solitude" in Mark Tucker's impressively accurate transcription, and the performance sounds too impressively accurate. Though Mr. Feinberg gets more of the notes in the cascading riffs that Ellington ever did, Ellington's playing had an organic flow that you can't learn by practicing.

Not quite true. The problems of both musicians and the fourth dancer in MacMillan's group can be mastered—*if they become conscious of the problem*. It would appear that this discussion is veering away from the area of choreography to the problem of performance. There is an overlap, but any number of choreographic statements can be blunted if the choreographer is not aware of what is a most subtle but potent factor in the musical phrasing of dance movement.

All musical notation is only an indication. In the playing by an artist, the beat is not an absolute. The "organic flow" mentioned above by Tommasini is a function of a barely perceptible anticipation of the beat, or the dragging of the beat or coming clean down on the heart of the beat. If their critics are correct, Ms. Huang and Mr. Feinberg are being "good," too good. They were playing what they read accurately instead of assuming the artist's prerogative of driving the beat, dragging it or landing clean into its center.

Working "before, after or on the beat" can create an endless list of different metaphors. The list is limited only by the imagination. Anticipating the beat by a hair can evoke an overflow of abundant energy; the music seems to spring out of the dancer's body; there is a frenetic nervousness; aggression is the motive; the dancer is challenging the musician to play faster. It could be the action of a Broadway show-biz kid trying to attract attention. Ahead of the beat is a very good Broadway characterization. They're fast and usually ahead of the beat.

Pulling the beat by coming in a hair late can give the sense that the dancer is being carried along by the force of the music; it can communicate a sensual longing, a loss of energy, an uncertainty, a withdrawal. Romantic movement is often behind the beat.

On the beat can be anything from a disciplined regimentation to a triumphant coming together of many forces. Is it because you and the music are one? A flamenco dancer, a guitarist and a *cante hondo* singer can create a roaring whitewater of tangled sound and unexpectedly line up in a unison climax that will lift you out of your chair. Don't even try to spell out the metaphor of that one.

I rarely have ever heard a teacher of dance technique or a choreographer make an issue of "before, after or on," and yet, any one of the three can radically change the intent and quality of the same phrase of dance movement. For the choreographer, a hyper consciousness of this factor in movement will illuminate his.her intentions. If and when the choreographer is clear that a phrase, a section or a dance is essentially active or passive, this relationship to the pulse of the music will be clear and expressive. Lacking this awareness and/or not actively exploiting the powers of rhythmic flexibility may flatten the contours of the choreography. "Before, after and on the beat" is the best kept secret of musicality. (See Before, After and On in Workbook 8.)

⌣

Live music? Recorded music? Electronic music? Who is to say? Erick Hawkins used live music for his performances and he believed that anyone who did not, betrayed the art of dance. Ideologies and theories that set up hard walls limiting the forms of expression carry that aura of authority and control which most of us hope will vanish.

Arguments: Not everyone can afford live music. Recorded music has preserved some of the most exquisite musicianship anywhere. Esoteric and exotic music present challenges that have inspired dancers. Some collage and electronic music can be performed live but much of it defies performance because of its complexity.

My first solo concert had the glory of one of the most gifted dance accompanists, the late Sylvia Marshall. I shall always be grateful to her for the freedom and strength I gained from her as she played and I would tear through *Spanish Dance*. In that same program, I performed *Indeterminate Figure*. It would take several pages of this text to make a complete list of all that went into it: water drips, the glorious voice of Jan DeGaetani, the floor boards of my West 73rd Street studio creaking, a wicked tango by Robert Starer, a razor-voiced operator telling the time, an explosion that could be *the* explosion and many more all assembled on tape. Sylvia toured with me in my first year. The expense was considerable. My income was floating on a few residuals from TV commercials. Preparing for the second season, Sylvia and I went into Robert Blake's Carnegie Hall studio and she recorded my entire repertoire that used solo piano. To this day, there is audible the short "frrrup" of a page turn in *Dance in the Sun*. Her recordings traveled with me all over the nation, Europe and the Pacific. I have no apologies.

In Chicago, a couple of men came backstage after a performance, appearing to be quite excited by my *Jazz: Three Ways*, but after a bit of talk, I realized they were more curious about the music. They were jazz musicians and, coming to the point, they wanted to know "Who was that incredible, funky pianist?" I used piano scores by Count Basie, Jimmy Yancey and Nat "King" Cole. Sylvia, a classically trained pianist, had listened to their recordings and learned from them how to swing. Would I have preferred touring with Sylvia? Undoubtedly. Would it have impoverished me? Undoubtedly.

⌣

Among my teaching notes, I found this: "I felt you were dancing to the rhythm of the music instead of to your own rhythm." Again, we are dealing with an overlap of the concerns of performance and choreography. In the sensibility that shaped the modern dance and contemporary dance, the life that flows *back and forth* between the dance movement and the music is dependent upon a vibrant inner life of the dance. That rhythm interacts with the music exactly as do lovers, friends and enemies.

# 11 Words and Song Lyrics

Over the years, I accumulated comments in my class notebooks when dancers used words with dance:

Before using words, ask the question, "Could I do this without the use of words? Would my vision be blocked, obscured, muddied without the use of words?" Yes? You must use words.

When you use words in a score or music, set up a relationship so the words and movement resonate, but do not copy each other. Why dance when the words say it all? Find the movement that the words don't say.

Notes on one who spoke as she danced:

When dancers adapt the style of synchronizing words with their motions, that is, fitting emphatic words right in and on the beat with emphatic gestures *that mean the same thing*, there is a serious weakness. Not so here. She handled very well what too many speaking dancers fail at: the timing of words and action. Her words slipped in and out of the dance with a music all their own, yet counterpointed the physical rhythms. When they did coincide, it was startling. In ordinary human communication, synchronicity is the convention. On stage, it is gratuitous. Synchronicity of gesture and words becomes illustration. It is no different than the TV advertisements for the marvelous set of knives. The printing on the screen roars "Only $19.95!" and the voice-over exults, "Only $19.95!"

Words and motion should have the same relation as the sophisticated relationship of movement and music, complementing and counterpointing each other so that each enriches, highlights or even contradicts the other and only rarely and strategically concur. What is stated here is both a performance and a choreographic problem.

The iteration of the above notes is an indication that this fault is omnipresent and not only in student work. There is only one reason for a choreographer ever to use words and/or song lyrics: the words and/or the song lyrics say what cannot be said in dance. If this rule is accepted, then certain corollaries flow from that: a movement cannot duplicate the meaning of a word and a movement cannot illustrate a word or phrase. It can juxtapose a movement metaphor that exists in tension with the word or phase. The temptation to contradict these rules is great, for it rises out of the reality of human communication. When the father sternly admonishes the child, his forefinger rears upward as he says, "Now . . ." then it beats down in the direction of the guilty one three times, ". . . you behave yourself!" One beat for each word. The words, the vocal music and the finger are metaphors for a threatened stick for the guilty.

Humans, the world over, use their hands and bodies concurrently with the varying emphases of their verbal statements. Of course, the intensity, range and specific motions differ with each culture, from great restraint to vividly exuberant. But the unifying timing of speech and gesture is universal. The thumb and forefinger make a circle and the hand makes a short forward thrust and stops precisely on the downbeat of the "p" in "Perfect!" To carry this practice over into dance will only diminish the potency of the movement metaphor and give the dance a naive mode of expression.

In contrast, pervasive interaction, counterpoint and reflection make for a dynamic that is compelling and challenging to the choreographer and to the audience. Just as with music, spoken accentuation and movement emphasis *selectively coming together at carefully chosen moments can have great power.*

Linear logic in the evolving of dance movement is a trap that is discussed in Chapter 6, The Play of Metaphor. Still, regarding words used in dance, a logical flow cannot be dismissed out of hand. Song lyrics often have a logical flow, while poetry tends to more disjointed connections. The choreographer must be clear about what thoughts must be communicated with clarity and what is intended only to be felt.

Some choreographers, intoxicated by the moving beauty of a particular song or singer, will seize upon it as an ideal score for a dance. They will bathe in the rise and fall of the melody, discover movements that are energized by the pulse and flow of the music and not pay the slightest attention to the lyrics. Instead, they will pour out the most gorgeous movement of which they are capable. A good splash of virtuoso activity adds excitement to the choreography. This is the opposite weakness of those who might be illustrating the text of the words. What can one say to one who ignores the content of a song only to exploit it for the glories of her.his technique?

There is a technical problem in the use of words spoken by a performing dancer: getting out of breath. The audience comes demanding something superhuman of us. Struggling to speak and gasping for air introduces an element of performer fallibility *that is of no interest to the viewers.* The matter is compounded by the fact that during rehearsal, it is not possible to know where or when a dancer will build up a significant oxygen debt. Speaking from personal experience, which I am fairly sure is shared with most dancers, in the early stages of rehearsing and performing a new work, I would often find it rough going two-thirds or three-quarters of the way through a dance. After a bit, this would disappear. Why? Unfamiliarity is exhausting. As soon as the sequence and energy flow of a dance become really known, the heavy breathing becomes a thing of the past. Thus, it is quite possible that where a verbal expression is initially near-impossible, in time, it may present no problem at all.

For the choreographer there is the responsibility to have all verbal expressions heard and understood clearly in all parts of the house. If the dancers are the speakers and have less than the professional skill required, they should receive training and coaching in vocal projection. If the text is to be recorded, the conditions of recordings must be professional in quality. Next to the piano, the human voice presents one of the most difficult recording problems.

I have used words intermittently throughout my career, but overwhelmingly in 1968 in *The Peloponnesian War.* That was an evening-length work that had a continual flow of taped words from the moment the audience entered the theatre to just before the end, a span of almost two hours. The talk even continued through the intermission. It was the text of *The Peloponnesian War* read by Frank Langella. If the house was opened at 7:30 PM, the tape carrying his voice was activated at 7:29 PM. It took up the text by Thucydides towards the end of the history and ran without a stop right into the dimming of the house lights to black. As people entered the theatre and took their seats, a subtle war would ensue. Some were fascinated by the text (one of the great historical accounts), not wishing to miss a word. Others, plainly irritated and finding it uninteresting or not be able to follow it, would begin to talk loudly enough to be heard by their companions. Sitting in the dressing room, I would hear louder talking coming from the house than I had ever heard from backstage.

When the theatre went to black at 8:00 PM, audience talk would cease as the reading continued for two and a half minutes, bringing the book to a close by recounting the devastating defeat of the Athenians by the Spartans. Still in darkness, this was followed by thirty seconds of silence. I have been told by members of the audience that that was the longest thirty seconds they had ever experienced in the theatre. The silence was finally broken by the voice of Langella: "*The Peloponnesian War* by Thucydides the Athenian, Book 1, Chapter 1. . ." continuing on for another two and half minutes in the blackout, during which time the audience remained silent and listened to a description of how the war started. Then the stage lights came on and I entered. In time, there was music and in time I began to dance. At times the voice was drowned out by the music and at times both were audible. At no time was there any attempt to match the stage action or the music with the text.

What did the audience see? Fifteen dances, each of which in one way or another indirectly referred to the time that all of us were going through in the late sixties. Sometimes the words had an uncanny reference to the stage action and much of the time they had none except that they were all about thirty years of war that took place almost 2400 years ago. There was no question that what *The Peloponnesian War* delivered was overload. In New York, people would come to see it three and four times.

Why did I do it? When I read the book many years before, I often came close to weeping over the pathetic silliness of this havoc that ultimately helped bring the amazing civilization of Greece to its ruin. More, the parallels with that far-off time and of the concurrent Cold War were chillingly close. All I did was juxtapose us to them, the Athenians and the Spartans. It was a rare performance that did not drive some out of the theatre. Those that stayed gave me as warm a response as I ever had. I doubt if it ever made clear sense to anyone who witnessed the evening. Why should it? The entire madness of our time made little sense to me, so *The Peloponnesian War* could make no sense, except for all of us to know that we were witnessing a global stupidity and that we wished we could do something about it. There was no way I, personally, could make this statement without the words of Thucydides. Thus, I danced in an ocean of words.

# 12 Virtuosity

A disappointment: I just looked up "bravo," expecting to find that it meant "brave." No, it derives from the language of Italy and means "fine." How much more appropriate it would be if I had been right, for true virtuosity calls on the courage of a performer. What cannot be denied is that regardless of whether it is relevant or irrelevant, in good taste or really quite vulgar, virtuosity is just plain exciting. Regardless of context, virtuosity is, in and of itself, a metaphor for human daring. We are thinking, "That's one of us up there," as we tilt our heads back to breathlessly observe Philippe Petit stroll across a wire stretched high between buildings with no net and nothing but a long pole to keep him company. The circus is frankly and simply dedicated to virtuosity. It makes no pretensions beyond that, though of recent, Cirque du Soleil and its imitators have been challenging that simplicity. They are on the verge of saying more than the demonstration of apparently impossible stunts.

On the concert stage, it is distressing when banal and/or shallow content is filled out with staggering tricks of dance. There are dance companies who inflate what little they have to say with near-impossible physical accomplishments and yet they find space on many of the major concert stages. As indicated in Chapter 7, Modern Dance Choreography—Ballet Choreography, for a variety of reasons, most modern dancers are not preeminently virtuosic. And yet two of its major artists, each in her own way, gave a simple and powerful prescription for *acquiring virtuosity within the context of modern technique*. Helen Tamiris constantly held forward a rule, "Follow through!" Anna Sokolow was even more concise. To innumerable students, she threw out the puzzling command, "More!" As I read them, if a soloist or a choreographer finds a powerful impulse, the proper exploration of its potential is not to check it within the bounds of good taste or caution. Finding out what would happen if . . .! Is there risk involved? Of course there is. But there is crazy, foolish risk and there is the calculated risk that a canny, skilled dancer will take.

By canny, I mean wearing knee pads, elbow pads, a liberal use of body padding, floor mats, approaching the tiger of danger with all senses alert but never losing connection with the initial impulse and the presence of a "spotter," a skilled person who stands by ready to break a dangerous fall when an iffy maneuver is being attempted. It also makes sense, in performance, to wear any kind of protection that can be concealed gracefully in a costume. This I did whenever I wore pants for a dance that demanded weight on the knees. It is good to note that any number of recent choreographies defy convention and wear highly visible knee pads over tights when protection called for it. After the initial surprise, it becomes an acceptable convention.

Modern dance has given rise to some extraordinary healers, most of whom have been dancers and some of whom have suffered serious injuries that limited their careers and turned them first to their own recovery and then to a profession of understanding the body with a view to avoid injury. They teach, heal and illuminate for us a better insight into our awesomely complex bodies. A few, however, have extended their understanding to a guiding principle of dance based on a foundation stone that has carved into it the word: CAUTION! I believe that there is a definite inroad of this kind of thinking into some technique classes, rehearsal studios and stage works. I believe this mindset vitiates the vitality and possibility of the virtuosity that is our obligation as artists. I am not talking of gratuitous stunts. I am pursuing the challenge put forth by Tamiris and Sokolow. How far does the inner action take the dancer? What further extension of the movement would not just produce virtuosity but a more vivid and *truthful* revelation?

If we are to present ourselves in the theatre, we must be aware that it is an arena of life and death. We are there to take risks for the audience. They hunger to see our strength and our daring. Seeing that gives them strength and daring. It is up to the choreographers to challenge their dancers to extend themselves. Foolish gambles with the bodies of the company are stupid and cruel. Caution is required when taking risks.

Needless to say, risks should only be entrusted to highly skilled dancers. It has been said that fifty percent of successful direction lies in casting. The original remark was about theatre but it is just as true for dance. You owe it to your choreography to get the best available dancers to do your work and if you realize that one or more of your dancers cannot fully realize its technical demands, get dancers who can. It is at this crisis that some young choreographers will sacrifice the integrity of their own creation in order to be liked.

Speaking of casting, there are some female dancers who may give an exquisite audition but when the work gets underway, the choreographer senses a weakness that is hard to define. Boys grow up learning to hit. Most girls don't. There are some adult female dancers who can do everything but one thing. They lack force. They conform to a secret image of what a woman is supposed to be and do: not too much, not too strong and not too emphatic. These days this is becoming much less of a problem as young women are engaging fiercely in sports and drill teams where the dynamic of hitting is a must.

A personal note: In my performing career, no matter how many times I was praised for my brilliant and virtuosic technique, I would be startled and confused. I came to dance late and I always felt a profound technical insecurity. The slightest wobble felt like a building coming down in an earthquake. Before my performances I would run over my worries and after, I would vividly recall every inadvertent divergence from the choreography. It was only when I began to teach my dances to highly skilled dancers that I got the faintest perspective on what I had achieved.

As a young choreographer-performer, I was desperate to acquire the kind of skill I thought was absolutely necessary if I was to make a go of it as a professional. My first action on graduating from college was to enroll in ballet classes, foregoing modern dance study. Every ballet class sets its sights on virtuosity as a goal. The second was spending long hours working alone, hammering away at the elusive turns, elevations, extensions and balances. The third was hours and hours of improvisation to music that charged me. Finally, there was the meeting with Tamiris from whom I learned not to think of the technical feat but of the inner action that *required the accomplishment of the technical feat to succeed.*

Once I had a grasp on this way of working, and it came easily to me, the most amazing things began to happen. I developed an intensely personal vocabulary and without being conscious of it, much of it was virtuosic. I had a glimmer of this when my understudies studied my Broadway roles or went on for me. These were all brilliant men, some from ballet companies, many of them soloists, with the full battery of ballet skills far beyond mine. And yet, they were struggling with what seemed so obvious to me.

This material is here, in a book on choreography, as a challenge to modern solo and group choreographers to examine how they can extend the technical limits which have hemmed in some of the accomplishments of modern dance. Actually, the challenge is being met—to a degree. There are half-a-dozen young choreographers who are pushing the envelope. Additionally, there is the welcome surprise of the large number of current professional modern dancers who are graduates of university dance programs, many with Master of Fine Arts degrees and virtuoso abilities. All have had, in their course of study, intensive ballet training along with modern technique.

A by-product of all of this is the increasing number of ballet companies which are absorbing some of the modern dance repertoire or commissioning new work from modern choreographers. The rivers flow parallel but sometimes the banks overflow and there is a commingling—and that is to be celebrated.

# 13 Direction

A good director is an invisible follow spot

As a youth, to be a writer was one of my many ambitions. I avidly seized any article about writers who would speak of their methods. Obviously, I was always seeking the holy grail of "the way to write." After coming across a half-a-dozen of these "the way to write," it became apparent that there was no "the way to write." There were only writers, each of whom had found *their own way to write*.

Choreographers? Some prepare far ahead of the actual rehearsal period. Both Jerome Robbins and Agnes DeMille would gather a group of dancers months ahead of a show's rehearsal time and do many studies. Anthony Tudor worked on *Romeo and Juliet* for almost a year and yet on opening night, he had to step before the curtain to announce that the last scene had yet to be choreographed. On rare occasions, Tamiris would do a few studies with me but most of her prerehearsal energies would be to read and reread the scripts of the Broadway musicals she choreographed or, when she was preparing her concert material, she would fill notebooks with her ideas. Otherwise, she would twist her hair for hours on end thinking ahead. She would arrive in the studio without a single phrase choreographed, but without any doubt as to what she was aiming at.

Tamiris was fast and nothing short of spectacular. We would rehearse at full tilt observed by an eye that could spot the slightest deviation in rhythm or motion. Thus, she was polishing as we rehearsed, catch an error, stop us and "Back to the top," to go again and again until suddenly she would be up on her feet, pick up from the last phrase and blast into a new phrase of movement which she had never done in her life. Speculating on how her mind was working, I assume that as she watched us dance through what had been done, she would keep us dancing in her head. One half of her mind was critiquing every gesture and the other half was dancing into the future, the unknown. When she rose to dance, there was no caution or uncertainty, only a fully danced new phrase.

Some face their dancers with done choreography and some come into the studio a blank. You have to find your own way. A talented colleague, Cliff Keuter, told me he would dream dance phrases, wake, remember them and bring them ready-made into the studio. For myself, ideas come at any time, any where, but dance movements, whether for myself or others, come only in the studio. I do not find movement in my mind, only the concepts are birthed there. It is only when my body is warm and ready to dance that those concepts come alive as sensations that flash through my body. I get a "feel" in my body that has no name or shape, I wait a bit and then go. It takes several "go's" before I find something I want to do or give to the dancer(s). Nothing here can help anybody. You have no choice but to flounder along until you find your own way.

The critical nexus in this matter of direction is how the choreographer relates to her.his dancers. They present a profoundly complex problem. Tubes of paint are passive. A good musical instrument is passive. A blank sheet of paper is passive. A good motion picture camera is passive. I never met a passive dancer. The quietest is a seething mix of eagerness to please, fear of inadequacy, an ego as sensitive as a radar detector and for some, a virulent critical sense plus a heated ambition to be standing in the place of the choreographer. It is all too obvious that when there is such a dependency, the choreographer gains by heightened sensitivity to the capacity and personality of each dancer.

How one deals with the creative contribution of the dancers is again an individual matter. In some situations, it would be unthinkable for the choreographer to invite creative input from the company. At the other end of the spectrum, there are those like Tamiris, who would challenge us by giving us a sense of what was needed next, allow us to work by ourselves, view what we had come up with and then accept, reject and/or edit it. None of us ever said that "we" had choreographed this or that. We knew too well her capacity to pour out relevant and beautiful movement and we knew that the problem we had been entrusted with was conceived by her and could enter the flow of the work only if it meshed with her concept. These little assignments were always for our own individual moments. She did not ask any of us to work on choreography for the group as a whole.

Included in this matter of "the creative contribution of the dancers," is the matter of style. How much performance individuality should be allowed to the dancers? Some works and some styles demand strict adherence to a specific way. On the Japanese Noh stage, conformity to rigid standards of performance would appear to be the rule. And yet, knowing so little of that world, what is it that makes one a star in that setting if not some strong individual take on what was given? One would think that the ballet would have little tolerance for personal variations and yet there are countless stories of how Balanchine would modify his choreography to realize the talents of the dancer who happened to be before him in the studio. This is a delicate matter and it behooves every choreographer to tread lightly on this business of impressing *all* the details of a style upon a dancer, particularly when dealing with a talented one. There is a balance to be sought between the vision of the choreographer and the temperament of the performer.

How much does the choreographer tell the dancers? Some directors communicate in detail and some shudder at the very thought of such an action. In my prejudiced view, it is astonishing not to include the dancers in the vision of the choreographer, and yet this is fairly common practice. Tamiris, and I too, believe that there is an extra flow of energy from dancers who know what they are dancing about. They bring not only energy but a living intelligence to their performances. This calls up a remark I may have heard or read, "Real learning only takes place when you are emotionally engaged." I think that is an exaggeration, for some of the best learners are like icicles, but *what* they learn is very different than what the heated ones learn.

Being out in front, being the "boss," brings with it the possibility that one or more of the company would also like to be the "boss." Some dancers are quite objective about this ambition and bide their time before making that play, usually by leaving and starting up their own company. Others are not so objective and consciously or not, begin to inject some form of negativism. The choreographer has several ways of coping: counterattacking, confrontation, charming and gaining allegiance and finally, if these do not succeed in restoring order and a good working atmosphere, "OUT! OUT!" The one way that will produce nothing but heartache and misery for all is to try to ignore the threat and hope it will go away. No strong director is at a loss when one or more of the company is cool or hostile. If the director is one who has to be loved by everyone, she.he is in a terribly vulnerable place.

Is a collective of creators possible? The only two that come to mind are The Grand Union and Pilobolus. The Grand Union had a short life in the early seventies and Pilobolus has a had a long and successful life since 1974. It obviously has worked for them. The Grand Union was a collection of power houses: Yvonne Rainer, Steve Paxton, Trisha Brown, Douglas Dunn and a few others, each of whom went their own way. I can't imagine a more difficult structure for creative work in dance. When I directed the Workgroup, there were some members who yearned for a collective way. I always opened up the discussions on what we had done and what we were going to do but I resolutely held to the position that the last word had to be mine. All work in the arts is difficult. I think the cooperative path compounds the problems which is not to say that it is not possible or under certain circumstances preferable.

To take course work and/or workshops in choreography can make for a good beginning towards acquiring your craft, but usually, a bit more would help. Find a choreographer whom you admire and do everything you can to gain entry into his.her company. Obviously, being intimately enmeshed in dance creation would bring with it insights into the craft. Being the assistant to the choreographer will bring you even closer to the gritty details needed to produce.

∽

It is said that books are not written, they are rewritten. It takes strength and the kind of objectivity that every choreographer needs to face up to a moment when it becomes apparent that something is not quite right. The time comes to pause and examine and be willing to go back and revise. It is not permitted to fall in love with your creation. If it is lovely but not really right, "OUT! OUT!"

The curse of our time is the lack of it. For most people in the universities studying choreography, the constant complaint is the lack of time. Course work can be overwhelming, intense competition for the services of fellow dance students, limited studio space and time combine to force creative work into a pressure cooker. Once into the profession, the constraints simply change but also multiply: deadlines, the shortage of funds, the necessity of earning the dollars to finance the work, the limited availability of dancers who usually are holding down part-time jobs and the high cost of studio space continue what only can feel like a conspiracy against careful and deliberate progress.

There are solutions, but not many. A few wonderful foundations offer space and time to work slowly and without undue and premature public exposure. I mention none of them here because by the time this book appears in print they may be gone and/or replaced by others. A more important answer is that at some point early in the career of every choreographer, there should be every attempt to find a year or two when several creative projects can be worked for *all the time they need. By which I mean, time to make mistakes, time to revise, time to start all over again, time to throw out false leads and time to polish and refine what is working.* A couple of years of this will give the young choreographer a secret library of resources and alternatives to the problems that inevitably arise in professional work and *require quick solutions.*

∽

What follows is a personal observation about the strange detours that direction and style take from the director to her.his dancers. One of the miracles of Martha Graham's performance style was that in the welter of her passion and her incredible range of motion, I could not sense any muscular effort. For me, it was as if I were witnessing a play of light. The eminent characteristic of the wonderful dancers she has trained is their intense muscular involvement.

Witnessing Merce Cunningham perform, I am constantly aware that *he* is seeing ghosts, leprechauns and a world of great complexity. His arms ward off, embrace and swat personal, specific and detailed things. His dancers are all different but hardly any of them deal with his specifics and details. Some are like geometric ice, others have a ferocious intensity and some seem to be having a lovely time. They seem to stay with whatever they have locked into from the beginning of an evening to the end. Merce changes from second to second.

Alwin Nikolais's dancers lost their individuality in the guise of concealing costumes and overwhelming props and yet his protegé, Murray Louis, is one of the most vivid and striking personalities to step into the modern dance arena. The implication of this theory is that artists breed their opposites!

↬

Directing is a rare talent, difficult to analyze, to teach and to do. Some of the best directors are tyrannical horrors and some are supportive angels; no matter, style or decency are not on the agenda of this chapter. The ideal director regards each dancer as a singular entity requiring a particular kind of incentive. Some dancers need only a hint in order to work out the inner life of a role. Others do best when they are given a good deal of information. If the desire is to work in the ways outlined here, choreographers and directors cannot roar at their dancers, "Move it!" "Feel it!" "Come alive!"; generalities that can only inspire banal performances. Something specific must be given to direct, lead or inspire the minds/hearts of the dancers. Treat them like muscular automatons and expect either the performances of automatons or a stage full of performers each infused with a radically different point of view distantly related to the thematic material of the dance. Or, have the good fortune to collect a group of dancers who can intuit the intentions of the choreographer. I have often heard from dancers that the choreographer never told the dancers what the dance was about or who or what they were in the dance. Movement was given plus various exhortations about quality, energy or loyalty and that was it. This is true not only of my student choreographers but of any number of professional choreographers, some of whom have produced major dance works. Style and method are a matter of philosophy and taste. You take your choice and you go your way. In summation, there is the choreographer's metaphor and there is the dancer's. They are probably different and sometimes radically so. If they appear to be identical, what more can be asked?

Some dancers are quite evil and competitive. Finding a choreographer who is not sure of her.himself, these dancers will challenge the leadership, break discipline and be openly critical in a way that deflects the authority that should hold the group together. To get work done, either find a way to reach them or throw them out.

Question: Is it productive to open the door to comments and criticism by the company members? There is no answer. This is a matter of temperament. Assuming that it is in the cards to speak up, the next question is when? Unless the director or the choreographer pauses during rehearsal to ask for an opinion, after the rehearsal is the proper time to speak up. A discussion during rehearsal, particularly one initiated by a company member, breaks the rhythm of the work and that rhythm is the most precious tool of the director/choreographer.

# 14 The Stage

THE COSTUMES

THE LIGHTS

THE SETS

THE SOUND

The ensuing discussion may appear to be going far afield from the ostensible focus of this book, choreography. On the contrary, there is no single factor in the entire chain of events that goes to make a performance of a dance that is not capable of ruining the end result. Anyone who has the arrogance and nerve to assume the responsibility of creating dances owes it to him.herself to be thoroughly knowledgeable in the matters of the costumes, the lights, the sets and the sound. Further, with each day, advances and complexities in technology and techniques are developing at an exponential rate. Even if the latest method of digital recording seems irrelevant to what you are doing, know enough about it to be certain that you do not need it.

## The Costumes

It is all too obvious that as dancers, we work to be seen. Our physical statements must have the impact we hope they will achieve. If our clothes camouflage our intent, in essence, we vanish. Face it. You always look like something. The question is, "What?" Dancers who present work in a choreography class dressed in such a way that what they look like is severely contradictory to the intent, style and the character of their choreography succeed in being their own enemy. There are a pair of opposites in this matter of poor taste dressing: super-casual, raggedy, survivor work clothes that conceal the body's configuration or svelte, skin-tight, high rise, low cut, nylon erotica. Unless clothes are appropriate to the choreography being shown, they distract from the work at hand, attracting attention to the *person* rather than to the dance. Teachers who slip into either of these modes of dress are misleading their students.

A critical question facing every choreographer is how "dancey" the costume(s) should be. Whenever students are introducing a new piece, giving the title, the composer, the light scheme, etc., I almost always interject the question, "Will you (or your dancers) be wearing 'dance' clothes or 'people' clothes?" The question of costume cannot be raised too early. What is worn affects the movement and if it is at all possible, wearing bits and pieces of a possible costume will help create the style and integrity of the moves *as they are being created and certainly when presenting the early versions of the choreography.*

Learning to do without has been one of modern dance's greatest contributions. It would be simplistic to say that those early pioneers resorted to this severity because they usually lacked the dollars. Actually, their aesthetic called for stripping away what they considered frivolous decorativeness in costume as well as in movement. In the program of her second New York concert, January 29, 1928, Helen Tamiris wrote a "Manifest"[17] in which this appeared:

> The dance of today is plagued with exotic gestures, mannerisms and ideas . . . Will people never rebel against artificialities, pseudo-romanticism and affected sophistication? The dance of today must have a dynamic tempo and be valid, precise, spontaneous, free, normal, natural and human.

Personally, I hold no brief for simplicity as a general rule. There are statements and cultures that are best expressed in the most elaborate costumes or in nudity. As the wise man on the mountain top said, "It all depends." What are you saying? And what about nudity? A bright young man in a choreography class at the American Dance Festival asked all of us to come out into the hallway when he sent word that he would be ready. When we were called, we arrived to find him *im ganzen nackt*. With super-sophistication, we observed his dance as if it were a common occurrence. When he finished, he dressed and returned. In the discussion that followed, I asked him why he chose to be nude. He said he could not think of an appropriate costume, so he chose to wear nothing. With answers like that, he should have been a Talmudic scholar. "Ray, 'nothing' *is* a costume and an exciting one at that. The question is, are we to be excited about your dance or you?" In the fall, we had a little follow-up correspondence:

> Dear Ray,
> Conceptualizing is not a weakness but it can be a trap when it glosses over reality. Nakedness is not only a costume but I can only wish for you that in the rest of your career you are costumed as well as you were in that hallway. You are a handsome and well formed man in the glow of your youth. Any costumer will be hard put to top

what you were "wearing." Admiring daring artists and trying to understand what it is that they are doing is admirable. All the more reason for you to emulate them by hooking into the passion of *your own concerns* and never letting ideas—concepts—a school of thought—a particular style—dominate or cloak the gritty specifics of your own vision. Creatively, all the rules of art—if there are any—have to be re-established with each work—each time.

What makes a good dance costume? I am in no position to make any answer to that awesome question. At one end of the spectrum are the yards and yards of silks that encase a Noh dancer and ironically, on the other end is the occasional paired nakedness of Eiko and Koma. A partial answer to that question would be a critical history of the clothing worn by dancers through the years. It is a project that is waiting to be done.

One cavil in regard to today's dance stage: the vinyl floor is generally black and many times the stage is backed by a black velour! For my taste, this means that black costuming and black shoes lose color vibrancy. Being blotted up by a background color is a poor fate for a dancer. Videotaping against black exacerbates this disappearing act.

In 1958, I spent one thousand dollars on one dance! The triple underdressed costume for *Three Happy Men* alone cost seven hundred and fifty dollars—in 1958! Something clicked in me after that, resolving to do without, to rely primarily on movement. For the next solo program, *Spring '65,* I made six dances, never leaving the stage. I danced in the same costume, wearing a mask for one dance, changing once from a soft slipper to a character shoe and using a comb, tissues and a glass of water spread out on a table on stage right with the tape recorder which I alone started and stopped—all in full view of the audience. I thought, "Now I've done it! Stripped it to the bone!"

In the next solo program, *The Peloponnesian War,* I started out with a hat, a grey business suit, a dress shirt and tie, stripped that off to appear in ratty, but once elegant ballet tunic with puffed velvet sleeves, satin slashes and white tights, removed the tunic to a sleeveless white top, then added a pair of white pants, a black belt and a mustache, then into a white pullover, then stripping to a bare top and picking up a ten pound 30-02 Infield rifle and bayonet, firing that straight at the audience. Intermission. Act II, I appeared in a tweed toga, with that off, I was back in the opening business suit, dress shirt and tie. A few dances later, I slipped into a brown velvet and gold pajama dress surmounted by a full head mask of an exotic woman with outrageously long eyelashes, then back to the business suit, followed by a red, white and blue sequined jacket, then back to the white shirt, tie and grey pants. Next, to nothing but a dance belt and finishing off gloriously draped in still another toga, this one of coarse, white homespun.

So much for stripping to the bone.

# The Lights

When I first began to tour the university circuit in 1957, the hardest thing to achieve was side lighting. The stages were equipped for drama, not for dance. There were rarely any light poles for positioning in the wings or for hanging lamps that had the precise and hard-edge definition required by dance. Once in a while, as in Ibsen's *Ghosts*, a theatre designer would throw a shaft of the golden light of a breaking day to come through the wings, otherwise, most of the light came from overhead pipes and from the balcony rail of the house. I would have the crews hang side lights on steam pipes, ladders, chairs—anything in the wings that was sturdy enough to support a Leko lamp. Over the years, light poles in the wings gradually proliferated, until now, it's a wonder that a dancer can make a safe exit without crashing into the welter of equipment in every wing: wires, poles and appropriately labeled "shin-busters."

The end result of this evolution is that now, most wing poles have a minimum of three and often four side lights each and dance has a style of lighting that dominates the field: heavy washes of color from the sides, little or no light from the pipes overhead except for back light, and little or no light from the front of the house. The principle behind this development is that if the edges of the body are heightened by light, as is the case with side and back lighting, motion will be emphasized. In fact, shin-busters, in their most sophisticated use are placed as low as a foot and a half to two feet above floor level and focused flat across *so that no light touches the stage floor*, giving the dancers a floating, airy quality.

This is all undoubtedly effective in heightening the awareness of movement but there is an additional effect which is exactly what certain choreographers seek: the faces and the individual identity of the dancers are squashed into anonymity. Reader, at the next dance concert which you attend, look carefully at the *faces* of the dancers. If they are lit by the contemporary style of heavy washes of side light, you may note that their cheeks are highlighted and puffed up a bit, while their eyes uniformly seem to be set very close together. What's going on? A light source impacting a face from the side casts a deep shadow in the pit beside the nose and on each side of the nose. The eye itself creates these shadows. They are not unlike the pieces of coal used to make eyes for a snowman. The little black pits create the effect of crossed eyes. Facing front, all the dancers have a shadow stripe running down the center of their faces from crown to chin. Whatever intelligence and personality is present in that face is overlaid by this abstract mask created by the harsh, unimpeded side lights.

For choreographers who are primarily movement oriented, none of this presents a problem but for those who are creating dances wherein the specific humanity and *differences among the dance figures on stage* are equally critical factors, anonymity and abstract multiplications of identity deny the intent of the work. Dances that depend upon the audience being sensitive to the reactions and development of characters being danced need *face light*. Face light is of course a prime requisite for drama and *is equally so for dances that have elements of drama in motion*. (The light plot on the next page is, at best, a generic version of this thinking about light for dance.)

There is something else overlooked in this lighting scheme of washes of light from the wings and little from overhead except for back lights: if Dancer A is seen moving from upstage left to downstage left, *there is no light change on his.her body*. If Dancer B crosses from mid-stage right to mid-stage left, there will be a change in intensity but no color change since the color behind him.her will remain constant, as will the color coming from the wings being approached. Even the back lights are usually constant in color all through the stage space. One of the significant events available to a choreographer is motion from one place to another. We are not in an unlimited space out of doors. We operate in a limited arena and our task as choreographers is to open up the stage until it resembles the world. Color washes diminish the impact of movement in space.

It is possible to make every change of location *an event* with light. My method is to divide the stage into nine areas, checkered with alternating cool light and warm light. In addition, cool and warm lights alternate from the wings, thus avoiding washes. Ironically, there is one flaw to this neat scheme. During a diagonal passage from upstage to downstage, the dancer is always in a cool light area but there are color changes from the wings. Here too, the color in each wing faces its complementary opposite on the other side of the stage. Thus, every time the dance travels in space, *his.her body changes the lights*.

I had a basic scheme which I think may be helpful in many circumstances. My strategy was as useful as it was demanding. I toured alone, which meant that though I mailed my light plot on ahead, it was quite often barely or incorrectly hung. Without a stage manager it was necessary for me not only to direct the hanging and focusing of the lamps, but to teach all the movement or music cues. Occasionally, this provoked a degree of resentment from the local crew, since it gave them more responsibilities than when a dance company arrived with a stage manager who knew all the cues. In most cases, their interest and involvement doubled when they became aware that I was knowledgeable and that I had some unusual ideas about light and sound.

The checkerboard of light mentioned earlier was at the heart of this scheme. Many years ago, a teacher of stage techniques at Yale University, George Isenhauer, suggested a basic nine area light plot for the stage. Each area was to be lit by at least two lamps from the pipes coming in at ninety degrees in respect to each other's position. The pipe for each row of areas was to be about six feet in front, focused at an angle of about thirty degrees. The logic for that sharp angle is that it is just steep enough to cast shadows, giving a sculp-

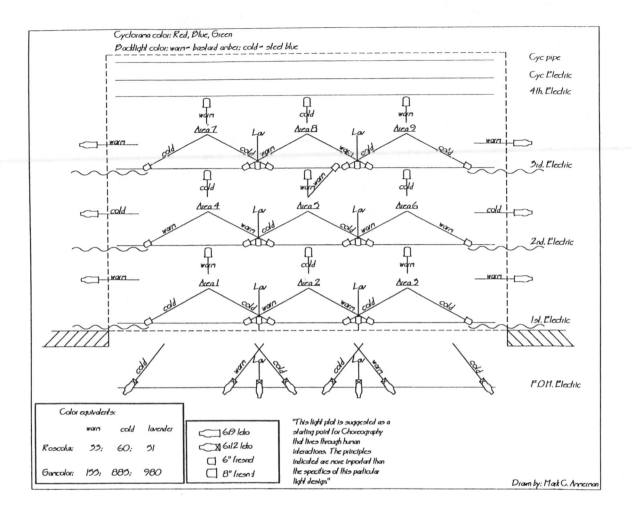

Cyclorama color: Red, Blue, Green
Backlight color: warm - bastard amber; cold - steel blue

Cyc pipe
Cyc Electric
4th. Electric

Area 7   Lav   Area 8   Lav   Area 9
warm       cold              warm

3rd. Electric

Area 4   Lav   Area 5   Lav   Area 6
cold       warm              cold

2nd. Electric

Area 1   Lav   Area 2   Lav   Area 3
warm       cold              warm

1st. Electric

F.O.H. Electric

Color equivalents:

|  | warm | cold | lavender |
|---|---|---|---|
| Roscolux: | 33; | 60; | 51 |
| Gamcolor: | 155; | 885; | 980 |

6x9 leko
6x12 leko
6" fresnel
8" fresnel

"This light plot is suggested as a starting point for choreography that lives through human interactions. The principles indicated are more important than the specifics of this particular light design"

Drawn by: Mark C. Anneman

tural definition to facial and bodily features. This is important for dancers as well as for actors. A even steeper angle is best reserved for very dramatic situations.

For dance, a low angle from the balcony rail in the front of the house will flatten the face and body of the dancers and destroy the sense of stage depth, since the same light is defining the dancers upstage and downstage. By and large, balcony rail lights are murder for dance, unless we are dealing with musical comedy where the entire energy is to be in the laps of the audience. The best source of front-of-house lighting is a pipe that is no more than eight feet in front of the downstage positions of the dancers. Again, for dance, in most cases, lights from this pipe should not be used for anything but the downstage areas.

To finally get to the matter of colors. Lighting for actors tries to bring the actor forward, particularly his.her face. The general solution for this is to use "natural light." This means using colors that are not pure and making one side brighter and *different* than the other. The classic colors are, specifically, bastard amber for one side of the face/body and steel blue for the other. Here, the less than "pure colors" diminish the distance of the actors from the audience (a close up), which is precisely what the directors desire.

I took the skeleton of this plan and twisted it to fit the needs of dance and particularly of a solo program that needed variety from dance to dance. Furthermore, it kept the need for specials to a minimum. In this light plot, each area had a pair of Fresnels coming in at ninety degrees with the same color and, usually, the same dimmer. I very soon hit upon two pure colors for the warm and the cool: a light flesh pink, often labeled pale rose and a daylight or no color blue. Sadly, there is no common terminology among the makers of theatrical gels and this often led to unnecessary confusion. The light plot diagram in this chapter illustrates the checkerboard of colors. I learned to make one addition: a blending color along the edges of each area, a pale lavender. With this three color stage, aside from covering every portion of the space, I could push the emotional tone this way or that. Toning down the cool and pushing up the warm, including the special lavender, heated up the air. Reversing that gave an icy astringent look.

Of course, there was a strong use of side lights but rarely at the expense of what I call "face light." This preserved the clear definition of the face and body and above all allowed expression to be visible. It is these two points that are being ignored by too many choreographers who have works that involve individual expression. They are caught up in a style that is so pervasive it is not questioned. Most of the lighting designers are similarly swept along by a fashion. Basically, it is the choreographer who has the responsibility to divine the nature of his.her work and communicate its needs to the lighting designer.

A generation ago, computerized light switchboards were not available. Their possibilities should be explored and exploited to the hilt. Every choreographer could profit from a crash course on their resources. Of course, the awesome fluidity possible with these instruments presents a problem. How closely should the lights pursue the actions and changes of the choreography? With computer controls, there are very few limits. Again, as with music and speech, I am of the school that prefers the mystery that appears when there is contradiction between the danced action and what accompanies it. Light that remorselessly pursues the focal point of a dance with specials, color changes and dimming controls telegraphs to the audience what it should be expecting and feeling. A plethora of light cues could very well make the lighting designer the principle focus of the dance work. This style of lighting flattens the imagination of the audience. Artists who do this have little faith in their audiences and less in their own creations.

## The Sets

Anything that amplifies the choreographer's intentions and the actions of the dancers is wonderful. Anything that is not absolutely necessary is a burden to the eye and to the budget of any touring company. A close-up analysis of sets for a dance is always in order: do they help the choreography or the reputation of the scene designer? The bigger the budget available for sets, *the greater the temptation to use them.* It is not possible to cast out any generalizations about the value and the hazards of sets for dance.

## The Sound

In sound, the number of links that can affect what we hear are too many to think of. The first step in order to achieve optimum sound reproduction is to check the volume balance between the speakers. Sitting in the center of the house should expose this relationship. More volume might be pouring in from one side than the other for a multiplicity of reasons: differing speaker efficiencies, an asymmetrical configuration of the house, weird wiring, poor connectors.

Next, starting with the first dance, check the volume for each dance separately. This immediately opens the door to extreme differences in taste. We have a generation that has rarely heard live instruments, unless they are amplified as is the case with rock groups. Their ears recognize music is something that is amplified. The classic, folk or jazz music they might love, they know only through electronic amplification and loud—really loud —is good. This is true not only for the sound technicians but for the choreographers and probably for a younger portion of the audience! And who is right? As the choreographer it is your call. I have a simple criterion: if there were an actual piano being played, how loud would it sound? The same with a cello, a string quartet, an orchestra or a vocalist. Time and again, I have heard recordings of these played at grotesque and even painful volumes. Of course, if the recorded score is of a rock group, very loud would be right.

There are persistent mythologies about the effect of the presence of a live audience on volume. "It's too loud," complains the choreographer. "Oh no, the audience will absorb most of that!" says the sound engineer. Actually, if the seats are cushioned and covered with cloth, the audience will make little or no difference. If the seats, particularly the seat backs, are hard, find the correct levels and then add just a bit to anticipate the effect of bodies and clothing blotting up some of the sound. A simple test is to stand on the apron of a stage and clap the hands sharply. A house that is very "lively" in its response will give an audible reverberation of about a second and a half. A "lively" house will lose some of its volume to the presence of an audience. The opposite, a "dead" house, will give back almost nothing and the presence of an audience will have almost no effect of diminishing the volume of sound.

As soon as I find the volume I deem correct, I check, for each dance, the treble/bass balance with the same intent: to hear once again the actual texture and sound of the instrument. Once the best possible treble/bass balance is found within the limits of the system available, some further adjustment in the volume level is usually necessary.

Stereo reproduction presents an odd problem in the theatre. In the home, the distinction between sound from one speaker and the other is easy to make out. In the theatre, those seated in the center are getting equal volumes of sound from both sides of the house and thus the stereo effect is apparent, but for the majority of the audience, seated further to the left or right of center, the message from the far speaker is weakened by distance. When I toured *The Peloponnesian War*, I needed two tape recorders, one for the music and the other for the voice of Frank Langella reading Thucydides's text. I quickly learned that a stereo effect would frustrate all those sitting on the far side of the spoken voice. Aside from being weakened by distance, the voice would be always drowned out by the music. The solution, forget the stereo effect and have each tape recorder feed a different amplifier and *pair of speakers*, one on each side of the stage.

Another lesson from that experience was that next to the piano, the most difficult sound to reproduce accurately was a male voice. Thus Langella always got the better sound system.

This little essay on sound is directed not only to choreographers but to technicians. First, it helps if the choreographer knows what he.she dreams of and finds a way to communicate that to the sound engineer. Second, the choreographer must leave *time* to hear, judge and direct *all* aspects of the sound from positions throughout the house. Leaving major acoustic decisions to the audio engineer is not recognizing the profound impact of sound upon the presentation of any dance work. Ideally, the technician should also be in the house. He.she would be in a better position than the choreographer to detect certain problems such as the location of the speakers, the *choice* of the speakers and weaknesses due to the equipment. It is for this reason that I think that sound requires at least two skilled technicians, one at the controls and one to prowl the house listening for problems. It is worth noting that in several Broadway houses, where every seat is precious, about six seats are gouged out of the rear of the orchestra to make way for an open sound control center. This is ideal.

## The Stage

Proscenium? In the round? Site specific locations? Much of the time, we take what we can get. A few of us push the envelope of the given. For the Workgroup, in the round was best since our energy was never directed out to create a stage picture for a witnessing audience but concentrated on each other pursuant to the interactive nature of what we did. Twyla Tharp, at the beginning of her career, started in gymnasiums but is now filling proscenium stages with her work. Was this a retreat or a change out of her own necessities? Ask her. Once again, I am proposing a piece of research: spaces for *and against* dance, how they evolved, which worked and which were obstacles and what lies ahead?

## Conclusion

The Costumes! The Lights! The Sets! The Sound! There's so much to know! And it's going to get more complicated as the technical marvels multiply. No, we are not dancing around a campfire. It is not going to get easier. In fact, this chapter has left out one of the of the most significant developments of the last twenty-five years, the ease and availability of videotaping our creations. Yes. But to what end? Simple recording has value for archiving and recreation of the choreography but it is all too apparent that *the dance, as we know it and love it, vanishes in these flat images.* The challenge for all in our business is how to make a videotape of a dance a work of art that takes its inspiration from the dance it is imaging. How? The videographers have to open themselves to the power and mysteries of dance. The choreographers have to learn the new poems that are possible within that tight rectangle—the stage—that flat floor boxed in by hanging cloths. Thus far, we are only at the beginning in this endeavor. In *How to Dance Forever*[18] there is an extended essay on videotaping dance.

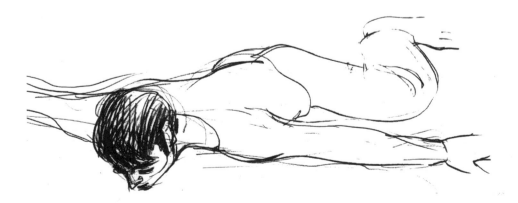

# 15 Choreography for the Theatre, Musical Comedy and Opera

The memory of a most radical decision contains a particular moment when "everything became clear." We go along in life and sometimes things begin to pile up. We take vague notes, but take no action and then when least expected a minor moment is transformed into a momentous summation and we discover we have changed.

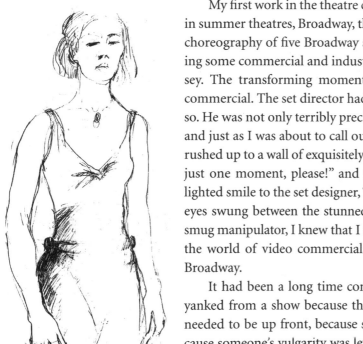

My first work in the theatre came in 1940. In the years that followed I danced in summer theatres, Broadway, the Rainbow Room, films, TV and assisted in the choreography of five Broadway shows. In 1956, I was performing in and directing some commercial and industrial films for an adventurous outfit in New Jersey. The transforming moment came as I was directing a L'Oreal perfume commercial. The set director had put in a long morning making everything just so. He was not only terribly precise but very good. I finished directing the actors and just as I was about to call out, "Roll!", the client, a representative of L'Oreal, rushed up to a wall of exquisitely displayed glass shelves of perfume bottles, "Oh, just one moment, please!" and rearranged the bottles, turned and with a delighted smile to the set designer, "That's so much better, don't you think?" As my eyes swung between the stunned tight face of the designer and the face of that smug manipulator, I knew that I was on my way out of commercial art, not only the world of video commercials and industrial films but all of it—including Broadway.

It had been a long time coming. I had seen too many beautiful moments yanked from a show because they weren't super smash, because someone else needed to be up front, because someone's vanity needed a little power play, because someone's vulgarity was leveraged and given free play. The bitter fact was and is that almost every moment and gesture in the commercial theatre was and is filtered through the sensibilities of too many people, some of whom can be quite gross and some quite sensitive and creative.

In art as well as in science one always risks failure. In commercial dance, failure or even partial success is unacceptable. There are several reliable hinges that ease open the door to success. The ambitious choreographer will choose from the following "Menu for Success":

- Present nothing that demands extensive thought or complex speculation.

- Avoid weighty, "serious" thematic material.

- Pay close attention to current audience tastes and do all that is necessary to satisfy those demands.

- Create material drenched in variety, surprises, novelty and inventiveness.

- Don't forget sex.

- Feature staggering virtuosity for the men and impossibly high extensions and penché arabesques for the women.

- Call for lush, elaborate and/or chic costumes, sets and props.

- Call for erotic costuming and actions.

- Call for smiling at the audience.

- Train your dancers to look seductively at the audience.

- Mickey-mouse the phrasing and the strong beats of the music.

- Stay ahead of the beat to underline high energy.

- Engage young and physically attractive dancers.

Probably, the above will appear to be a cynical and contemptuous putdown. It is not. The "menu for success" is a perfectly valid way of working *if that is the choice*. Many of our finest and most exhilarating choreographers have chosen this path. I worked in that field for sixteen years, learned a lot, earned good money and gained something of a reputation doing it. For me, it just wasn't a good fit. Between shows, I was in the studio making "serious" dances that refused to pursue any of the above clues. Without being conscious of it, I was building a bridge away from Broadway to the concert stage. While I worked on Broadway I constantly crossed and recrossed it, and then in 1956, crossed and never looked back.

One phenomenon deserves a bit of attention here. About twenty-five years ago, when the market for modern dance began to open up, nationally and internationally, several dance companies arrived on the concert stage observing in one respect or another the above "menu for success." They gained attention, great reviews, bookings and substantial grants. Just as no one ever said that the king had no clothes, no one ever noted that they were presenting the craft, the ambitions and the culture of "show business"—of commercial theatre.

A few more commercial dancing notes, descriptions and/or tips: As a youngster living in Brooklyn, going to the movies on Saturday afternoon was a big deal, particularly since there was also a vaudeville show. I loved the tap dancers and I noticed that they made a big thing out of doing all difficult sequences and tricks twice, first on one side and then on the other. They were saying, "This is no fluke! Not only do I have absolute control over this difficult stuff but I can do it on both sides!" I, as audience, agreed and I think most of the audience joined in the excitement at this triumph. Two things were proved: the dancer could do it again and again and she.he could do it *on both sides.* Without consciously assessing the fact, all of us know that for most people, abilities and strengths are not the same for both sides of the body.

This shared belief has had a very strong effect on choreographic structures. Countless ballet phrases, particularly the virtuosic ones are automatically done twice and sometimes three and four times. One of the ironies is the naive and consistent use of this pattern straight out of vaudeville in Denis-Shawn choreography, regardless of whether a phrase had virtuosity or not. They used this device as a given. Ironically, Martha Graham used phrase repeats extensively in her choreography but in her work, every repeat is something of a shock and an actual intensification of emotion. Why? Her choice of moves was both shocking and laden with emotion.

When the sophisticated choreographers invaded Broadway in the forties, this ploy was dumped. Repetition was a rare device. Instead, the dancers would usually do something on one side, look as if they were going to repeat a phrase but rather "pull a switch," by syncopating, making a variation or simply taking it to another place. The same material might be used and reused but rarely in a simple undifferentiated repeat, thus following the example of good old Johann Sebastian Bach or the devilish Wolfgang Amadeus Mozart or the sophisticated Duke Ellington.

A trick that is not a trick if it is integral to the structure of what you are saying: if a section of a piece demands a prolonged, quiet and sustained passage that risks being boring, introducing a violent, sharply accented moment early will keep the focused attention of the audience for a long time. This will work even if the eruption is not integral, though that would be an unscrupulous solution. This device works in "serious" as well as "commercial" dance.

High energy is a given in commercial theatre. As mentioned earlier, pushing the beat is one way of conveying that quality. In "serious" dance, energy level is not a matter of augmenting audience attention but is rather a function of expressing the content and spirit of the choreography.

Slow or fast, high or low energy, active or inactive, every section of a dance work should have an inherent pervasive rhythm which is its lifeline. Among the many talents that enriched Tamiris's choreography was her unconscious sensitivity to this critical matter. Everything she did was marked by a vital propulsion energized by this rhythmic sense. Viewing her work, one was never sure where it was going but certain that this train was on its way. This ideal deserves thought and attention from anyone seriously committed to choreographing dance *in any medium*.

How should we put it? Art versus Entertainment? Art and Entertainment? Or, is the distinction unnecessary and false? In 1975, I had a residency at the University of Nebraska. During my time there, I was invited to do a piece for the educational TV station based at the University. I thought an unlikely marriage would be to pair *Strange Hero* with *Path*. The former is quite accessible; *Path*, the dance with a twelve-foot beam of wood carried in the same repetitive phrase for what seemed like forever, appeared opaque and obscure to many, while some claimed it to be the best of my solos. This is what we taped. When I finished both, I sat on a stool and talked on art and entertainment. A bit out of breath, without a script and in the sweet flush of having just danced, I managed to speak coherently on this subject that provokes so many. The whole business was fairly successful and is part of the educational library of the Nebraska Educational Television Council for Higher Education and a part of my own library of videotapes. The title is *Dance as Art and Dance as Entertainment*. What follows is the conclusion of the talk:

> I think that art is very much like science. It is a probe into the unknown, in fact I think that art is like the advance guard of science. We go to places where science does not have the equipment with which to deal. Many, many millennia ago, the poets and the flute players and the dancers probed the moon. They did dances, they wrote poems and created all sorts of mysterious rites to reach, to touch, to understand that exquisite, strange waning, expanding, disappearing phenomenon. Now that our healthy young men have put their heavy, hob-nailed boots on the face of the moon, I don't think many poets will be writing about the moon. We led them there. We led those space men to the moon. We will have other frontiers.
>
> To pose the other word and then to shuffle back and forth between them. I think that the essence of entertainment, or rather the necessary given about entertainment, is that everything is given. There are no questions. Someone comes out with a playful smile, a bit of a wobble and a hiccup and we think, "Ah! A drunk." We know that right away. Someone does a flashy step and it's fun and what's wrong with that? It's best when it's virtuosic and we are given answers that have been given and they are given sweetly, with inventiveness, and surprises by beautiful, magnetic people.

I know when I get through with a heavy day, it's fun to pick up a mystery that is not a mystery. There are no mysteries about a Bond adventure or an Agatha Christie mystery. There are only ingenious automobiles and tricky plots. There are no questionings of who they are or who I am or what my place in the world is. I don't want that. There are times when I just want to let down and not think about those things. I adore the comic strips though some of them are quite artistic and poetic. Everything can be easily contradicted and I can contradict it all myself.

On the other hand, I think art is not unlike a thesis that men and women prepare when they are trying to get doctorates. They study an area of life that has not been observed or they examine a certain field that has not been approached from that particular point of view. They spend a long time at it—a year—two years—three years, and there comes a point when they know more about, say, a certain aspect of Aaron Burr's life, or they know more about a certain crystal that is found in granite than anyone else in the world, and they are aware also of the further information that they lack. Then they take the results of what they know more about than anyone else and they put it into a coherent shape and they carry it to their fellow men and women and say, "This is what I found. This is as much as I know, say, about viruses. This is as much as I have discovered. Now with this little step, can we proceed further?" I think artists do this with human experience. Beckett, the man who wrote *Waiting for Godot*, was once asked, "Why didn't Godot appear?" He said, "Well, if I knew who Godot was, he would have appeared." The anguish that the audience feels when these two men wait for Godot to appear is the anguish that Beckett is speaking about.

Very often I am asked, "What does this dance mean? Why do you carry this wood for so long? Why do you do the same step over and over again?" Any number of questions, and I have always refused an answer. I refuse an answer because I am convinced that I would destroy your poem because you, looking at this dance and what happens there, will relate it to this and that in your experience and in your life. If I were to tell you what it was for me, I would destroy what it was for you since there can be no greater authority on my work than me. And so most important is for you to trust your own reactions and when you see something that baffles you and gets you nervous and you don't understand, be excited and let it churn up all kinds of energies and it will provoke little half answers about the mystery of what it is to be. Entertainment avoids ambiguities that demand thought. Art, if it is not ambiguous, is teetering towards entertainment.

Another way of expressing this point of view: great art surreptitiously draws us into a more intimate contact with some part of our life. For a bit of time, great entertainment draws us out of the welter of our own existence. Both serve profound needs. Both are rarely purely one or the other but rather a mix of each.

Concluding this chapter are the thoughts of three brilliant movers from musical comedy, drama and opera. Their works successfully blend art and entertainment. They were asked to speak to the problems that young choreographers should be aware of if they consider working in these fields.

꘎

### The Broadway Musical

*Susan Stroman*

As far back as I can remember, I wanted to be a choreographer. I knew that when I came to New York, I couldn't just come and "take over." I had to come as a performer first. I was lucky to be able to make a good living performing. One of my most memorable jobs was the national tour of *Chicago*. It enabled me to work with Gwen Verdon, Chita Rivera and, of course one of the greatest choreographers, Bob Fosse. His work greatly influenced me. Every beat he did was motivated by some piece of imagery. The use of imagery strengthens the dancers' ability to move.

About twelve years ago, I decided I only wanted be known as a choreographer. In New York, you can't have a split focus. So I stopped performing, crossed my fingers and put myself out there as a choreographer. I took every choreography job that came my way. The pivotal project came when a friend and actor-turned-director and I created an Off-Broadway revival of John Kander and Fred Ebb's *Flora the Red Menace* for the Vineyard Theatre. The space held fifty people. I made about four hundred dollars for the rehearsal time, had a terrific time creating it for the small space and assumed that few people would come. It proved to be a summer hit. This one production led to the formation of personal and professional relationships that have proved artistically fulfilling. Liza Minnelli engaged me to choreograph *Liza Stepping Out at Radio City Music Hall*. Hal Prince invited me to choreograph his production of *Don Giovanni* for the New York City Opera. Kander and Ebb allowed Scott Ellis and me to create a revue based on their music, *And the World Goes Around*, which became a critically acclaimed Off-Broadway production.

It is very difficult to get that first big break. These three shows opened the door to *Crazy for You*, the most memorable and fantastical theatrical ride of my life. At the heart of that success was the collaboration of the entire creative team. Going through the entire show with the director and the whole team is critical. No page is turned without everyone knowing his intention and vision.

The more shows we do, the more we learn about other people's departments. It always strengthens the collaboration if you can articulate clearly to the costume, lighting and set designers. Talking in their language is the key. What they do makes your work stronger. The most incredible step in the world lit badly will miss. A choreographer needs to be sure of his work by the time he gets into technical rehearsals. That is the time when the design team takes over. Collaboration of all the departments is the real joy of the process. When something is not working, another department might be able to save the moment.

Musical numbers have to come from a scene and go back into a scene. In *Crazy for You*, the characters are able to sing "I Got Rhythm" because two scenes earlier, they sang and danced to the tune of "Slap That Bass." The act ends with the lead female character, Polly, showing the lead male character, Bobby, how he gave the town rhythm. The script is designed to 'allow' the characters to sing "I Got Rhythm." Choreographically, everything then becomes believable. We not only see entertainment, it all makes strong plot sense. The days of blackouts after each number are over. Choreographed transitions from one set to another set can be magic. The evening must become seamless.

A dancer has to act to be able to work for me. There's nothing more boring than watching someone dance without the breath of a character. In *Steel Pier*, the wrestler does a fox trot very differently from the vaudevillian or the socialite. They do the same step but because of their character, the step looks dissimilar. The dance needs to propel the plot forward. It can't do that if someone is going to stop acting. The way they act in the scene has got to go right through the dance and out again. When I speak of choreography, I am not just talking about steps, I am talking about character. That combination is what makes the choreography rich.

The work one does before entering the rehearsal studio is probably the most important in the process. A lot of people think that choreography is just doing steps when in fact the steps are the very last thing that I do.

When dealing with musical theatre the choreography has to service the many elements of the book. I have to research the time period, the geographical areas, the particular class system of the various characters and the other sociological and psychological events that might relate to the story. The research that I do is quite extensive. When I find the one particular piece of information that is going to inspire me choreographically, it's like finding gold. For example, I had no idea that the black race invented the Charleston until I read about it in a book entitled *Black Dance From 1619 to Today* by Lynn Emery. That piece of information became a key element in my choreography for the second act montages in *Show Boat*.

I agreed to do *Show Boat* because of what I imagined Hal Prince might bring to that story. Everything that Hal is involved in is very political. He directs with an emphasis on sociology. I knew this would be an important *Show Boat*. The team wanted to do a show that would be palatable to a 1994 audience. The show became about family, forgiveness and the passing of time during a historical period of America. There was some flack from several groups during rehearsal that forced us to have to cross picket lines. The public controversy surrounding the show's subject matter made me go even further into my research and find out what I could do to make this a different *Show Boat*. The dancing and musical staging in *Show Boat* call for realism. There is no place for "dream sequences" or a line of beautiful show girls. The choreography exists in *Show Boat* to heighten the plot and accentuate the character activity.

In the second act, Hal Prince asked for a montage to show the passage of time. When he first said it, I thought, "Well, this is just going to be a big fashion show. I've got to get through twenty-seven years here." But then I thought, "What else can I bring to this montage that will make it more important?" I used the information that the Charleston was developed by the blacks in New Orleans on the levee to set me on a choreographic concept for the passing of time. I already had a big Charleston number done by white dancers in the last scene of *Show Boat*. I wanted to show that the whites learned how to do the Charleston from the blacks. The montage takes place on the streets of Chicago. I was able to incorporate not only fashions of the times, but also street dancers, panhandlers, a one-man band, gamblers, jazz trumpet player, etc. At the last section of the montage, I have three black Charleston dancers having a wonderful time dancing for coins. They do a Charleston against the music, "Hey Feller" and "Old Man River." A group of white folks watch them enthusiastically and try to pick up the steps. When the scene comes later with the white Charlestonettes, some of the same moves are repeated that were done by the three black dancers earlier. The choreography poetically shows the contribution that blacks have made to music and dance during that time.

Because the Kern estate allowed me the freedom to not only develop the music for the dance but to interpolate other Kern melodies, I was able to incorporate more dance based on the history of America. The aspect of poetically portraying the contributions that African Americans made to music and dance separates this *Show Boat* from any other ever produced.

*A Christmas Carol* has now become an annual event at Madison Square Garden. Again, because the choreographer was part of the early conception of this show, *A Christmas Carol* dances from beginning to end. My mission was to present varied examples of dance styles that would be believable in the period of Dickens, and yet be very much an invention of my own. The close collaboration with the creative team and designers, Jules Fisher, Tony Walton and William Ivey Long made this musical event a success. Collaboration in the musical theatre is the key to victory.

If you believe in and have a passion for a particular project, then you need to give it all you've got. Imagine yourself succeeding. When I was younger, I used to imagine when I danced that I could fly. I don't feel that any more because I'm a little older, a little more earthbound. But, because I imagined it, I really did fly. You have to keep your mind open and not let anybody zap your faith in yourself. The job will not come to you. You have go out and get it. If I hadn't gone out and created *And the World Goes Around* I wouldn't be here right now. Chance favors the prepared mind. You need to be able to take a chance. Many people say, "That person's lucky." Luck has something to do with it but luck is really the ability to seize the moment. One needs to be alert, adventurous and feel the timing.

Even when I was very small, as I listened to music, I would visualize the music, as I still do today. I always wanted to be a choreographer ever since I could spell it. The idea that it's actually come true is really a dream realized and I know I'm very fortunate. There's nothing greater for me than standing in the back of a theatre and seeing and hearing an audience being affected by a movement that I created. It brings me enormous joy to move an audience to sigh in *Show Boat*, cry in *A Christmas Carol* and laugh in *Crazy for You*.

Susan Stroman created *Blossom Got Kissed* for the New York City Ballet and *But Not For Me* for the Martha Graham Company. She has been honored with London's Laurence Olivier Award for her choreography of the National Theatre's production of *Oklahoma!*; the Tony Award, Drama Desk Award and Outer Critics' Circle Award for *Crazy for You*; and the Tony Award and the Outer Critics' Circle Award for *Show Boat*. She choreographed the Broadway productions of *Big, Steel Pier* and the revival of *Picnic*. For Off-Broadway she choreographed *Flora, the Red Menace* and *And the World Goes Around* for which she achieved the Outer Critics' Circle Award. An Emmy nomination was gained for the HBO program *Liza Stepping Out at Radio City Music Hall* starring Liza Minnelli. Ms. Stroman choreographed *Don Giovanni, A Little Night Music* and *110 in the Shade* for the New York City Opera. For television she directed *A Tribute to Leonard Bernstein* and co-conceived and choreographed *Sondheim—A Celebration at Carnegie Hall*. She has choreographed *A Christmas Carol* for Madison Square Garden and the dance movie, *Center Stage*, for Columbia Pictures. For the 1999–2000 Broadway season she directed the revival of *Music Man* and conceived, directed and choreographed *Contact*, which gained her the Tony Award for Choreography. In 2001, she won Tony Awards for Direction and Choreography for the Broadway hit, *The Producers*.

### Choreography for Opera

*Elizabeth Keen*

Choreographing for opera can be a rewarding experience. It is enriching to be a part of this vibrant artistic arena, to exchange ideas and be stimulated by others, and to find just the right choreographic solution for a particular scene. It is a wonderful challenge, but this silver cloud has a grey lining. A choreographer's work may be integrated into the staging of the entire opera, but more commonly it is limited to a single scene. While an opera usually lasts several hours, the movement work within it rarely extends beyond ten minutes. These moments are first and foremost in the choreographer's mind but not necessarily in anyone else's. In opera, dance can be something of a step-child. What is it like to join this nonetheless vital field? What follows is an attempt to lay open the opera world, how it usually operates and how best to prepare to function well within it.

Opera companies, like the communities that support them, come in all sizes. The older and better established the opera house, the more complex its internal organization. Each department has its own needs and its own turf. Though the director, in tandem with the conductor, reigns on the artistic front, it is the stage management department that is responsible for the coordination of all aspects of the production itself. Scheduling is extremely complicated. The practicalities of scenery, costumes and lighting, the budget and union rules constrain and, at times, take precedence over creative concerns. The priorities depend on the values of the administration. Production stage management then calls the shots. To someone coming from the field of concert dance this may seem to be a case of the tail wagging the dog. It is, however, important to know up front what these limitations are and not be surprised by them.

Within the structure of opera production then, what is the choreographer's place? It lies in the chain of command that extends from the director, through the choreographer to the performers. Whether the choreographer is used in a very limited way or is asked to attend to anything that moves within the production, (i.e. gestures, use of capes or crowd scenes), all artistic decisions stem from or refer back to the director. Having said that, though, how it all works out is another story. The myriad ways in which directors and choreographers collaborate vary according to personality, clarity of vision, knowledge of dance/choreography, organizational ability, sense of authority, modus operandi (detailed planning versus a more improvisational approach), degree of competitiveness, willingness to work in partnership and, most exciting, artistic empathy. By definition, directors like to be in charge. Some may welcome suggestions; others like to dispense orders, sometimes even when they seem to invite your participation. One of the best directors I have worked with always had a specific idea of what he wanted to happen in a scene. In pre-production meetings he would indicate in the score how far his staging would go and exactly where the performers would be when a dance was to begin. This kind of clarity was very helpful, unlike the director for whom I choreographed at least a dozen versions of a dance only to be asked to return to the very first sketch she had seen and rejected. Some bosses hover over your shoulder as you work; others are more trusting and leave you alone.

In preparation for work on an opera, here is a checklist of choreographic concerns:

- What is the story of the opera?
- What purpose does the dance serve within the work:

    how does it anticipate, advance or celebrate the plot?

- What seems to be the style of the director:

    realistic, imagistic, flamboyant, constrained, fantastical, traditional, highly
    personal?

- Will your use of space be similar to the director's or a contrast?
- What is the appropriate movement style?
- What special research and training are needed?
- With whom will you work and what are their movement abilities:

    dancers, extras, principals, soloists or chorus members?

- How might set and costume influence your staging?
- What is the music; how danceable is it:

    are all the repeats being used, or are there cuts?

- How much rehearsal time do you have; how much do you really need?

When you first meet with a director, it is critical to understand his or her approach, and to assess the implications for your choreography. Some directors prefer a natural style, or what might be termed the untrained look. Others want a specialized movement vocabulary that is either invented or that requires specific knowledge of period style. For example, I have been asked for "inauthentic flamenco." Translation: untrained singers would be dancing and they needed to resemble the real "stuff" without appearing foolish. Yes, I used many pure Spanish dance elements, but did I compromise? You bet.

Before going into official rehearsal, invest studio time in working out movement ideas with a few dancers, even if their pay comes from your own pocket. Some choreographers choose to walk in with every step already set. It is my experience that this only saves precious time when you are working on a set piece, to be inserted into a scene. Pre-production preparation is essential but your choreography needs to be in sync with the director's emotional tone, dramatic and spatial choices and particular production style. The chore-ographer must be sensitive to this and, therefore flexible and ready to adapt. It is most helpful to attend rehearsals other than your own to discern specifically how the opera is unfolding. It may be difficult to grasp the actuality of style from pre-production meet-ings, and a director's words are surprisingly easy to misinterpret. Observing scenes as they are created also provides a chance to understand the personalities of those singers with whom you may be working. This is useful information because working well with your cast is as important as choreographing well.

You will often work with non-dancers. The trick is to find simple and effective move-ment phrases that are not too frustrating to learn. Remember that performers want to look their best. Singers can resent staging that is beyond their training or lack of it, and rightfully so. It is important to respect their accomplishments, to appreciate how much they have invested in their art, and to discover how movement can enhance their artistry. When working with soloists and principals it can be helpful to observe what they do nat-urally and build from there. If they originate even a part of a movement idea, it will feel right to them and probably look right as well. This technique also holds in working with a chorus. Once their self-confidence is established, singers settle down and more easily learn actual steps and patterns. Whatever the movement vocabulary, make certain the dramatic motivation is clear; if the intended feeling is right, the steps will fall into place more easily. It is often interesting to blend dancers and non-dancers, reserving the more difficult passages for the dancers, who can also serve to cue in or lead the others. Be flexible and keep a friendly atmosphere. Bruised egos will make life tough for you and not help your work. In opera the egos justify the extravagance of the art form.

Your work will be affected greatly by that of the costume, set and lighting designers. In fact, one of the great perks of being in opera is the opportunity to meet designers in related areas. Their contributions to the production reflect their own discussions with the director. You may or may not have been a party to these conversations. Ask to see the costume sketches for the dancers as soon as possible. What are the fabrics; will they move well; is there enough room in the armpits and in the crotch; will the garments enhance or conceal the movement? An experienced designer will know all about these pitfalls, but it doesn't hurt to double-check tactfully. More than that, the costume can suggest movement possibilities. How much can the skirt swirl? Can the cape be used to enfold a partner as well as hang decoratively from the shoulders? Sometimes the clothes are absolutely essential to the dance, as in the *Dance of the Seven Veils* in *Salome*. In my choreography for Maria Ewing, the Salome of Sir Peter Hall's production, the costumes, designed by Liz Bury, were a great asset. The extraordinary way they draped, and the sinuous manner in which they flowed, floated and then fell instantaneously to the floor, was inspiring. Ms. Bury provided an enormous eighth veil made by joining three wedding saris. I used this to frame the dance by having two handmaidens (whose original function was merely to pick up the costumes after the dance) manipulate it into fantastical shapes. In this production, a complete set of rehearsal clothes in inexpensive fabrics was made available. For these costumes to have arrived as late as the dress rehearsal would have been a disaster. Whenever possible, ask to have key garments, or substitutes, and shoes for use early on.

The use of space is critical to choreographers, a concern shared by scenic designers. These designers always provide three dimensional models of their sets. Study them carefully. Will you be working within a proscenium arch, or with an audience on three sides or totally in the round? How can your dance make use of the set; what kind of spatial patterns does it suggest? Beware the set that seriously obstructs the dance. A set designer is unlikely to have choreography uppermost in his mind and may unwittingly make your life difficult. I remember a production of *H.M.S. Pinafore* that had an entranceway from a lower deck plunked dead center. Every dance would have had to circle around it. I argued successfully that it be moved much farther up-stage.

The switch from studio to stage almost always necessitates unanticipated adjustments.

It may take longer to climb a stairs unit than expected, or to exit stage left and re-enter from stage right; a sense of immediacy and significant details may be lost. Even if you have been lucky enough to rehearse in a space the size of the stage with the entire set in place, some weaknesses only reveal themselves in the theater. You will also have to check the sight lines to ensure that your staging can be seen from all points of the house. Peculiar to opera is the placement of video monitors at angles around the stage so that singers needn't always face front to glue their eyes on the conductor. Your staging must not block their view of the conductor whose image appears on the screen.

Lighting can make or break a dance. Cues are set in the theater before the performers are on stage. The choreographer should be on the spot and should have requested people to walk the space. It's really important to have invited the lighting designer to see the choreography ahead of time and to have spoken about the important moments in the dance. It's not just the practical questions of brightness and placement of lamps but the timing and quality of the illumination that will enhance the dance. Sometimes designers are interested in what you have to say and sometimes they are truly intransigent. Failing discussion, if you really feel a change is essential, you may have to go to the director to get it, but if you are over-ruled, learn to suffer with ingenuity. After all, we all win some and lose some. At least you have been articulate about your needs.

The one person who is the director's equal is the conductor. They are not called maestros for nothing; their word is law. The musical interpretation of the production is literally in their hands. Like all people, some conductors are approachable; some are not. The choreographer often has learned the dance music from a particular recording, and has choreographed to its phrasing and tempo. These may or may not gibe with the conductor's reading. Find this out as soon as possible, or you may find yourself re-choreographing. If, as may be the case, the conductor is not on the scene until the last weeks of rehearsal, check with the assistant conductor whose business it is to know these things. A few words about final orchestra rehearsals: they are very expensive given the number of participants and there is much to accomplish. The conductor's first consideration is to connect seamlessly the playing in the pit with the singing on the stage, no small accomplishment. Hence, rarely are conductors able to run the dance more than once; yet the dancers need to be secure in what they are doing. The wise choreographer will try to get on-stage time for the dancers apart from the singers and before the final orchestra dress. It is also important to realize that both piano and orchestra dress rehearsals are extremely trying times. Be prepared for heightened sensitivity all the way around, as the performers deal with their nerves and become accustomed to their costumes, the stage and back-stage areas and the sound and tempi of the orchestra. While dance companies usually rehearse up to and including the day of performance, in opera, the final orchestra dress is followed by a forty-eight hour break prior to opening night. Since dancers don't seem to need to rest their bodies as long as singers their voices, it is often possible to get extra movement rehearsals in this time slot, though the stage may not be available.

For the sake of convenience recorded music may be used in dance rehearsals, but usually a pianist plays for these sessions. Musical lines of particular instruments don't always appear in the piano reduction of the score. Make sure the pianist is playing the cues the dancers need to hear, but also that the dancers listen to the orchestral version of their music. The two can sound disconcertingly different. The musical score has sections that are marked by numbers or letters. It is smart to note these markers so the accompanist will understand where you are in the music. Some pianists are sensitive to dance and will comprehend what is meant by "Take it from run, run leap" or "from those fast notes." Others will not find your ignorance endearing. It is far better to be able to say, "I need to begin four bars before rehearsal letter B." Also, you must know the difference between musicians' counts, where numbers refer to beats in a measure, and what are called dancers' counts, which can refer either to a series of movements or to a series of notes in a rhythmic sequence. Dancers' counts drive musicians crazy. Choreographers must know the difference and be able to count in measures.

Ignorance is not bliss; it may even get you fired. Before joining the opera world, be reasonably familiar with the historical development of opera. It is extremely useful to have a working knowledge of the following:

- Dances from different centuries (including appropriate manners, bows and curtsies).
- Ballroom dancing (early 20th century tango and present-day Argentinean tango differ).
- Various folk traditions (Poles, Hungarians and Russians do not all dance the same).

There are experts in movement styles of all varieties who often give workshops in their specialties. Seek them out. Since an opera choreographer is often involved in staging crowd scenes, make a point of studying how groups move and react; observe when and how an individual stands out against a crowd. Photographs and figurative paintings can be wonderfully instructive about the arrangement of people in space. Begin your own picture collection. Knowledge of art and music history, the ability to follow a score and to hear phrasing and rhythms are all of paramount importance. Read plays, go to theater, as well as to the opera. Notice how plot develops; how a director paces a production. What effects are visual, which ones are emotional? Try to sing; try to move while singing, dance in an opera. Study acting; dance in a play. Choreograph anything you can. Fool around in the studio with friends. Volunteer in community performance groups and college productions. Work as an intern with a professional company in administration or stage management. Acquire multiple skills; you'll use them all.

Most of the information discussed thus far relates to artistic decisions and activities, all of which take place within a particular work structure that falls under the umbrella of stage management. Stage managers are responsible for the day-to-day organization of rehearsals of all performers from principals on down to supernumeraries (non-union extras). Additionally, they schedule vocal and language coaching sessions, chorus and dance rehearsals, costume fittings, and they co-ordinate orchestra rehearsals, the assembling of props and the installment of scenery and lighting equipment, all according to the rules of different unions. Further, during any given performance they call all the cues that allow the production to unfold. Just like performers, stage managers and their assistants need time to practice their routines. It is not difficult to understand how complex the situation becomes and why last-minute requests from choreographers are not appreciated.

Needless to say, a choreographer should maintain a good working relationship with these organizers, not just so they will be inclined to be helpful to you when you need them (and you will), nor simply because you'll be in daily contact with them, but out of respect for all they accomplish. It is important for everyone's happiness that there be open communication and good-natured appreciation not only for the performers who are applauded by the audience, but for those who function behind the scenes, including the crew and wardrobe. It's all integrally connected. Part of the choreographer's job is to provide stage management with explicit notes of the choreography. If the opera is repeated in subsequent seasons the choreographer may be asked to return and recreate the work; however, in larger houses there is usually a ballet mistress whose job it is to maintain, recast and rehearse revivals. The notes the choreographer has provided, as well as videos made at final dress rehearsals, if permitted by the union, are used for this purpose.

It is important to make known during contract discussions that you wish to audition the dancers yourself. In the United States they are usually hired per production. The dates of the auditions should be early enough to ensure that you have time to find the dancers you need. You also must indicate to the opera company how many rehearsal sessions are necessary to set the dances. If you are creating new work, this is not easy to assess, so ask for maximum time. If dancers are hired by the week rather than per session then this won't cause a problem. Whatever the arrangement, you cope.

Opera has awakened to the notion that singers should be trained to act; perhaps the time has arrived for a more concerted effort in movement training as well. No longer is it enough for artists to stand still on stage, sing, and occasionally gesture. Many opera programs are aware of the need for adequate movement studies, but some of them could take it far more seriously. Audiences as well as choreographers would be grateful.

If dance in opera does not have the best of reputations, it is because it has been slighted, sometimes by the short-sightedness of management, sometimes by budgetary concerns, and sometimes by embarrassingly poor choreography. Opera is a conglomerate of the arts. To be truly successful, each part must fulfill its potential. Dance needs to be as strong as the other links in this artistic chain. For those who lend their choreographic talent to opera, the experience is its own special journey. I have found it well worth the trip.

Elizabeth Keen began in the concert dance field performing in the companies of Paul Taylor, Helen Tamiris–Daniel Nagrin, Katherine Litz and Mary Anthony. From 1966–1981 she choreographed for her own group, The Elizabeth Keen Dance Company, which toured nationally and performed annually in New York City with support from the NEA and NYSCA. Since then she has choreographed primarily for opera and theater. Her work in opera includes: *Carmen*, *Falstaff* and *La Traviata* (Glyndebourne Opera Festival), *Carmen* (the Met) and *Salome* (Los Angeles Opera, Covent Garden, Lyric Opera of Chicago and San Francisco Opera) all directed by Sir Peter Hall; *L'Ange de Feu* (Los Angeles Opera, L'Opera Bastille and the Netherlands Opera) directed by Andrei Serbin; *Candide* (Central City Opera), *Porgy and Bess* (North Carolina Opera Association), *Johnny Spielt Auf* (Long Beach Opera), *The Gondoliers* (Chatauqua Opera) and *Romeo and Juliet* (the Washington Opera at the Kennedy Center and the Seattle Opera) all directed by Peter Mark Schifter. Theatre choreography includes *Animal Farm* (Associate Choreographer), *Yonadab*, *The Tempest*, *Cymbeline*, and *A Winter's Tale* (Royal National Theatre); *A Winter's Tale*, *Hamlet*, *Romeo and Juliet* and *As You Like It* (American Shakespeare Theater); *Guys and Dolls* (Goodman Theater); *Kiss Me Kate* (ArtPark); *A Comedy of Errors* (New York Shakespeare Festival); and *A Doll's House* (The McCarter Theater).

Ms. Keen recently returned to the concert field with a new solo, *Abstract Expressionism*, for Dance Theater Workshop's Founders Celebration. Ms. Keen is currently on the faculty of the Julliard School, the José Limon Summer Dance Workshop, the Alvin Ailey School and the Lincoln Center Institute. Previous faculty appointments were at Sarah Lawrence College, Princeton University and NYU's Tisch School of the Arts. She is a graduate of Barnard College and holds an M.A. from Sarah Lawrence College.

### Choreography for the Theatre

#### Donya Feuer

His name was Arion of Lesbos and he was said to be our first Choreographer,
  creating movement for the chorus 400 years before Christ,
  with a text sung or spoken in a highly stylized language,
  his actors on platform shoes with masks that heightened the role,
  the voice and the actor for a public of many thousands of people,
  with the sky as their ceiling and the earth their stage.
His task—to concentrate the eye and focus of the public,
  to see, hear, and follow the actors acting the play,
  to strengthen the tempo and the rhythm,

enhancing what they did with movement.

The choreographic material from then on became a precise support system
for the entire performance and its meanings.

I can imagine him climbing the endless steps up to the very last row
"to check it all out,"
not once, but many times!

Seen from here in our time, it seems to have been a profoundly inspiring job
Addressed directly to the gods in whose honor these plays were performed.

So, to briefly describe how I see choreographing for the theatre some 2500 years later:

Generally speaking:

You do not have to like the director but it is better if you do, as mutual respect
and a good speaking relationship is the "abc" of it all.

Good also, if you feel it is a place for you to learn and gain knowledge.

Read the play many times—really knowing it before you begin.

If you are working with a condensed version, check out the original to see what
has been done and try to understand "why."

So much gets done before you are in the picture, including the sets, costumes,
shoes, lighting, etc. All of these demand that you know their "why."

And above all, the music: learn it, sing it, improvise to it, etc.

Really try to understand the intentions, goals of the director.

Ideally study him working with the actors. There you have a unique chance to
see them both interacting. That experience will enrich what you do later
on. Let them inspire you.

Do not compete! That is difficult, because you are enveloped by creative energies. Rather enhance what is already there, or latently there.

This will make actors feel at home and gives you the possibility to ask even
more of them later on. It establishes the ideal quality of a working and productive ensemble. You will also have a happy director and there is nothing
like being trusted.

Practical and basic

Space

Make the actor aware of the body as a surface that disturbs the space it goes
through.

Heighten awareness of the others on stage.

Hands

They always articulate the carriage and the intention of the body.

And

Not in the least, Martha Graham's unforgettable, *"This bone, your collar bone is God's necklace. It is a gift and you must learn to wear it well."*

Auditions

The actors are primarily not your choice though definitely a part of your responsibility. Whenever possible, be a part of the audition process, not only for dancers, in the event that there will be some in the cast but also the actors. Giving a brief movement section will tell the director that this talented actor has no sense of rhythm, a potential disaster if the role calls for some dance.

When choosing your dancers be sure you really look forward to working with them and can freely share and entrust them with the vision of your work, a personal but important note.

Warming up

Movement training is possible with the actors and the dancers.

Design it for the tasks of the specific production you are doing.

Do it everyday before rehearsing.

This will be the making of an ensemble and it is pure gold.

More thoughts

You are extending an art or expanding it, maybe both.

Transitions from acting to dance and back again, there will be the test of the ins and outs of your choreographic sequences.

Any dance number in a play is potentially dynamite.

It will demand all of your attention.

As will every entrance, exit and crossovers.

Choreography for the theater involves every move made on the stage. The acting scenes help define and often open the door to the choreographic work. That is the way to reveal something special, a dimension hard to define though it is visible. It brings to the play, or rather should bring to the play, a kind of weaving that includes everything—the actors, the dancers, the lighting, the sets, everything. Movement language coordinates feeling, emotion, the lie, etc. It does not express, illustrate or explain anything. It complements, it enhances, it supports the visible and invisible and is often best when it is difficult to say exactly what or where it is. However, the public feels it, the players rely on it and the producers are happy.

Summing up

It is not a lesser art but a different one. The demands are tricky but when we succeed the results can make a big difference. A difference that matters.

Donya Feuer is a graduate of the Julliard School of Music and worked early in her career with the Martha Graham Company. She went on to hold positions as Artistic Director of the Studio for Dance with Paul Sanasardo, Guest Pedagog-Choreographer in Stockholm and Choreographer for the Royal Dramatic Theater. Ms. Feuer has choreographed extensively for Alf Sjöberg, including productions of *Yvonne, Troilus and Cressida, The Marriage, Alcestis, Feud in Chiozza* and *School for Wives*. Ms. Feuer's work with Ingmar Bergman includes choreography for *The Magic Flute, King Lear, Markisinnan de Sade, Peer Gynt, The Winter's Tale, Misantrope, Bacchae* and *Maria Stuart*. Feuer's own productions include *A Midsummer Night's Dream, The Tempest, Measure for Measure, If Five Years Pass, Blood Wedding, Easter, Soundings, God is Alive and Well* and *Ej Blott Till Lyst*. In addition, Feuer has choreographed productions for the Royal Swedish Opera, the Netherlands Opera, Stockholm's Music Dramatic Ensemble, The Norwegian Opera, Fact Theater and others. Feuer's work in film includes the *A Life* and *Rekviem for a Dancer* (with Nijinsky); *The Dancer*, which was honored as Best Scandinavian Documentary of 1994; and the 2000 film, *The Working of Utopia*. Ms. Feuer inaugurated "Dance on Film" at the New York Film Society and was nominated for an Oscar in 1995. She is also the winner of the Carina Ari Gold Medal and Stockholm's Prize of Honor. In 1990 she began "In the Company of Shakespeare," a vast educational project, in cooperation with the English poet Ted Hughes. This project has continued through 2001. Since 1996, Ms. Feuer has been a professor at the Stockholm Institute for Education.

# 16  Mindsets

Early morning, after a commuter trip to Stamford, Connecticut, standing before a group of young students of acting poised to take their movement class with the New York dance guru, I muttered sourly, "How is it that you all are so filth . . . Oh, I'm so sorry!" and quickly removed my eyeglasses to clean them carefully. Some laughter and we went on to begin the class. A little joke, but not really funny. It is not at all possible to perceive anything without a mindset that gives a coloration and a character to all that we behold.

Over the years, I have heard teachers of choreography evaluate the choreographic efforts of a student and in the doing, plant in his.her consciousness and unconscious self-awareness a view of what is possible and what is not acceptable in the fine art of dance. A brilliant young dancer, after several years of good experience in New York, returned to Arizona State University as a graduate student. In my technique class, she absorbed everything in no time and could do most anything asked of her, yet her dancing was flat. One day, I said, "You dance like a ball point pen. You do everything so well, but it all comes out in the same thin line of energy. It's as if you have no opinions and no personal taste or are fearful of expressing them. Buy a fountain pen with a flexible point and practice writing with light pressures and strong pressures and then tell me what you think."

Was there a change? Yes. Gradually, a zest and playfulness slipped into her work. She was dancing like a fountain pen. A few months later, she told me that early in her study of dance, "X," a well-known and revered teacher of a "cool" technique, turned on her asking, "Why all the melodrama? Just do the movement."

In most of my choreography classes, I hand out several sheets of paper to let them know where they are and who they will be dealing with. The first one is my attempt to free them from what might be their past.

*Hazards Facing Students of Choreography*

There is an unfortunately long list of brutal trips which some teachers of chore-ography lay upon their students. I have heard these criticisms glibly dispensed by un-talented and talented teachers alike. It is even possible that on occasion their remarks have had weight. Personally, I find them simplistic, suspect and, even worse, they im-plant creative inhibitions which persist and hobble the work of some professional artists long into their careers:

- You are being self-indulgent.

- It is too personal.

- It is literal.

- It is literary.

- It is theatrical.

- It is pantomime.

- It is political.

- You are emoting.

- You are acting, not dancing.

- It doesn't use the space.

- There is no change in level.

- There is no change in dynamics.

- Why are you trying to convince an audience of what they already believe?

- They never say, "nothing happens," because they do not want anything to happen.

- Upon eliciting what a particular piece is "about," the one sitting upright in the chair says to the one sitting on the floor, "I don't see that at all."

- Sometimes there is talk of the work needing a beginning, middle or end. It is not easy to know what they mean, but often they say "It has no climax." The problem is, some things do not have a climax, therefore all works do not need to have a climax.

- "What I want to see is . . ." is a favorite phrase of some and it is an indirect way of solving your problem for you.

For students who have studied with teachers who speak in this manner, it would not be surprising for them to assume that this is *the* way to give helpful criticism. They may have felt wronged by the criticism inflicted upon them, but perversely for that very reason, it might be too easy to slip into that frame of mind in the years that follow when they will be sitting in that chair, delivering judgement upon the one sitting on the floor.

⸻

To return to the matter of eyeglasses, those of us who live with them know too well that they are never perfectly clean. They always need attention. There is a useful metaphor here. It is not entirely fanciful to say that everyone wears "eyeglasses" if you believe that all that we see is glimpsed through the prism of our personal experience and mindset. If we regard our self-awareness as the distorting dirt that clutters up our vision of what is out there, it behooves us to continually wipe our eyeglasses as thoroughly as possible. Those whose "glasses" are heavily encrusted with self qualify as neurotics and/or bigots. Some examples: Any who are unremittingly preoccupied with immaculate tidiness in every detail of their lives see dirt everywhere. Or, those who have a continual frantic concern with time are panicked by the slightest delay. Those who believe they are under siege see enemies everywhere. They qualify as neurotics with their rigid response to most situations. Wherever they look, that portion of themselves that smears their "eyeglasses" bends their vision in a particular way. And then, there are those tragic ones whose consciousness of self is so overwhelming that their "eyeglasses" are opaque. They look and see only what they have created and they qualify as mad.

Picasso remarked at an exhibition of children's art, "When I was the age of these children, I could draw like Raphael. It took me many years to learn how to draw like these children." Being adults, we do have serious obstacles when it comes to being creative. We know too much. Children are raw and, at a certain stage, produce art that is quite stunning and perceptive.

What are the obstacles? Before anything, we as dancers have in the course of our training accumulated a mass of neuromuscular patterns. Without them, we would be untrained —unskilled. With them, it becomes a challenge to come up with fresh and personal movement. I came to dance out of the restlessness of an adolescent body. I would shut off my homework, snap on the radio and rock about. In time, I got caught up in the excitement of moving to music, particularly and strangely enough to Armenian folk music! *Never having had a dance class, let alone attended a dance concert, what did I do then?* Knowing nothing, I could work up a joyous sweat. Lost. Lost. Forever lost. Years later, I choreographed a solo in thanks to that Armenian music, calling it *A Gratitude.* I did not pretend to be an innocent. No. It was quite sophisticated: tricky rhythms to the tricky Armenian rhythms, a sequence of double air turns and a delicate, lyrical closing with slow balances. I didn't even attempt to reach for that innocence, which of course was lost in time.

As we enter the studio, not only are our bodies preprogrammed, so are our minds. What to do? In almost all of the exercises, games and structures that we evolved in the Workgroup, we began with some form of meditation to clear our minds. It is the practice for many artists of Asia to precede creative work with meditation. Achieving that quiet sense of emptiness as we turn to plow into a new space in the work keeps us ready for the unexpected and expands our peripheral vision.

In this business of meditation, there is a word to be wary of: "centering." This was a favorite concept back in the sixties and seventies. It carries the aura of focus, of knowing where you want to go and directing all your energies to that point. Hunches, intuitions, wild guesses and the unforeseen may not thrive in that atmosphere. Creatively, we need every one of those possibilities. If we are too focused, we only see what we have *put* there instead of what *is* there.

Aside from meditation, there are dozens of ways to open the horizons of the mind:

- A dream book. A collection of your dreams.

- Knowing what the others are doing—not only in dance but in all the arts that excite you.

- Having a delightful time fooling around to any music that gets you going or to music that irritates you.

- Gardening or studying physics.

- Reading the newspapers, the classics and the comics.

- Two exercises that will be found in the Workbook: Backdoor and the Hub Meditation.

- Try not to take Martha Graham, Balanchine or Merce Cunningham into the studio with you. Giants are noisy and take up too much room. Minor artists have a place of honor in the history and practice of art. Subjecting yourself to the major-minor test is sterile masochism.

- Speaking of sterility, it is fertilized by perfectionism.

- Accepting the premise that you will always be beginning; that as you begin each new work every "principle" you had previously accepted will need to be re-established or *discarded*.

- Accepting the principle that a great hazard to an open mind will be your last success.

- Demanding success at all costs can be very expensive, while being open to the permissibility of failure gives you the freedom to take risks. The opposite of not taking risks is being safe. Safe sex? Yes. Safe art? Please no!

- Accept uncertainty. It is the best guarantee against the shock and disappointment that follows on the heels of being sure of almost everything.

- Living with all your senses wide open and ravenous.

In the creative process, it is almost inevitable that there will come the day when you see with stunning clarity that what you have made is hopelessly inept, unoriginal, misshapen and best described as "garbage." If you can get through that day and continue with the work, you may very well produce something quite beautiful.

In the making of dances, there are times of great heat where everything seems to flow effortlessly. Oppositely, there are stretches that can only be crossed with cool, careful detachment, concentration and *prolonged tedious labor*. Strangely, there are choreographers who have difficulty with passionate eruptions, not trusting their unpredictability and disorderliness. They prefer to be in control all the time. Their opposites are those who cannot cope with the inevitable tasks that demand composed thought, analysis, tenaciousness and all too much time. The artist that emerges and survives *is balanced, ready for whatever comes up, the flood or the freeze. The others, in spite of talent, will produce only a fraction of what they contain.*

For some, the great incentive is to be the best; to be better than all the others. This is inevitably an exhausting business. Aside from the labor of producing their own work, they have to constantly study the competition, i.e., look over their shoulders. (I wonder how many races have been lost by this maneuver?) Perhaps the real terror should be that they are not as good as they might be.

From where do the ideas come? From where does the inspiration arise? I used to do a lecture-demonstration, "The Symbol and the Object in Dance." It consisted of five studies, all involving the act of sewing from an abstraction to the concrete. In the last study, I literally sewed up the hole in one of my dance slippers, at which point I would drop the sentimentious remark, "All art comes about because of a hole in a shoe. A hole! What to do? Save the shoe and fix it up? Buy new ones? Create a shoe that will never get holes? Stop wearing shoes?" Certainly, a provocative way of making the point that the seed of the art object is a difficulty, a tension, a need, a contradiction, a defiant hope. What we do about that tension defines us as artists.

There is that in humans that cries out to right things. Who can resist straightening a picture hanging crookedly? Imagination springs from the concrete: a hole in the shoe or some other difficulty. As soon as an ache rears up in the heart, the mind turns here and there looking about—and within. Solutions appear and disappear. Reason rejects, sorts and considers. The British have an appropriate phrase for dealing with this turbulence. They "sort things out." Every artist has his.her own technique for "sorting" in this dance between heart and mind. There are times when the idea, the solution, the concept unrolls with a simple logic. More often than not, the vision gains clarity in shards that, at the most unexpected moment, come together to make a whole. It's called inspiration and it rarely appears without prolonged probing, guessing and mulling. There are those naive ones who think it is a gift because it is said to come unbidden. No. Most artists continue to bruise their fists against the blank walls knowing that predictability is not part of the bargain. Their devil and their angel have one thing in common, uncertainty. They work and they work and they work and they hope.

There is no "way." Some keep extensive notes. Some just mutter quietly to themselves. Some find what they seek in dreams. Some meditate. I had a giant bulletin board upon which I tacked index cards inscribed with the multiple ideas that flowed into *The Peloponnesian War*. I'm certain that someone out there has plastered their refrigerator door with brilliant notes on post-its. Just never trust your memory—find your own way or ways of gathering the elusive ideas that may someday propel your work.

One of my life partners used to subtly bait me by insisting that she had the more active inner life. This justified the fact that she often broke dishes as she washed them because her mind was "elsewhere." Obviously, having one's mind "elsewhere" was of a higher and more poetic order. Can we say that there are two kinds of artists: those that use the material of the objective world and the others that use what is "within"? I believe this is a muddy and useless dichotomy. Drawing material from the outside world is the work of a mind whose internal life is charged and altered. Building work from internal sources means encountering and being affected by the outside world. Whatever the source, unless you are dealing with what is vital to you, that stirs you, you probably won't provoke that searching energy that explodes into "inspiration." You must really *need* the solution—and of course there is no "solution."

The rarest of artists are those who can mature and locate their own centers without knowing the work of other artists. Most artists need the awareness of other artists, both those that came before and their contemporaries. In this respect, dance has an inherent awkwardness compared to the other arts. It is not easy to be seen dancing or to see dance. Actors can function in the most miserable spaces. They are easily filmed or televised. Musicians can dispense ecstasy on a street corner or be available with a Walkman. Record stores contain in their aisles almost the entire history of music. The visual arts have museums, galleries and magazines that can keep artists far from New York City or Los Angeles aware of what is happening in the their world. Dancers out of the major metropolitan centers are lucky if they get to experience a few of the significant dance movers or view the infrequent and inadequate showings on television.

Traditionally, dance has been the most ignorant of the arts—ignorant of its past. Sculptors can study the works of fellow sculptors who lived thousands of years ago. Painters can be overwhelmed by prehistoric paintings found in the recesses of Spanish caves. Their eyes can feast upon the walls of ancient Egyptian tombs and the villas of Pompeii. Musicians are poorer. Not until the medieval manuscripts do they have any music that can be studied. From the time of the Renaissance, there have been a few written and scripted social dances and promenades. As for creative performances, dancers have, until this century, survived with little better than what amounts to the equivalent of an oral history supplemented by engravings and photographs. In the recent past, we have lived with a demonstration history—a history preserved by the living bodies of demonstrators who recalled the past for us.

Finally film emerged as a viable but inordinately expensive technology. Mickey Mouse and Fred Astaire have been memorialized but except for a few snippets, not Isadora Duncan, not Pavlova, not Nijinsky and too little of the major works that shaped the birth of the modern dance. Now finally, we have a technology most of us can afford and even operate! Is there a concert that is not videotaped? From the most professional work to every Master of Fine Arts thesis there is now a recording. Granted the full truth and visceral impact of dance movement is barely approximated on videotape. Give us time. Note how long it took the recording of music from its early days to achieve the startling fidelity available today. Daily, we are acquiring a history. We are no longer the illiterates of the arts. It behooves every dancer and every dance department to take advantage of video resources not only for personal records but to open the awareness of what has happened and what is happening in dance.

# 17  The Criticism of Choreography

Back in 1957, I was, for a few weeks, in the Rockies, in Steamboat Springs as a guest artist at Perry-Mansfield, a summer arts camp. Apart from my teaching work, I was putting the finishing touches to a long and complicated solo, *Indeterminate Figure*. The large space I needed for many hours was not available at the camp. A wonderful and awkward space was found for me. It was the Veterans of Foreign Wars Hall, a former garage converted to a hall for folk dancing. The wonder of it was the enormous space and the new hardwood floor, resilient as a diving board. The awkwardness was that the surround of wide-open industrial windows coming down to waist level exposed me to all who passed along on the main street of Steamboat Springs.

But no one stared. A startled glance would last for an instant. Once I looked up to face the windshield of a truck, becoming transfixed by six pairs of eyes: two cowboys, two lit-

tle boys between them and two horses over their heads. One of the men seemed to utter a command and the children looked away as did the other man. I was safe from becoming an odd spectacle, until one day in the middle of a cross to "stage right," I came face to face with the bluest pair of eyes. Ignoring him, a boy of about ten, I continued the rehearsal, only to realize that this was different. His gaze was unrelenting. I kept on for another twenty minutes, stopped to get some water and sat on my relax bench directly under the window with the blue eyes. Ignoring him, I lit a cigarette.

Silence for a bit then, "What are you doing?"

Grudgingly I replied, "I'm dancing."

Again silence. Then he said, "You're a good dancer."

Criticism is the one thing which choreography never lacks. Everybody is a critic: the professionals, every member of the audience, the stage crew, the dance company, friends, lovers and enemies, mothers, fathers, relations, colleagues, teachers and sometimes, the nastiest of all, the choreographer. Where to turn? Who to listen to? Why listen? What to do with it when it is given? This is a bundle designed to mess up the mind of every choreographer.

Criticism enlightens and confuses, gives strength and injures. Along with all the complex requirements of this profession, every choreographer would do well to form a philosophy and a technique for making criticism serve rather than destroy the months and years of work that go into the product.

While still working on Broadway, I created and performed five solo dances. These first appearances were treated with considerable critical respect. Thus, I felt encouraged to continue creating. Then came the time when I ventured to share an evening with another choreographer. A review in a major publication dismissed my work as "Broadway slick." To this day, I blush when I acknowledge the fact that I did not create another new dance for the five years that followed. I was clobbered and I took it. I wonder how much longer I might have continued to hold back if it were not for a few colleagues: José Limon, Paul Draper, Jane Dudley, Louis Horst and of course Helen Tamiris. In a subtle way, they helped me to a fashion a distance from criticism. I might rise up in an indignant rage at what I believed to be an obtuse and insensitive review of my work, but in time, I learned not to collapse into a wallow of self-doubt.

Personally, I think it is dangerous for an artist to produce in isolation without any feedback, (a soft term for criticism). What is needed is a friend, and I use the term advisedly. I think every artist needs a friend with a complex mix of qualities: one who is genuinely supportive; one who feels free to speak negatives about the work and one who shares with the artist fundamental aesthetic perspectives.

There is a radically different kind of critic that can make a genuine contribution to assessing the values of one's work. Some of my early solos were created in the studios of Michael's School of Acrobatics on Eighth Avenue in New York. The studios were small, not at all clean, each one equipped with a built-in 78 rpm record player and cheap to rent. There was even a free warmup room for those who came early or were low on cash. Hanya Holm, Alwin Nikolais, Tamiris and some of the best tappers and Spanish dancers filled the three floors of studios. Michael himself was a small, stout man with a thick Russian accent who took on handsome young women, ambitious to become successful "exotic" dancers and taught them walkovers, splits and seductive routines.

I was working on a new dance on an upper floor and had reached an uneasy plateau. On an impulse, I tore down the steps to find Michael at the reception desk. "Mike. Do you have a minute? I'd like to show you something I just did." "Jerry! Take the desk," and off we went. I set out a chair for him and performed, full out, the two-thirds of the dance that had been choreographed. He sat there quietly and then with a half-smile said, "Dot's neat Daniel." I thanked him and off he went.

I had learned all I needed to know. It was one thing to dance alone in the studio and another to dance with a representative of the human race observing me. As I was performing, I could immediately sense the soggy sections in the choreography and the passages that felt strong and connected to the inner line of the dance. Being seen helped me to see. Whenever I could manage it, I would take all the new dances out on tour before presenting them in New York. The road would teach me what I needed to know.

The first rule in coping with criticism is to develop a sufficient distance which obviates the possibility of bleeding with each bad review and close enough to appraise its value. It will help if the artist accepts the premise that *all criticism contains in its folds a critique of the critic.* Listening or reading, some part of the mind must be asking the question, "What's her.his problem?"

⌐

You can't come into a restaurant and hand the waiter your menu. Too many people do just that when they come into the theatre. Objectively, there are no rules—only the ones we make up, and yet it would be false for me to deny that I maintain some kind of structure that accompanies me as I enter a dance theatre. At a certain point while I was on the faculty of the Arizona State University Dance Department, as discussions arose about evaluating the work of both students *and* faculty, I found I needed to put into writing thoughts and criteria that had hovered in my mind without being called to account. Next is what I submitted to the others:

### An Attempt to Examine What Actually Takes Place in My Mind When I Look at a Dance

I am in the theatre and viewing the work of a professional. What are the hinges on which my values and reactions swing? Before anything is the question and I suppose the criterion: Am I moved? Am I emotionally involved? Secondly, am I challenged? No matter how well-crafted a work of art, be it a dance or art in any other medium, if it projects a thrice-told statement, attitude, content and/or form, it is not only a bore but defeats the purpose of art as I see it. I come to the theatre to learn the news. "What's happening out there where you are?" is what I am asking the artist when I go to the theatre.

Following that, I am beguiled by craft, good taste, shocking "bad taste" that opens up my sensibilities to other ways of looking at life and dance in particular. Personally, I am more interested in "life" than in "dance." Craft includes everything that goes into the assembling of the work; the dancing, the casting, the dancers and their performance quality, the music, the relation to the music, costuming, lighting, props, etc.

I no longer have any preconceptions of what dance is. Anything that moves in a manner that causes me to sit up and wonder about myself, the world or dance itself, emerges as a vital artistic statement. *I do not demand that I understand what I am looking at.* The obvious bores me and conversely, if something baffles and even upsets me, I tend to regard that as a work I consider worth seeing again.

### Values that Help Me to Evaluate the Quality of Choreography by My Lights

- It captures my attention throughout the work.

- It has an emotional impact for me.

- It is intellectually challenging.

- Its structure is innovative at best and convincing at the very least, meaning the thread or the path of its development is not torn.

- I take on the concerns of the work and am drawn into the life on stage, i.e., I do not sit back watching what seems to be the dancers' problems.

- I am not continually wondering what the dancers are doing.

- It is not a rehash or a regurgitation of the work of other artists but rather, it is in some vital aspect, somewhere along the line, new.

- The accouterments of dance technique, music, costume, lights, props and set, if they exist, are skillfully assembled with obvious craft.

- For me, not understanding a work is quite different from spending much time wondering what the dancers are doing. With a strong work, my mind, memories and imagination clothe or invest each move with a particular import though it may be radically different than what any another viewer is experiencing or what was specifically in the mind of the choreographer and the performers. This is so even if I am mystified by the meaning of the entire work.
- There is good taste which drowns a work in boredom.
- There is bad taste which may simply be the howl created by cutting a new door through the wall of the past.

What of the teaching of choreography, which of course involves criticism of student work? Here the teacher has the choice of electing to be a god or a collaborator. I choose the latter, though because of my personal emphatic style of expression, some students back off from that and paint it as domineering. Well, I am not humble and I beg my students not to assume that posture either. An inherent facet of every class in choreography is the observation of student work and its evaluation. What follows is the design of my classes and workshops:

1. Since choreography is not improvisation, what is presented in class cannot be improvised, i.e., the student must assume full responsibility for every move, that is, being able to repeat what has been shown.

2. The presenter introduces his.her work with all of the information that would be available to a theatre audience: the title of the dance, the composer, a description of the anticipated costume, particularly as to whether it will be a "dance" costume or pedestrian wear and the sense of the lighting scheme. At no time, before the performance of the work or after, will the choreographer explain the work, give its rationale, justification or scenario. Unless the dancer plans to have extensive program notes, no audience would have access to these explanations. The issue of program notes could be a chapter in itself. Over the years, I came to avoid them.

3. After the verbal introduction, the dancer asks the viewers to close their eyes and to open them when an audience would begin to see, by calling out, "Curtain up," "Lights fade up," etc. Similarly, the dancer will call out "Curtain," or "Lights fade to black," and the group is asked to accept those remarks as instructions to close and/or open the eyes. The reasoning here is simple. In looking with a view to evaluating a dance, a blurred idea of when it actually starts and ends is no help at all.

4. When the dance is done, the choreographer places her.himself before the group. They make their observations first and then I speak.

5. Fundamentals of the critique session:

- The viewers tell the choreographer what it is that they saw and felt; what was conveyed to them. The focus of course is the choreography, but it is not necessarily irrelevant to bring in the matter of performance, since that can profoundly affect the effect of the work.

- They point out where they were drawn into the life of the dance and where they seemed to be looking at it from a distance.

- They note of the quality and continuity of the choreography and call attention to the particular points at which the dance life may have stopped—even for a moment.

- They observe how well the choreography relates to the music.

- Comments have great value if they are specific and tend to be unhelpful when they are generalized.

- At no time does anyone, including the teacher, attempt to contribute a solution for what they perceive as a problem. Critiques beginning with the phrase, "What I would like to see is . . ." are discouraged. The gift of the group is feedback, positive and negative. Solutions, if needed, are the sole responsibility of the choreographer.

6. Attitude:

- Kindness is crucial and necessary. This does not preclude being critical.

- There are those who feel that one should begin with the positive responses to the work, before raising any negatives. Personally, I tend to do that and out of respect and sensitivity, most students do that too. I have a resistance to laying down a formulaic manner of expression. I say nothing on this score.

- Anyone may ask the choreographer to repeat the work. Almost every art form, except dance, permits easy revisiting of the experience. How many times have we seen the same Van Gogh, heard an Aaron Copland score, seen Rodin's *Thinker* and read or seen *Hamlet*? And how much richer we were for those revisitings. Dance has an inherent awkwardness, requiring a large space, music and rehearsal. There is usually value in an immediate repeat performance of the work for the viewers, unless of course, the physical demands upon the dancers are too much for that one session.

7. In some of my course outlines for choreography I include a passage on the matter of participation by all in the critical process:

> An integral part of your work in this class will be participating fully and consistently in the discussions of each other's presentations. We need each other's viewpoints, since critique at its best is subjective and only a wide range of opinions will help each of you gain a perspective on which criticism you will respond to and which not. Further, articulating your reactions to the work of your colleagues is an important step in clarifying your own perceptions and values regarding this difficult work of making dances.

> One of the most important things you are going to develop in this process of articulating observations about each other's work is a taste. As you watch the others you might hear yourself saying "That is so right!" and suddenly a door will open to a way of working that you know you will find valuable. Conversely you may think, "Not only is that awful, but I think I've done it myself and more than once." This is one of the most subtle things that you can learn here—what is right—for you. What is taste? It is your sense of rightness.

8. Researching in my class notes for this chapter, I came upon a comment written by one of my students regarding other students' reactions to critiques:

> It was especially interesting to see how students reacted to your comments and whether or not they were able to separate their egos from their "dance." There were a number of students who never could and seemed to think that you didn't like *them* for some reason. They were not yet capable of giving their "dance" or any dance the honor that it deserves as a separate entity. I remember that in hermeneutic studies there are theorists who talk about the "text" having a life of its own once it is complete—that the author has been separated from it.

> Kerry Kreiman

I deeply regret that I never gave what she wrote more thought. It is true that among my choreography students there were, on occasion, emotional reactions to my teaching that amounted to resentment. I never could understand their response to what I thought was caring and considerate mentoring. Now I see that how I spoke was difficult for some students to deal with. It is too late to undo the past, but now I will have a new ground rule for *all* criticism by me and by students in my classes or workshops:

*Direct all criticism to the work and none of it to the choreographer.* This means finding a discipline of thinking and speaking in which we learn to say, "What the dance says to me is," or "What the dance neglects to do," or "The dance movement in the middle passage seems unrelated to the music."

Speaking in this manner achieves two things. First, it recognizes a premise which I subscribe to and which I urge upon my students. The work of art is an entity that exists in the space between the artist and the audience; that the work of art is separate from the artist; that judgement is directed to the art work, not the artist. Second, it makes it more probable that the choreographer will really hear what is being said in the critique sessions.

On one point, there is a radical difference between Tamiris and myself regarding what would be asked of a student presenting a choreographic study. I never put to a student the question, "What is your dance about?" I prefer to deal with what I see, not what is explained to me. As soon as I am told by the choreographer what a dance is about, I begin to perceive what I have been told, not what I experienced. Occasionally, Tamiris did ask that question and some of her critique dealt with how successfully the student expressed that content. She did not say, as many teachers of choreography do, "Well, I saw none of that in your dance," thereby proving conclusively that "the dance was not clear." Tamiris never led her students to attempt achieving literal clarity. She would label such efforts as "too close to the bone." For her and for me, to say that a piece of choreography "is not clear" is to offer a compliment. Neither poetry, nor dance, nor art in any form is about what is clear but is about what is mysterious, elusive, ineffable, demanding thought, mused over, wondered about and provoking. Mystery is the arena of art. To keep talking about "the lack of clarity" is contra-indicated and misleading to young artists. The goal she set before them was always to find metaphoric gestures and designs. Her critique would guide the student in terms of her.his declared intent. I prefer not being a partner, as it were, to the "intent" of the choreographer, but rather a witness.

I do break my rule of not asking when I think the person is so far from understanding what I am trying to give that nothing less than an exposure and comparison of his.her thought process and mine will help. If I have the impulse to do this, I let the student know that I am breaking my rule this time and that she.he is free *not to tell me the content and intent of the piece, if that is her.his preference.*

꙳

There is an arena of criticism that leaves me cold. Early, I was invited to participate in a dance series with some of my colleagues. I accepted readily until I learned the format. We were to dance and then, when finished, we were all to come out on stage, with the house lights up and were to sit on the edge of the stage. (The oh so intimate charm of that gesture gave me quick queasies.) We were then expected to answer questions about our work and listen to comments from the audience.

I cannot imagine the existence of one audience, anywhere, without at least one evil sadist, one habitually contentious intellectual and one scene-stealer. To be subjected to the chance evaluations of individuals whose taste and values could be completely out of my orbit was unthinkable, particularly since we were expected to bring new work to that series. I didn't join.

There are collectives that foster critical sessions attended by other dancers and choreographers but again, one is exposed to a chance collection of people some of whom have values alien to that of the artist. Such criticism is potentially harmful. A new dance work is no different than a newborn infant. It is vulnerable and easily damaged. I go back to that invaluable friend who has taste, can give it to you straight and loves you. These mass critique sessions are potential quagmires that can suck the energy out of a creative effort.

ꜝ

After the work is done and performed publicly, one must expect responses from all sides. How to survive and gain from that is the next question. In fact, there is every chance that what you do will be detested by some. Following the pendulum in the other direction, you may find some underfoot, knocking their heads on the ground, groaning "Hallelujah!" There will be a range of responses and the weight of them will be in a certain direction, positive or negative. To whom do you listen? There is value in being aware of your environment. Listen to everyone and read every review. Pick your way through the mine field, being very careful not to allow yourself to be injured *by those whose values and motives you neither share nor trust.* Be equally wary of praise, particularly checking out its source. Finally, when all is reviewed, make all your own decisions. Allowing another to make a final choice for you is to abdicate your title as the artist of the work. In all of this, you are permitted to weep, rage and call dire curses upon the denigrators. Sooner or later, it pays to calm down and get the perspective needed to move on.

ꜝ

There is an element of creative work that many critics thrive upon—style, particularly whether it is consistent or variable. There are artists who hit upon a style early and explore that for their entire artistic life. Critics love them and relish labeling them with precise titles and descriptions. They are very suspicious of artists who resemble chameleons —artists who make radical shifts in the course of their career. The labeling process gets too messy for them. Most painters in hanging their work for exhibition tend to group what they show with a high degree of consistency. They assume that wide swings in style within the same show will be viewed negatively. I think there is an unwritten assumption that such a showing indicates a capriciousness—a lack of sincerity. How? Why? I know not why, but I suspect that critics who are disconcerted by the mercurial find it difficult to assign and locate such an artist to a particular place in their own spectrum of styles. Do choreographers do this? Not having made a study of this, I have no answer. Personally, I never made any effort to plot one course or the other.

Disregarding this speculation about critics, is one of these ways of developing better than the other? I believe the question is moot. Either way can produce a career of great value and beauty. To adhere to a certain style over the long run gives the artist the lifelong task of plunging deeper and deeper into a specific area of existence and developing a continually honed and refined vision of that focus. Conversely, consistency may be the mark of a timidity that will not budge beyond the first ways of success, exploiting what has *worked* rather than facing the danger of the unfamiliar that might not work.

Shifting styles may be the mark of one who is constantly in touch with the changing times of existence, and we do inhabit a period of dazzling accelerations. Still, the question can be asked: does the apparently versatile artist avoid the full developmental challenge of each thrust only to move on to another direction and still another, trusting to his.her talent to validate the variety but never achieving the depth demanded of a single-minded way of working? Probably this question has confronted every artist who has had an extended career. My feeling is that the wise artist does not consciously pick either one way or the other but rather moves ahead one step at a time, possibly looking back to see where she.he has come from but avoiding plotting a future stylistic growth. The future happens, regardless of critics, and best of all without conscious control.

꙳

In one session of a choreography class at the American Dance Festival, I did the unpardonable. I fell asleep while a student was showing her work. I woke just in time to see the end and hoping that the dozing was not noticed, I covered up by asking her to do the dance again. As the dance progressed, I could see exactly where I fell asleep. When she finished, I confessed my embarrassment to the student, apologized, and then, in a sense defended myself by pointing out that I nodded off when the dance came to a stop, as it were. It was standing still. True, there was motion but there was nothing new that would justify its continued length. I confessed that my observation was subjective and thus vulnerable to disagreement. She listened and seemed to assent to my remarks, but then one can never be sure of what the other is thinking.

Can one say that falling asleep is a form of criticism? Probably the most repeated quote in dance came from Doris Humphrey: "All dances are too long." In one summer at the American Dance Festival, there were a couple of choreographers from South America. I recall one who launched into a most outrageous and exciting solo, but after a very long time, it seemed that she was spinning out a brilliant five-minute solo into infinity. It actually ran for twenty-five minutes. In that season, there was another very similar piece of choreography, a duet with a hair-raising beginning and then much, much more of the same. Bewildered, I turned to my neighbor, the dear man, Woody McGriff. He smiled, "They're very talented, very young and they get enormous grants from their governments and so feel obligated to deliver massive gobs of choreography. A short dance would never respect the size of the grant."

In all of this talk about "too long," I am not ringing in the matter of repetition. There are repetitions in dance and in life that can build a continuous level of breath-taking excitement. The serious question that the choreographer must place before her.himself is, "When have I said what I have to say? When is my dance finished?" This is not an easy question to answer, but it must be answered. If the dance is really finished, tacking on reams of moves and configurations will do nothing but flatten whatever good dance came before.

ᕦ

There is a variety of thinking that arises from some critics that is, to say the least, humiliating to artists. The painter, Ben Shahn (1898–1969), in *The Shape of Content* quotes from a 1956 report by the Committee on the Visual Arts at Harvard University:

> It is a curious paradox that, highly as the university esteems the work of art, it tends to take a dim view of the artist as an intellectual . . . one encounters the curious view that the artist does not know what he is doing. It is widely believed and sometime explicitly stated that the artist, however great his art, does not genuinely understand it, neither how he produced it, nor its place in the culture and in history.[19]

There are critics who gravitate towards this view of the artist, viewing her.him as an innocent who is incomplete without explication by the professional analysts of art. They hold that neither the public nor the artist can possibly grasp a definitive perception of the work of art without the intervention of the critic. If you see one of these coming, start moving or better still, say nothing and use a copy of *The Shape of Content* as a fan to drive off the hot air.

ᕦ

There is something called "feel good choreography." The dancer gets a feeling and starts a dance with that feeling. Very soon, or later, a phrase emerges that is a reflection of that feeling. The dancer then does that phrase several times: three, four, five, eight times and comes to an impasse. Another feeling emerges—a variant on the original feeling—and with a little transition a new phrase develops. It feels right, and then, armed with these two phrases that feel good, he.she does them several times: three, four, five, eight times and finally comes to another impasse. Sooner or later a new phrase develops and if it feels right, it joins company with the first two and this augmented sequence is repeated several times: three, four, five, eight times until it comes to an impasse. Finally the dance is finished and the dance feels very good to do.

In this snide little recital, I am taking on the role of a critic myself to which I have no right. It's a big world. If you and I go to the supermarket, when we arrive at the checkout counter, your cart and mine will have very different contents. I suspect that some very engaging pieces of choreography have been created exactly this way, that I have witnessed them and even enjoyed the experience. Actually, when I suspect that such a process produced what I am seeing, I tend to back off and go cold. Why? I think it is because this kind of artist is too close to that view of us expressed in the quotation above from that Committee on the Visual Arts at Harvard University. Art with only a modicum of feeling is repellant to me. Similarly, art without an intellectual framework carries the weight of irresponsibility. For me, leaning too far in either direction denies the awesome power potential in art.

↜

Kerry Kreiman, a dancer based in Ft. Worth, Texas and a particularly bright person, was in my choreography class at the American Dance Festival and many of the notes that enter this text she made in the classes. Following is a point she picked up and amplified.

> One aspect of your class that I found reassuring was that you emphasized the fact that there are many ways to do the "same" dance. I have always felt this way and have been annoyed by choreographers who became inflexible in regard to changing the choreography for a different cast or a different performance space.

It is a small mind that believes what has been done must be done precisely and exactly the same in the future. The giants, like Balanchine, Cunningham, Graham were constantly bending the repeats of their works according to who was performing and where the dances were being done. This very point raises a serious problem for young choreographers. All too often, the value of what they have created is not apparent because they are dealing with their own lack of directorial experience and the inexperience of the performers available to them. It is all too probable that some very good choreography is concealed by inadequate performance. The teacher of choreography can help by opening up the critique of the choreography to include this aspect. On more than one occasion, I have, upon sensing a weak delivery of the given material, taken the choreographer and/or the performers aside to suggest a cast change to bring the material alive. Whatever happens, the "same" choreography is thus seen in a new light.

↜

Grants: The giving of grants is implicitly an act of criticism. So-and-so gets a $25,000 grant. So-and-so receives $2,500. There is no escaping the assumption that one of these is the better artist. So many factors enter into these decisions: experience, track record, who knows whom, the appraisals of critics, the taste and opinions of the deciding panels. Inevitably, some will get hurt and the sun will shine on others. There is no perfect system. At this distance, the best solution available is the panel of peers reviewing as best they are able the work of their fellow artists. I have participated in these, unwillingly, it is true, but sensing the obligation, I join and we review too much material in too short a time and sometimes we compromise, giving up our favorite for the one who can command a consensus. On occasion we are all happily triumphant with our mutual choice.

What if you create with great vigor and are ignored by the grant givers? Do you give up? Few givers have roiled me more profoundly than the New York State Arts Council. Their grant applications were so detailed and complex that only with the assistance of an expensive accountant could they be completed. Further, one report a year was not enough for them. They asked for several. This charade meant that one had to spend at least ten percent of the received grant to pay the accountant preparing the reports. Bitterest of all, they had the temerity to pop this question at the very end of the application form: "If you do not receive a grant what will you do with this project?" Whenever I would come across this moment, I would pray for a magic voice, one that could roar all the way to Albany, "You know all too well that in spite of everything, we will plow on, so why do you push us into a corner and think that denying a grant will not make a significant difference?"

For many years, I received no grants from the National Endowment for the Arts. It hurt. Did I doubt myself? I always doubt myself, but that never stops me from working and producing. Then one day in 1980, my then manager, Keith King, announced that he was filling out a grant application to the National Endowment on the Arts for 1981. "They want to know what you would do with the money." As close as I can remember, I dictated the following:

> I plan to do a dance about Spring—or not about Spring. You might think that I am joking. I am. I never discuss my creative ideas with anyone, not with my bedmates and certainly not with a group unknown to me in Washington. Further, I have been making up an answer to that question year after year despite the fact that I have no idea what I am going to work on in the next year. I sit here and concoct what might appear to you as a worthy project and still I do not earn a nickel out of you. I lie and all I get is humiliation. Enough. I am going to do a dance about Spring—or not about Spring—of indeterminate length and for this I will need $5,000.

The best joke of all—I got the $5,000. I am guessing that I struck a nerve among the choreographers on that committee and regardless of what they thought of my work, they connected to what I had said.

A grant should not be based on an evaluation of a planned project but rather on the work produced in the past by the artist. Planned projects may sound ridiculous on paper. They are often written months ahead of the creative time and may easily decay on the shelf.

And then there are those who have an extraordinary ability to write up glorious sounding projects and that is their major talent.

Finally, a critique of professional criticism of all the contemporary arts as practiced by newspaper and magazine writers: when one compares the labor that goes into most works of art with the time and effort that goes into the criticism of art, there is quite a disparity. But beyond that simplistic point which proves nothing about the validity of what is written, there is the question of power. When one compares the number of people reached by a writer for a major newspaper or magazine with the number of people who experience the art object being reviewed, the impact of the professional observer is enormous in comparison with that of the artist. Going further into the future, what the critic has written will be ensconced in libraries around the world and soon on the internet. The critic's every word will exist long after the artists and the audiences that witnessed them are gone. That has to be called power, and what happened to your opinion?

Art in the nineteenth century was a garden of profound yearnings for the absolute, the pure, the true and the highest ideals. Hopeless despair or boundless optimism gave the times deep and vivid colors. True, there were weeds in this garden, harbingers of the next century. The twentieth century saw the delivery of one body blow after another to Romanticism. Picasso, Stravinsky, Joyce, Duchamp, Graham and those influenced by them set up a constant attrition that loosened the foundation of every certainty that had sustained artists, audiences and critics in the previous century.

If this view of what has brought us to this point in history has validity, what set of artistic standards can sustain and give authority to what any contemporary critic has to say? They have the perspective gained by history and a wide experience in an art form and a consequent taste derived therefrom. *So do you.* Let us assume that you, who may not be a critic, have a wide experience in the art form of dance and have consequently developed a taste of your own. Seat yourself beside a professional critic in a theatre where a new dance is being presented. What happens? You go home, get on the phone and call your best friend to tell her.him what you thought about the event you just saw. The critic goes to a keyboard and taps out what she.he just saw and thought. It is conceivable that the two visions are close *and just as probable that there are major divergences.* Visiting about, going to work and social events, your slant will be communicated to less than a hundred people. Some critics reach half-a-million readers. Talk about power and, again, what happened to your opinion?

I have a solution to this imbalance of one voice prevailing. It is a good one, completely impractical and will never be implemented anywhere. Years ago I read in the *Village Voice* something I had never seen and never expect to see again. Three of the paper's drama critics recorded and published a discussion about a play which they had all just seen. The sense of what that play was and the depth of awareness given by the contrasting three voices was richer, more rewarding and *convincing* than any criticism I had ever read. What newspaper or magazine would hire three dance critics to attend and discuss the same performance? None. Even the readers might have a resistance to reading what would appear to be a mish-mash of opinions. It's so much easier to deal with one oracle at a time.

↜

No artist can afford to avoid self-criticism. Fred Couples, a major player in the game of golf: "I try to picture the shot, then I step up and hit it. But I don't try to analyze my game while I'm still out on the course. If I hit a bad shot, I don't stand there and attempt to figure out what went wrong. That may come later." That's his way. Every artist must find their own, but he makes a point that should be considered. A continuous stream of self-criticism would be stifling. Make a hunk of work before backing off. This "backing off" is easier for almost all the other arts. When I write, I wait for a substantial section to appear and then I send it into my printer. Reading the hard copy is almost as if it's been written by another. The typos, of course, jut out from the page but the organization, logic and economy, or lack of it become visible. Composers can listen to tapes. Painters can walk away or turn the painting upside down. Sculptors can walk around and away. Playwrights have as much trouble as choreographers gaining perspective on their work until the actors take over.

One would think that with the advent of videotape, this "backing off" business would work for choreographers. Not a simple solution. Video and even film of dance is almost always a distressing come-down from the original. To come close to the spirit and impact of original choreography of any dance demands a technically complex production supervised by a creative videographer of camera operator. Not easy to pull off with a work in progress.

Tamiris had a deceptively simple way of "backing off." She would squint fiercely while twisting her hair and seem to know immediately what was wrong with the choreography. I never had a conscious method beyond what it felt like. Self-criticism is a tough one and I realize I have little to say about it. Among my notes there is only this:

> Analysis is necessary but must be limited. Pervasive appraisal of one's work is a burden that would act as a drag on the creative process. When you're producing, do everything to let it flow. Once you have something, there will be time enough to back off and look at it critically. Actually, that is a step that should not be neglected for any of your works.

↜

At Arizona State University, all the high school dance departments are invited for a day of master classes and a performance. From one such day I saved this comment made by a high school student after viewing a dance work by Shane O'Hara, a very talented dancer-choreographer and graduate student at A.S.U.

In high school, our dance teachers tell us that the theme of our compositions must be clear to an audience. Not being sure of what we were seeing today was fun.

# 18 Anecdotal Material

There are classes and workshops in choreography and then there are books on choreography—which is to be preferred? With no further thought, I lean towards a good class or workshop. That living situation reveals, in the most vivid way, insights that can give the young choreographer a few guidelines in the pursuit of their visions in dance. In all of my classes, the students spoke first when the time came for the critique of a new work or study. As I stated in the preceding chapter, the point was made that for students not to participate in this part of the class would be a serious omission. Putting into words the weaknesses or the virtues of what they were observing would serve to clarify their own aesthetic. Not to speak up would leave their thinking vague and unformulated.

The special wonder of these living situations is that there is no way to know what will emerge. Thus, even the instructor is continually faced with a particularity that does not permit the theoretical generalizations that deaden teaching. What does a book offer? The ground is covered more thoroughly. A point of view is preserved in print for now and in the future that can serve as seeds for thought and discussion.

What follows is a weak substitute for a living class or workshop. It culls a few specific moments from years of teaching that hopefully will clarify some of the theoretical material that has been offered here. The notes for what follows were not complete. At best, there will be a description of the dance being discussed and at other times, that was not recorded and thus there is only the commentary.

*Dancer A* presents a work in progress. It begins with the formal placing of six cameras on the ground. Simultaneously a text is being stated. She was told by her husband to record "every detail of our lives." She has kept a notebook, all the letters and all the photographs. Then there is a sequence of almost militaristic or compulsive movements gathering up the cameras and finally some more anxious and compulsive phrases.

*Daniel:* "At the edge of which cliff is X standing? What is the pain and/or the anger of X? The dance only engages with what X thinks she should be doing. It only points toward something. It never goes there or tries to go there. There's no blood anywhere."

She comes back with an opening that unzips the cool original beginning and gives a brief glimpse of an agony that will lurk behind all the strong compulsive movements that followed.

*Dancer B:* From behind a screen a foot appears and is quickly withdrawn. A hand repeats the action. He steps out upstage right, head bowed. Religious music while traveling forward on his knees. Stops down right and abruptly runs to a standing full length mirror that is up center. Facing front there are a series of discrete events: applying lipstick, a paper bag over the head, covering the genitals, etc.

*Daniel:* "Except for the traveling prayer section, this is a series of tableaux. You are showing pictures of your shame but nowhere do you go through what you feel about your plight." Reading this, I have an uneasy feeling that I was dead wrong. The act of assembling the tableaux and showing them to us may have been as vivid an expression of his feelings as we needed. The fact that the tableaux have little or no movement, i.e., no "dance" is really none of my business. Delivering judgement that something performed "is not dance" is a tricky business. The history of dance and all of art is marked by time mocking such self-assured verdicts. Also, there was the error of saying "your shame," rather than the shame of the figure in the dance.

*Dancer C* has a strong range of movement with an assured elegant line. She presents a dance of a mother and child in wartime. It is full of gestures of tenderness for the infant, heroic stances against the threats surrounding her and strenuous attempts to ward off the danger. Everything is done with a strong frontal design, beautifully executed. There are many arabesques and stunning extensions in second.

*Daniel:* "Is this woman a dancer?" "No." "Does she have an audience?" "No." "Then why have you constructed a dance that more than anything tells us how good a dancer you are?"

Subsequently, she never changed a thing.

*Dancer D:* This dance referred to Kerouac's life and writings and Neal, who is one of his characters. There is a moment when the dancer, as Neal, is sitting on the ground and he suddenly bounces up into the air. There is a time, upstage right when his head flips about violently, he turns and comes about with his hands pointing as if with a gun. In one passage he is looking straight forward and it's very like tap dancing. (Is Neal entertaining us?) Then he stops everything and for want of a better description just horses around. But for all of that, nothing happens.

*Daniel:* Your dance is being performed with extraordinary vitality and electrifying images. We are given a series of illustrations of a state of being but not one of them is developed. A lot of things are started but none are pursued.

After a while a question arises: are you, Shane exploiting your personal facility for moving quickly and violently, rather than dealing with Neal? What is Neal doing? Is he trying to kill himself, be an entertainer, trying to get to heaven or is he masturbating? The lack of clarity could be the most interesting part of the dance. It could all be part of Neal's confusion about life. The most chaotic, schizophrenic life has a thread, albeit a secret one. You, as the artist plunging through the landscape of this life owe yourself—and him—intimation of that connection. How? Some aspect of that apparent anarchy must needs be developed. You can't just do each exciting thing, drop it and then go on to the next.

By the time he did his Master's Thesis concert he pulled it together. I am not sure how he did it, but he did.

*Dancer E:* Unfortunately, my notes for the next critique have no mention of the dance that provoked the comments but it has a point worth examining:

*Daniel:* There is a subtle trap possible in choreography wherein you have created something that has very clear logic for you but strangely, it doesn't work for anybody here. You understand perfectly what has taken place but you haven't done it physically. You know what it's about, but you leave something out. There is a neat parallel here with manuals that are written for computers and software. The hard-wired heads that write those manuals know everything and just can't help assuming that you know that "dump" is a common term that needs no explaining because everybody knows that! Unfortunately, beginners in that world encounter a stone wall created by *the assumption that they know what they do not know.*

The problem for the choreographer, and for all artists, is to determine what it is that the viewer *must know in order to direct his.her attention to the mystery of what is being danced, sung or written.*

*Dancer F:* This dance presented a problem similar to that of D.

*Daniel:* I have an uneasiness about the connection between "X" being suddenly and so easily erect after being knotted up on the floor. Then again there was the change from looking left and right hysterically to suddenly dropping to the ground accompanied by heavy, audible breathing. The fact that "X" appears to be schismatic, doesn't mean he.she lacks an organic life. When a schizoid person veers abruptly from one action to another without apparent connection, it doesn't mean there is no connection. I have an air conditioning system that is also a heating system. The warm weather comes, click a switch, move one vent and whoosh, in flows cool air. The whole character of the machine changes, but it is the same machine. The big question is how to get from one thing to another. How to make a break that is not really a break, without it all appearing to be a pair of structures and not a pair of separate entities?

My suspicion is that there is a heavy dose of conceptualization on your part. It's as if you are not burrowing into that person the way a worm goes into an apple. No, it is more like a person neatly cutting an apple open, taking out the core and observing, "Oh, there's a worm inside." Though there is a vitality through the dance, you acquired an idea, found this and then that and put them together but it all smacks of a precise construction rather than an animalization. With this criticism in mind, would you take a moment, and get your head together and see if you can do it again—right now? Feel free to interject any improvisation that might help you respond to the criticism.

*Daniel (after the second showing of the dance):* Surprise! This was the same dance but utterly different. There was a sense of danger. Even the indecision about coming back had a sense of, "What do we do now?" You wrestled with the choreographic problem in terms of the character and that gave it a life where the other one had an intellectualization. Straddling the previous structure and the new challenge given you gave it all a fierce energy, but best of all, all of the pieces became part of the whole.

*Dancer G:* Here, I have notes on the response but not the description.

*Daniel:* It is possible to imagine you in the studio choreographing. "This is good, and that's good, and that's good"—put it all together and you have a dance but you don't have a piece of body music. It is this, this, this and this but more seriously, the fact that you muddied up a solo dance with more than one character is the most dangerous ploy of all. Unless you play with different hats, we have no idea when you are who. You would have to study with that shape-shifter in *Deep Space Nine*.

*Dancer H:* The figure in this dance seemed to be vulnerable and possibly hunted. It was clear that the character in the dance was not a dancer.

*Daniel:* Dancing is one of 10,000 metaphors that can be brought to life by choreography. Many fine dance works have no one "dancing" in them. This woman wasn't dancing. She is not a dancer. And if she were to dance, it would be vulgar and not the elegant configurations of this dance. Some of the movements are inappropriate to a woman in those circumstances, but they are in the choreography because you have hemmed yourself in with a limited conception of what is permissible in a dance. For dancers, the most irrelevant thing in the world is to be a dancer unless it is a dancer who is being danced.

*Dancer I:* Again, here is just the response.

*Daniel:* The figure can't move freely because his.her hands are caught together, but then they are released to flutter about and then they get caught again. In other words, "X" can be in prison when "X" wants to be there. That's being a dilettante. In the midst of this, there is the projection of what appears to be grave distress. At the same time you are aware of us, the audience and are arranging the entire gestalt of your design, your shape and motions for us to see you do it. Your spatial consciousness is not in relation to the environment, the ambiance, the terror of this person's agony, but is designed to show us you looking good in agony. While "X" appears to be in trouble, you, the dancer look good and skillful. Who do you want us to look at? You or "X"? How can you do this and make us believe it?

You have too many different things going on at once. There is a thematic material of someone in grave trouble. There is your gymnastic skill which has little or nothing to do with this person in trouble. There were elements completely beyond the range of your metaphor of entrapment: the handstands and the walkover. You do an exquisitely controlled développé and lose the painful situation of this creature in such dire straits. You are toying with "X's" agony.

*Dancer J:* In this dance, again, it seemed that the dancer was not completely connected to the person being danced.

*Daniel:* "X" rises so easily but initially there was established a premise of great weight in that initial crouch. You know more about "X" than anybody here. Without telling us anything about who or what your "X" is, is it easy for "X" to straighten up? Is it easy for "X" to go from point A to point B? Crouching in a deep squat and then rising to fully erect represents a big change. Is it easy to make big changes? Why is it not easy? Does it require power? Does it require a long time? Is it dangerous? Are you afraid of using up too much time?

Did you ever see Diane's turning dance? (See Chapter 6 for a full description of this dance.) Perhaps the most important thing about that dance is that it tells us to take the time to do what we have to do. You should take all the time you need. Never worry that we will become restless. *We are only restless when we don't believe you* because you don't fully believe in your "X." Your crouch was a strong beginning. It was like a curtain going up and very powerful. We were prepared to wait until something happened to make you change. We were more patient than you.

*Dancer K:* This dance had a powerful metaphor of four women leaning and clinging to a door.

*Daniel:* When they leave the door, the four women go into unrelated conventional dance movements.

Responding to the criticism of this failing, they come back and now everything they do is shaped by the relation to the door, even when they leave it.

*Dancer L:* An ingenious dance inside a plastic shell that looks like the nose cone of a bomb. He gets in it, disappears in it, walks around with only his feet showing, gets laughs with pigeon-toe and duck-foot travel and that's it.

*Daniel:* If "X" doesn't have any place to go and goes anyway, there might be a few laughs on the way but the dance is being betrayed.

*Dancer M:* The dancer begins with a strong, beautiful phrase repeated about eight times and then goes on to another rich phrase which is repeated about eight times. The pattern continues with new material cropping up throughout. All movements had a textural or intentional connection. Only once did he go back to an earlier movement. The obvious: he works with an Afro-American dance company whose stylistic structure is to do precisely this: a movement phrase repeated four to eight times and then move on to do a new phrase four to eight times, and so on through the entire work.

*Daniel:* Implicit in what you are doing is a repetition that can go on for days but because you are dancing for an audience far from that original culture, you feel the necessity to make it interesting for us. So, you do repetitions in very brief sections, making each of them as interesting as possible and finally presenting them in such a manner that they build to a climax by becoming more complex and more virtuosic. Do you think you could accept the actual premise of the original situation and really do a repetition of a single phrase, a phrase that has an intent and implicit within it a wish to arrive at a certain state of being. Do that phrase to a point of exhaustion or to a place where what is inherent in it *forces* a change, moving you closer to the goal of the phrase?

*Dancer N:* A ritualistic dance to music that sounds Arabic. Intermittently he opens his mouth in what could be a silent scream. Everything is in control in its movement and symmetry, even the scream.

*Daniel:* The silent scream is a wonderful juxtaposition against the formality of the rest of the dance but it is an aspect of the dance which is not pursued. The dance will fill out when you allow the implicit chaos of the scream to take over your movements, for a short or longer time, but limiting it to that one static gesture leaves the dance unfulfilled.

*Dancer O:* A student uses one of Meredith Monk's vocal scores that is full of an unrequited longing. Her dance is an intricate choreography governed by a strong design. Her movement vocabulary is demanding, highly skilled but performed dispassionately.

*Daniel:* You are not taking the risk that Meredith took in that lullaby. I think you are playing it safe. You picked that music because it touched you and thus on some level you probably sense what is going on either with Meredith or with you, but you are not dealing with it. Are you being evasive? Are you not taking responsibility for what you think and feel? Is there something behind the facade of your brilliant dancing? Or is there nothing behind it? Is the only thing behind that wall a wall?

What you just danced is a wall—an interesting, well done wall. I find brick walls interesting, too. The woman on the other side of the room said she saw razor blades but she didn't see blood. There are times that I have walked past an estate wall and wondered what was on the other side. One can walk past a wall and not want to know. Did you want me to see more than I saw? There was a part, early, where you and the music come close to each other. Try starting from there and see what happens.

∽

*Student:* Do you do your choreography, think it's good and then add the inner light, or can you just work from inner light and the choreography comes?

*Daniel:* I have my answer to that question. Why don't you find the answer that works for you?

# 19  The Ethics of Aesthetics

A professor of philosophy at the University of Toronto, Francis Sparshott, wrote *Off the Ground: First Steps to a Philosophical Consideration of Dance*. He asks, "Why has dance played little part in traditional philosophies of the arts?" He examines the writing and thinking on dance by philosophers from Plato to the present. The arguments he presents are dismaying to a dancer. He wants us to recognize that we were either ignored or denigrated by all of the great thinkers as they probed and puzzled the problems of all the other arts. The most devastating evaluation of dance came from the philosopher, Georg W. F. Hegel. He would accept nothing as art that did not contribute to a civilizing endeavor. For Hegel, ballet was "a realm where we have left behind us the logic of prose and the distress and pressure of everyday life . . . mere dexterity has nowadays wandered into senselessness and intellectual poverty." Hegel also wrote, ". . . the expressive pantomime version of the art of dance, though it does indeed qualify as true art, never amounts to more than an inferior version of the art of poetry." And, ". . . as a symbolic art, dance is ineffectual and strange. As a classical art, it is imperfect poetry. As a romantic art, it is a degenerate form of poetry."[20]

For him, "civilizing endeavor" demands words, ideas and the energy of the intellect which the dance lacked. The following quote from Sparshott gave me a clue to the strange and unique evolvement of dance on the periphery of the arts. It is a classic statement that pervades much critical thinking about art and its development away from the principle of representation:

> Meanwhile, it may be claimed that at the hands of Balanchine, the traditional art of ballet dance has been reborn within this context of earnestness as the art of pure

dance that it always potentially was. Just as relief from *the burden of representationalism* has disentangled from extraneous tasks the pure art that painting always really was, so relief from story telling has set ballet . . . free to be the art of dance that it never managed to be before. But without the heroic example of modern dance, one doubts whether this could have been achieved: the eyes to perceive it as well as the power to sustain it could not be supplied from within the ballet tradition itself. (Emphasis added.) [21]

Representation is nothing if it is not imitation. From ancient times until the middle of the nineteenth century art had for its irrefutable mission, "To hold, as 'twere, the mirror up to nature," to quote Shakespeare. Aristotle gives imitation the central function of art. Beauty is only a part of art for him. But if one is to review thinking on art and aesthetics since the middle of the nineteenth century to the present, imitation has been gradually ushered out of the province of art. What happened?

In this period, tremendous advances in all the sciences, the mass production of reading matter in the form of books and newspapers and the availability of cameras cut the ground from under one major function of art, the dispensing of information. Not only is it no longer necessary for artists to convey information, they can no longer do it as well as the other forms of information providers. If you had photography, of what use was painting? Thus, the skills of imitation and representation emerged as archaic.

Émile Zola, the great French realist novelist, was an amateur photographer. For a while, his best friend was the painter, Paul Cézanne. Imagine for a moment Cézanne looking at Zola's portraits and landscapes all captured by the click of a shutter. The snapshots were more accurate than anything Cézanne could achieve.

From Cézanne on, the observed fact diminishes as a significant factor in painting. In fact, all of the arts, which were based on the premise that the observed fact and the successful imitation of that observed fact as central to art, take a beating. In literature, the attention shifts to the irrational in life, witness Dostoevsky, Melville, Whitman, Baudelaire, Pirandello, Rimbaud, Chekov. Stella Adler, the great teacher of acting said, "In Chekov, no one says what they are really thinking." Nothing of this mindset is picked up by dance until after World War I, and then, only by modern dance.

Actually, there were two responses to this displacement or as Sparshott puts it, ". . . *relief from the burden of representationalism.*" (Emphasis added.) One was a gradual turning away from nature to the act of painting itself—the road to formalism. The other road was the search to find meaning and significance below the surface of things. Once we accept the possibility that the puzzle of existence cannot be penetrated simply by logic, reason and the observed fact, we then must turn to a new kind of art. Dance is eminently suited to deal with uncertainty and what is not easily named and yet is present and potent.

My point is that "representionalism," "story telling" and "imitation" were not a "burden" for art, but rather were a dignified, worthy and vital function of art and one day technology found a better and more efficient way of performing that social act. Artists moved on to probe the other aspects of art—art which is not and never was—"pure." I give Sparshott grudging credit for his recognition that it was modern dance that cleared the way for Balanchine's way and take it back because he does not recognize how richly "impure" is modern dance and incidentally, Balanchine's art.

It is only when Isadora Duncan steps on the stage followed by what we know as modern dance in Germany with Mary Wigman and in the United States, with Martha Graham, Helen Tamiris, Doris Humphrey, Charles Weidman and Hanya Holm, that facets and aspects of our existence are probed, exposed and dealt with in ways which dance had only barely hinted at in the past. Probably not since the earliest time of dance have artists used it as a truly serious and profound mode of expression.

So perhaps in some way it is possible to face up to the fact that the philosophers were right not to consider dance on a level with the other arts. If imitation was part of the spine and substance of art since it was one of the prime ways in which people learned about their lives and the world around them, then dance was the weakest of the muses. Compared with the word, paint, statues, song, opera or the theatre, dance is weak in conveying information.

What was it that modern dance did that finally brought dance into the full dignity of the "fine arts"? It went into the space between the two poles of the ballet: the literal pantomimic gestures on the one hand and the abstract, virtuosic, spectacular vocabulary on the other. All through history, there were present in dance the subtle messages, hints, auras, clues, allusions, implications and traces of those things that elude reason and words. It took the modern dancers to make those the focus of their art.

You greet someone in the morning and ask "How are you?" The reply is "OK." But you immediately know something is wrong. What told you that? We are all at every moment pouring out reams of information about ourselves, through body gesture, metaphors, bits of clothing, the tone of our voices—the list is long. It is this vast library of human expression that is not reasoned and not spoken in words but is there for all of us to sense, feel and see. There is the vast sea of motion and emotion coursing unseen through our bodies waiting to be articulated. It is this that is present in all human motion, be it daily discourse, a classic ballet or the work of a modern dancer. It is the modern movement that recognized what modern art saw twenty, thirty years earlier: we no longer need to give factual information. We need to look at and unearth the more subtle vibrations and motions that lie within our being.

There is one more matter that profoundly affects our aesthetics and our ethics. Arnold Hauser wrote a series of books entitled *The Social History of Art*. His manner of entering each period affords an unexpected insight of great value. He examines how artists *earned their incomes and who paid them.* Can any artist—can any choreographer stand completely clear and uninfluenced by the source of his.her income? I was never unaware of how fortunate I was through most of my concert career to be a soloist most of that time. I could get by with very little. The one big expense was the Workgroup company and that was fed by the extensive touring and good fees that I earned performing my solo *The Peloponnesian War.* The board of my foundation consisted largely of individuals of modest wealth from whom I received hardly anything—financially. And then of course, I was touring when the National Endowment for the Arts was really alive and supportive.

When I look at the stationery of contemporary dance artists with their enormous boards, their lists of corporate sponsors and their implicit huge budgets, I feel compassion for them. The work, the time, the calls, the "development" officer, the exquisitely designed four-color slick stock brochures and the galas all add up to one monstrous irrelevancy. How they manage and yet produce the fine work they do is beyond my imagination. There is an unspoken question here: What effect does all of that have on the work? From my limited observation they represent a substantial amount of integrity which should command our admiration.

The thrust of this chapter and in fact this entire book would seem to encourage the creation of serious dance works and by implication disparage lighter, more entertaining material. So be it. When I wrote *How to Dance Forever*, the question of youth and the dance was an inevitable consideration and it led to a chapter, The Youth Conspiracy, not only on youth but the question of seriousness and the scarcity of it in dance. If you have the curiosity to pursue this, it is on pages 259–266 of *How to Dance Forever.*

There is a continuing, surreptitious attack on content—less so today than a few years back but still in there, chipping away. One of the classic slams at any art that attempts to confront contemporary issues goes like this: "Why are you trying to convince an audience of what they already believe?" Who doesn't believe in love and yet has anyone ever asked that question of *La Sylphide*? In the midst of this confusion called "life," we are in continual need of reinforcement. Every holy day the faithful of all religions reassemble to be once more convinced of the validity of their beliefs. Dance, theatre, music, art, each in their own way reaffirm either our faith or our doubts.

"The Ethics of Aesthetics." This euphonious title may give the impression of being flippant for such a weighty pair of subjects. It did, in fact, give rise to a glib remark by a prominent dance administrator, "The ethics of aesthetics? That's an oxymoron!" On the contrary, this chapter steps out on a limb with the premise that every aesthetic stance contains within in it an ethical vision.

One of the joys of teaching is the surprise. In the summer of 1966, I gave a six-week workshop at California State College in Los Angeles. It was a large heterogeneous group:

skilled and unskilled, professionals and amateurs, faculty and students. About a dozen were high school teachers with barely any dance background compelled by a recent curriculum decision to begin the teaching of some dance.

Towards the end of the session, I turned the group loose to create their own works with the hope that we could have a little concert in the college theatre. Came the time for showings, quite a few lovely works emerged. Among the last seen was a solo by a slender, unassuming woman.

She began by carefully laying out some props on the floor: a pillow, a light blanket, a clock, a pair of sandals and a few articles of clothing. She handed a cassette to the musician, slipped a sleeping garment over her leotard, lay down under the blanket, resting the side of her head on the pillow. A discreet nod from her and the music began: Debussy's *Prélude à l'après-midi d'un faune*. The first shocker was how long she lay there, at peace and unmoving as the music wove its sensuous path. Finally, on the release of a deep breath she rolled to rest on her back. Again, there was nothing for a long time until her eyes opened. After a time, tipping sideways, she sat up, looked about for a time and then tilted the clock to read it, rose and stepped out of the nightgown, laying it on a chair and picked up a blouse. Donning that, she found a pair of walking shorts, stepped into one leg with a bare foot and into the other with a sandaled foot. Only then did she wiggle her right foot into the remaining sandal. Lastly, she gathered up, in the same leisurely, unhurried tempo, a wide-brimmed hat, a large purse from which she fished out sunglasses. Donning them with a delicate gesture, she strolled out of the dance space, just as the lovely music breathed its last sigh.

What did she do? Nothing—for ten minutes! Some in the class were close to fury. Some sat there with a bemused smile and a far-away look. The lines of conflict were drawn and the ensuing discussion was heated. When my turn came to speak, the angry ones were astonished and I suppose dismayed. I was amazed that this high school teacher from Pasadena was pursuing a vein of thought taking place at the same time three thousand miles away among the avant garde of New York. Was it dance? Personally, it never occurred to me to ask. It was a compelling and original piece. Today, it would be neatly labeled a "performance piece." Isn't it wonderful to have a handy au courant word?

With fifty-five students in the workshop, a selection process was inevitable. I gave the group as a whole the responsibility of choice. With considerable debate, hers was included. As the rehearsals approached performance day, I saw a problem with the "awakening piece." I sought her out and said, "You know, the leotard is dead wrong. If you want to do your piece truthfully for the stage performance, when you take your nightgown off, what should you have on?" "Nothing." "Do you want to do that?" "I'll think about it." She found me the next day before class started. "Mr. Nagrin, if it is alright with you, I will be wearing a leotard under the nightgown. You see, I am not an artist. I am a high school teacher." Once more, her simplicity and directness awed me. Why should she take the rules of my profession for herself? I said, "Fine, do it your way." I never made her feel that she was lacking in courage. I didn't have the right. She was teaching in Pasadena, a conservative community, and if the performance had attracted attention, as well it might, it could easily have endangered her job. To her, it was clear where her responsibilities lay. How many artists even consider this? How many artists are so discreetly hermetic that the shell of their metaphors are completely opaque? That way lies safety. They can shout anything at all without making a sound. Expression without responsibility. Can one be an artist and do that?

In the perspective of the art of the last hundred years, the answer has to be, "Yes." Consider the following quotation from Georges Braque towards the end of his life:

> You see, I have made a great discovery: I no longer believe in anything. Objects don't exist for me except in so far as a rapport exists between them or between them and myself. When one attains this harmony one reaches a sort of intellectual non-existence—what I can only describe as a sense of peace—which makes everything possible and right. Life then becomes a perpetual revelation. *Ca, c'est de la vraie poésie!*[22]

Granted I am on thin ground when I take on one of the masters of twentieth century art. Regardless, I find Braque's belief troubling and by that token it find it impossible to deliver a book on choreography without speaking of responsibility. Few writings have gone to the core of this matter as the work of Martin Buber, particularly in the collection he edited: *Ten Rungs: Hasidic Sayings.* What concludes this chapter are quotations and commentary upon a few pages of this book. ("Rungs" are used here as a metaphor for the various steps or stages in achieving a pious way of life.)

Years ago, I was attracted to *Ten Rungs* because Buber was a major defining thinker in the consciousness of the sixties and seventies. Reading it, I was caught up in a completely unexpected connection between the musings on the convoluted relations between people and their God and the equally convoluted relations of artists to their art and their audience. Time and again, a paragraph would strike sparks in my mind until a most unexpected link appeared. So very many of the Hasidic sayings made another kind of sense if one substituted the word "art" for "God." Now, this may seem sacrilegious, particularly when it is coming from one who is an agnostic.

I find the thinking of the Hasidim strangely attractive, sensitive and very wise. Even if I do not embrace the fullness of their belief, I believe I have the right to borrow what has enriched my thinking, my work and my relations with others. In all of my choreography classes, I ask the students to read this book. Please read on before delivering judgement.

A note: In view of the publication date of 1947, it should surprise no one that in this text, human beings are referred to as "man," "he," and "him." If Buber were alive today, would he go for a generic that included women? No way of knowing, but here, his manner of writing will be adhered to.

≲

# From *Ten Rungs: Hasidic Sayings*, Martin Buber[23]

*Ten Rungs: Hasidic Sayings*, © 1947, 1975. Estate of Martin Buber.

## The Nature of Service

This is the service man must perform all of his days: to shape matter into form, to refine the flesh, and to let the light penetrate the darkness, until the darkness itself shines and there is no longer any division between the two. (49)

This could be as good a definition of the work of the artist as can be found. It comes very close to defining the task and the dedication that marks the profession of dance. It is somewhat optimistic on the matter of light shining into the darkness. I think that no matter how much light we shed on anything, it will always lap on the shores of the dark.

## Two Languages

There are people who can utter words of prayer with true fervor, so that the words shine like a precious stone whose radiance shines of itself. Then again there are people whose words are nothing but a window that has no light of its own, but only lets the light in and shines for that reason. (31)

This could very well be a comparison of two kinds of art. One comes out of an imaginative and virtuoso manipulation of the materials of art but devoid of personal connection. Another kind of art is sometimes called "artless," as it pours forth unhindered from the depths of a person.

## Who May Be Called Man?

In the Scriptures we read: "When any man of you bringeth an offering unto the Lord ..." Only he who brings himself to God as an offering may be called a man. (19)

Who may be called an artist? If you want to be an artist, how much of yourself are you willing to draw into that part of your being?

## In Every Man

In every man there is something precious, which is in no one else. And so we should honor each for what is hidden within him, for what only he has, and none of his comrades. (80)

It is not only important to recognize that there is something precious in others, it is terribly important—and this is one of the hardest things for a young artist— not only to believe that there is something precious within him.her but to recognize what that precious thing is.

## Each His Own

When a man leaves his own rung and takes that of his friend, he will not be fruitful on either the one rung or the other. Many followed the example of Rabbi Simeon ben Yohai, and their work did not succeed because they were not of his quality, but only did as he did, in imitation of his quality. (50)

Again, this teaching asks that each person respond to his.her own talent rather than being derivative.

## The Patriarchs

*Question:* Rashi expounds the words of God: "I appeared unto Abraham, unto Isaac, and unto Jacob" meaning "I appeared to the fathers." In what way can this be considered an explanation?

*Answer:* He who had a father who was righteous and devout is not apt to make a great effort to perfect himself, for he leans on the merits of his father. This is even more true of one whose father and grandfather were both holy men; the mere fact that he is their grandson seems to him like solid ground beneath his feet. But this was not so in the days of the patriarchs: Isaac did not concern himself with the merit of his father and his ancestors, for they did not want to be grandsons, but fathers. (50)

Here is an exquisite and challenging definition of the relationship of an artist to his.her predecessors.

## Originality

When a man embarks on something great, in the spirit of truth, he need not be afraid that another may imitate him. But if he does not do so in the spirit of truth, but plans to act in a way that no on else can imitate, then he drags the great down to the lowest level and everyone can do the same. (50)

In this, there is an attack on the opposite side of this question of creativeness. Trying to be creative regardless of what one has to say, trying to be an original rather than saying what one knows and trusting that and its uniqueness, draws one to a corrupt position. What is a corrupt involvement? Trying to be original—needing to be original. How can one be original without knowing what it is others have done and said before? A major portion of the energy of a person who must needs be original is to know what others have done and said before, rather than concentrating on the task at hand regardless of what others do or have done. It is entirely possible and even probable that the task at hand may call forth responses which have already been made. But if the artist does not look over his.her shoulder but hews to the task at hand investing all of him.herself, the solutions and responses will be original without trying to be.

## New Every Morning

Unless we believe that God renews the work of creation every day, our prayers and doing the commandments grow old and accustomed and tedious. As it is written in the psalm: "Cast me not off in the time of old age" that is to say, do not let my world grow old. And in Lamentations it is written: "They are new every morning: great is Thy faithfulness." The fact that the world is new to us every morning that is your great faithfulness! (51)

The Buddhists have a saying which is useful for every artist: each time you do something, it is the first time and the last time. The plié you will do in tomorrow's class will be the first and last time you will do that plié and to regard it as such is to regard it freshly and creatively and with a full awareness of what it is you're doing as opposed to taking it for granted. Many humans have no consciousness of the truth and beauty of this until they get a personal notice of death in the form of a heart attack or a diagnosis of cancer. Then the simplest act, brushing one's teeth and the clean, minty taste that follows suddenly becomes a treasured and exquisite experience.

I knew a photographer named Valente who told me how grateful he had been for his heart attack. He said, "Now, I get so much out of every day. I stand here and look out of my window, sometimes for an hour, relishing the gift of my eyes and the watching of those people striding up and down the street."

## In Water

Question: It is written in Proverbs: "As in water, face answereth to face, so the heart of man to man." Why does the verse read "in water" and not "in a mirror"?

Answer: Man can see his reflection in water only when he bends close to it, and the heart of man too must lean down to the heart of his fellow; then it will see itself within his heart. (79)

This paragraph asks us to come close to one another, to really pay attention to the other if we are ever to know ourselves.

## Two Kinds of Human Spirit

There are two kinds of spirit, and they are like backward and forward. There is a spirit man attains to in the course of time. But there is also a spirit which overwhelms man with great abundance, in great haste, swifter than the fleeting moment, for it is beyond time, and for this spirit the element of time is not needed. (74)

What is implied here is that there are things that one works for, states that one works for, places to which one directs oneself and then there are things which arise, unbidden, to overwhelm one. This could be accepted as a description of inspiration. And here it is said that the element of time is not needed. Time is not relevant because one works and works and works and when and how the heat of inspiration come upon one cannot be controlled in terms of time.

## Ascent

No limits are set to the ascent of man, and to each and everyone the highest stands open. Here it is only your personal choice that decides. (71)

I think the most awesome and frightening thing for any human being, and particularly an artist, is to have a full awareness of the awesome extent of one's potential and yet how far one is from reaching that potential.

*The Ten Principles*

From the child you can learn three things:

- He is merry for no particular reason;
- Never for a moment is he idle;
- When he needs something, he demands it vigorously.

The thief can instruct you in seven things:

- He does his service by night;
- If he does not finish what he has set out to do in one night, he devotes the next night to it;
- He and those who work with him love one another;
- He risks his life for slight gains;
- What he takes has so little value for him that he gives it up for a very small coin;
- He endures blows and hardship, and it matters nothing to him;
- He likes his trade and would not exchange it for any other. (55)

Could we amend this to say a little child, a thief and an artist—a dancer?

*Learn from All*

Question: In the *Sayings of the Fathers* we read: "Who is wise? He who learns from all men, as it is said, 'From all my teachers I have gotten understanding.'" Then why does it not say: "He who learns from every teacher"?

Answer: The master who pronounced this dictum is intent on making it clear that we can learn not only from those whose occupation is to teach but from every man. Even from a person who is ignorant, or from one who is wicked, you can gain understanding as to how to conduct your life. (64)

This one speaks for itself. Learn from all. Be open.

*With God*

You must know that every movement you make is bound up with the will of the Creator. That is why it is written: "Noah walked with God." For every movement is made through the impulse given by God. Noah clung to God with such very great devotion that it seemed to him that, whenever he walked, God was moving his feet. At every step it seemed to him that God was facing him and guiding him as a father teaches his little son to walk, and when the father moves further away from him, the child knows it is for his own good. (23)

The relationship of God to Noah is that of a teacher and the most significant thing that a teacher does appears in the last sentence. This is what a wise teacher knows. He.she knows when to move further away from the pupil.

## Into the Word

You should utter words as though heaven were opened within them and as though you did not put the word into your mouth, but as though you entered into the word. (28)

Here, as you will read elsewhere, there is a resistance to making something happen, to be deliberate and in control. The demand, the hope, the wish is that one can truly submerge oneself within the object, in this case when you speak. I can't resist at this point recalling a cartoon of Dennis the Menace in which he is standing in front of Margaret with his fingers in his ears and he is saying to her "Margaret, you should know better than to talk with a mouth full of words."

## Between Men

There are those who suffer very greatly and cannot tell what is in their hearts, and they go their ways full of suffering. But if they meet someone whose face is bright with laughter, he can quicken them with his gladness. And it is no small thing to quicken a human being! (44)

He talks about meeting one whose face is bright with laughter. It is no small thing to quicken another human being. Why is there so little humor in the modern dance? I, for one, view all humor as serious.

## Everywhere

God says to man as he said to Moses: "Put off thy shoes from off thy feet"—put off the habitual which encloses your foot and you will recognize that the place on which you happen to be standing at this moment is holy ground. For there is no rung of being on which we cannot find the holiness of God everywhere and at all times. (15)

No one can tell you where you'll find your art, where you'll find your vision, where you'll find your material, but be certain you don't dismiss what is near you, about you, or underneath your feet because it does not appear to be interesting or from a faraway place.

## "Get Thee Out of Thy Country"

God said to Abraham: "Get thee out of thy country, and from thy kindred, and from thy father's house, unto the land that I will show thee." God says to man: "First, get you out of your country, that means the dimness you have inflicted on yourself. Then out of your birthplace, that means out of the dimness your mother inflicted on you. After that, out of the house of your father, that means out of the dimness your father inflicted on you. Only then will you be able to go to the land that I will show you. (70)

The complexity here is the word "dimness." I think it might be worthwhile for each of us to try to fill out for ourselves what the word "dimness" signifies. Because on the one hand, from our country, from our mother, from our father, we get a tradition, our education, so forth. At the same time, we can consider what we get from them a limitation. Could this have a parallel with the Taoist thinking that says "No history"?

## Fulfillment

This is the secret of the unity of God: no matter where I take hold of a shred of it, I hold the whole of it. And since the teachings and all the commandments are radiations of his being, he who lovingly does one commandment utterly and to the core, and in this one commandment takes hold of a shred of the unity of God, holds the whole of it in his hand, and has fulfilled it. (54)

This asks us to note that regardless of which commandment or which particular task we are dealing with, we are dealing with the whole of it. It is something that is very hard for some very ambitious young artists to understand and so they force themselves to take on projects of inordinately large scope. They find it hard to respect what they might think a minor aspect of life's existence, or the narrowness of their own experiences. Instead they try to have an all-encompassing agenda, an agenda of great import and weight. Best not to try for a universal image.

## The True Love of God

To love God truly, one must first love man. And if anyone tells you that he loves God and does not love his fellow-man, you will know that he is lying. (81)

May we also say that "To love art truly one must first love man and if anyone tells you that he loves art and does not love his fellow man, you will know that he is lying"? Perhaps not. In the history of art-making there are a number of misanthropes who turned out compelling art.

## The Way

It is impossible to tell men what way they should take. For one way to serve God is by the teachings, another by prayer, another way by fasting, and still another by eating. Everyone should carefully observe which way his heart draws home, and then choose that way with all his strength. (54)

Students of art, aspiring artists and artists are surrounded by friends, lovers, teachers, enemies and critics. Out of love, concern for the art of dance, out of envy and even concealed hatred there is a phrase that continually obtrudes in the discussion and advice offered to the artist: "What I would like to see is . . ." We are surrounded by those who would tell us which way to take. Look out. Even love can crush.

## Two Kinds of Love for God

There are two kinds of love: the love a man for his wife, which should manifest itself in secret and not where there are spectators, for this love can be consummated only in a place apart from other beings; and there is the love for one's brothers and sisters and children, a love which does not require secrecy.

And there are two kinds of love for God: the love spent in learning and praying and fulfilling the commandments, which should be shown in silence and not in the presence of others, lest it tempt to glory and pride; and the love shown in the company of other human beings, when one hears and speaks, gives and takes, and, in one's secret heart, clings to God and never ceases dwelling upon him. (20–21)

There are two profoundly different activities in which an artist engages. One is a secret creative process; the other is the public one, the presenting of what one has gained and struggled for in private. They should not be confused. Many works that pass for post-modern art are the details and problems of the creative process that are really in the province of the artist's business and craft and should not be the concern of others. These are just the basket to hold a vision. The responsible artist's gift is what is in the basket. Some post-moderns are selling ingenious, startling, innovative, amusing and empty baskets.

## Only a Beginning

A man ought never to say that he is perfect in his fear of God; he should always say that now he is only about to begin to serve God. For did not Moses, after forty years of wandering, say to God: "Thou hast begun to show Thy servant Thy greatness"? (51)

Throughout her career, at some point in every project, Helen Tamiris would sigh, "I feel as if I am just beginning."

## No More Than This

Question: It is written: "And ye shall be unto Me a kingdom of priests, and a holy nation. These are the words which thou shalt speak unto the children of Israel." Rashi, our teacher, comments: "These are the words, no more and no less." What does he mean by that?
    Answer: Moses was good. He wanted to reveal more to the people, but he was not allowed. For it was God's will that the people make an effort of their own. Moses was to say just these words to them, no more and no less, so that they might feel: Something is hidden here, and we must strive to discover it for ourselves. That is why, further on, we read: "And he set before them all these words." No more and no less. (62)

This thought implies that it is possible for the teacher to say too much. It says that it is wiser for the teacher to say just enough to invigorate the mind, the heart and the sensibility of the student to then go on and make his.her own answers. Also, the artist must beware of saying too much and superguiding the audience.

## How to Say Torah

(Torah is the entire body of Jewish religion and law, including both the sacred literature and the oral tradition. A pious Jew will spend some part of every day studying the Torah.)

I shall teach you the best way to say Torah. You must cease to be aware of yourself. You must be nothing but an ear that hears what the universe of the word is constantly saying within you. The moment you start hearing what you yourself are saying, you must stop. (65)

In a time of floundering, I put down a few words to ease my confusion:
To find the self, lose the self.
Find the other.
Not a table, this table,
not a minute, this minute,
not a person, this person.
Words mark the place only,
eyes speak dark light,
words conceal, bodies reveal.
Walk into eyes, look inside bodies,
    very difficult,
    often painful,
    even dangerous,
but at least wet with life.

## The Growing Tree

Man is like a tree. If you stand in front of a tree and watch it incessantly, to see how it grows, and to see how much it has grown, you will see nothing at all. But tend it at all times, prune the runners and keep it free of beetles and worms, and—all in good time—it will come into its growth. It is the same with man: all that is necessary is for him to overcome his obstacles, and he will thrive and grow. But it is not right to examine him hour after hour to see how much has already been added to his stature. (74)

To regard oneself as a growing tree is a useful image for any artist, particularly a young one. If you are constantly examining yourself and constantly judging yourself, you will see nothing at all. But to attend to the details of the things that have to be done, to work on the chores of the day to day and the minute to minute necessities, one can trust in that more readily than continual judgement which in the long run, chokes one. And it is a hard thing for a conscientious and ambitious young artist—or even an old artist—to give up this game of constantly judging oneself. It is also hard for the teacher to rein in the urge to improve the student by constant and pervasive corrections, rather than giving the student enough slack to discover and solve what is needed to move forward.

## Two Kinds of Faith

Why do we say:"Our God and the God of our fathers"? There are two kinds of people who believe in God. One believes because he has taken over the faith of his fathers, and his faith is strong. The other has arrived at faith through thinking and studying. The difference between them is this: The advantage of the first is that, no matter what arguments may be brought against it, his faith cannot be shaken; his faith is firm because it is taken over from his fathers. But there is one flaw in it: he has faith only in response to the command of man, and he has acquired it without studying and thinking for himself. The advantage of the second is that, because he found God through much thinking, he has arrived at a faith of his own. But here too there is a flaw: it is easy to shake his faith by refuting it through evidence. But he who unites both kinds of faith is invincible. And so we say, "Our God" with reference to our studies, and "God of our fathers" with an eye to tradition. (13)

Every inspiring artist or tradition thrusts exactly the same problematic choice on the artists who come after them. Chinese artists were constantly confronted with a monumental tradition countered by the need for personal expression. In the *Mustard Seed Manual of Painting*, a seventeenth century document, there is this:

In the Sung period, Liu Tao-ch'un said:

- First Essential: Action of the Ch'i* and powerful brush work go together.

- Second Essential: Basic design should be according to tradition.

- Third Essential: Originality should not disregard the li—the principle of essence of things.

- Fourth Essential: Color if used should enrich.

- Fifth Essential: The brush should be handled with spontaneity.

- Sixth Essential: Learn from the masters but avoid their faults.

Six qualities are listed. The Fourth Quality says: To exhibit originality even to the point of eccentricity without violating the li** of things.

Can we then say that an artist needs a strong connection and cognizance of tradition balanced by the inner strength to arrive at personal choices gained through study, thinking, and feeling?

*"ch'i," an iridescent word, easier to sense than to define. An ancient book on painting says that a painted rock must have "ch'i." One can fumble for a direct translation: force, energy, breath, power, spirit, inner life and so on. **"Li" means at various times: good customs, natural law, the correct order of things.

## Participation

If I am not for myself, who will be for me, and if I am for myself, what am I? (56)

A double-pronged question. This is really at the heart of ethics. How each of us handles this in our lives is what defines each ethical being as a person and as an artist.

# THE WORKBOOK

# Workbook Introduction and Outline

As noted in the Introduction, two books preceded this one: *Dance and the Specific Image: Improvisation* and *The Six Questions: Acting Technique for Dance Performance.* This book lays out a mass of thoughts and tools for the act of choreography. The first book, on improvisation, organized itself by virtue of pursuing the continuous development through time of the Workgroup exercises, games and structures. A chronology determined the logic of its structure. In the second book, examining the craft of acting for dancers easily fell into a clean structure: moving from the fundamental qualities demanded of any performer, scanning the irrelevant baggage that performers need to unload, reviewing the basic six questions contained in each dance role and finally collecting the miscellany that might be useful in the preparation for and act of performing.

There have been more than enough books on choreography and almost all are marked by an elegant structure and a logical flow. If you have come this far in this book, you have experienced a collection of essays about choreography but held together by a minimal order. There is a some history, some "ground rules" and the multiple facets that reflect the problems of making—or rather of finding—dances. This section, the Workbook, has an organization of improvisation exercises increasing in complexity and specifically reflecting the problems and processes of choreography.

Should the sequence found here be pursued? Yes and no.[24] Yes, if it makes sense for you. I, for one, never knew from day to day what I was going to do in a choreography class or workshop. In my notebook, I would have a new sheet for each day with a line down the middle. On the right would be a list of the exercises we had been doing recently and a few I would like to start up. I always started with Gifts and as I watched, I sensed the mood and energy of the room and without too much thought it would be apparent what should come next. As we worked, I would enter on the left side of the page what we did. Before starting the next session, I would glance at that page and make up a new right column from which to choose. Just as easily, an idea not on the page or one that had never been done would become necessary because of something that happened or because of a remark or question arising in one of the discussions that usually followed a long session.

A suggestion: read through the Workbook, using the generous space on the left to mark it up with notes and questions. Highlight what appears particularly interesting. If you work on this material, who you are will shape your path. Nothing here is meant to prescribe an order of work. Follow the order of the Workbook or your own inclination.

Are there repeats from the first two books? Of course. A knife can be used to carve a wooden whistle, spread mustard on a pastrami sandwich, slice a filet mignon and play mumblety-peg. The Workbook is of course based on the premise that improvisation is a gold mine for the practice of choreography. Here the exercises have been selected, rephrased and grouped for one purpose, to open doors that sometimes seem to be locked to a choreographic intention. There are a significant number of teachers and choreographers who never or rarely resort to improvisation—and do very good work! And then, there are the others. This section is for the others.

For those who may have worked their way through some of the exercises in the two earlier books, there is this to say from the experience of teaching and *doing* them: the same exercise, game or structure repeated without preconceptions will always find a new direction with radically different results and unexpected insights.

It is too easily assumed that proper study is done in a group situation, either that of a dance company or a class. In fact, some of the most intense research, study and practice of our dance art is performed by solitary figures. I myself took fewer and fewer classes, spending hours and hours alone probing, testing new ideas and ways. All the Workbook exercises will serve groups of dancers. Some can be explored profitably by a dancer working alone; each of these will be clearly tagged by a superscript "s."

# Workbook Outline

## #1 Warming Up

Gifts
Medicine Ball
Outrageous Travel
Goldfish Bowl
Blind Journey[s]

## #2 The Rhythm Series

Breath Rhythm[s]
Pulse Rhythm[s]
Inner Rhythm[s]
Dedicate Your Motion[s]
Go Visiting
True Repetition[s]
Evolving Repetition[s]
Spinning[s]

## #3 Uncovering Sources of Movement—The First Steps

Circles[s]
Each Alone[s]
Backdoor[s]
Hub Meditation[s]
Visualization[s]
Gesture Permutations[s]
Gesture Rondo[s]

## #4 Metaphor

## #5 Sense Memory Sources

Faces
The Obstacle[s]
Passing through a Physical Object
Slalom

## #6 Sources of Movement Material

The Mind-Wash[s]
Not Naming[s]
The Other
A Duet
The Duet as a Structure

## #7 Finding Gold in "Bad" Habits

Cliché Rondo[s]
Your Familiar[s]
Possessed by a Mannerism[s]

## #8 Music Sources of Movement

Ambient Sound[s]
Rhythm Circle
Before, After and On[s]
Who or What Is Alive in the Music?[s]
Riff Cactus[s]
Using Music for Improvisation[s]

# | Warming Up

There is no question that dancers should never be expected to do *anything* in dance without an adequate physical warmup. There are a few strange ones who can plunge in without this and some get away with it for years. So be it. Good luck to them, but for the rest of us . . .

However, when the focus is a session laying the foundation for creative work, something more than a heated body is required. Warming up the psyche, the inner flow, the subconscious, the unconscious, finding the catalyst, connecting with inner resources, unloading the inhibitions . . . so many words but no short, simple way of saying what we all know is needed here. Why bother to define it further if we all know what is meant?

Whenever a section is indented on the page, it is presumed to be the voice of the teacher addressing the students.

**Gifts**

The first necessity in any session is to ensure the safety and the freedom of your bodies. Pick a partner and face each other, standing. The exercise is called Gifts. One will lead and the other will follow as in a mirror game. The leader has but one mission in mind—to get the other warmed up and on the way to dancing. That is the "gift," to free the body of the other, but the challenge is to fully take in who the follower is. "What does he.she need to get started? What is unique to this person, this body before me? Is there a nervousness? Would a bit of silliness be the right beginning? Would a formal, symmetrical opening center this person best? Are the shoulders lifted in a tense manner? Perhaps some easy shoulder rolls, lifts and drops would ease and lengthen his.hcr neck?"

Take your time to sense the specific needs of the person before you. Don't do what you think all dancers need—only what *this* dancer needs. You literally are trying to think yourself into his.her body. Can you *really know* these things? Never for certain, but you can guess on the basis of what you are seeing and sensing. All of us, whether we are self-aware or not, are constantly sending signals out to the world about ourselves. If you want to know about the other, the information is there right in front of you and if you really have to know, you will develop the skill, for it is just that—a skill, open to those who yearn for it.

When the leader has done a chunk of warmup work, he.she cues the other to take over the role of leader, and so Gifts proceeds, the roles changing from one to the other. It is vital that one person does not dominate by monopolizing the role of leader.

There are two negatives that should be respected. If you, in the role of follower, are given a motion or sequence that you sense is beyond your capacity, that in fact might be dangerous for you, *do not do it* and signal your reluctance to execute the move. The leader must respect this and go on to something else. The second negative says that the leader cannot do any move that loses eye contact with the follower for more than a moment. Any prolonged motions of turning away or bending far down or far back are oxymorons—a total contradiction to the whole point of Gifts. If the leader cannot see the follower, neither can the follower see the leader. The follower can be equally contradictory if he.she looks away or finds an internal focus. Losing eye contact loses the information needed to know what is happening with the sacred other person. The leader's paramount responsibility is to be constantly aware of every change in the follower to know how to proceed. The responsibility of the follower is obvious.

The rules of a good and a safe warmup are known but worth repeating now:

- Early stretches are wake up stretches and not for limberness.
- Go from slow to fast.
- Go from simple to complex.
- Feet, legs, pelvis, torso, neck, arms, hands all need attention.
- Grande pliés, deep knee bends—whatever, should be controlled, slow, limited in number and introduced midway.
- Introduce elevation late in the sequence.
- Introduce little jumps before big ones.
- Cool down should be followed by stretches for limberness.

Decide who will be the leader and start when you hear music. Find your freedom within your respect for the configuration of the space and the contours of the music. Be sure to continue if there are breaks in the music or if you hear me call out suggestions. If the leader chooses to cover space, travel abreast, not "follow the leader," thus keeping eye contact alive all the time. Go!

I find it necessary to always closely monitor what follows. Every group has its own predilections, strengths and weaknesses. Sometimes, I note a plethora of waving arms and have to call out, "Continue what you are doing and consider some big body motions." Or, if very few have done pliés, I will say, "Think of getting to demi-pliés." I sense when they are ready to move ahead and call out, "If you haven't done big leg motions, now's the time," or "Time for little jumps," or "Time to travel, to cover space," and then "Whenever you are ready, cool down and stretch." I *never* speak out when dancers are improvising except in Gifts or when the structure requires the calling out of the time for the next stage. All through Gifts, I stay en garde for injudicious choices such as violent jouncing of hams on heels, jumps too early in the warmup, ballistic stretches, etc., and will immediately enter the work space to talk quietly to the dancers concerned. However, the less aware dancers are of the leader/teacher/director while dancing, the better. Sometimes, I end it by saying:

Whenever you are ready, cool down, stretch down and then take a moment to discuss with your partner what happened. What worked for you? Where did your partner really locate your need? Where was a need ignored?

When time is tight, I say,

When you are both warmed up and ready to dance, let go of the leader-follower relationship and keep moving easily to the music on your own motivation as you both turn to face front. We will be ready to move on when all are facing front.

The wonder of Gifts is that it is perhaps the fastest and the safest warmup I've ever encountered. I've been initiating workshops in this manner since 1971 and have never witnessed a serious injury in any of them. Additionally, it is a perfect introduction to the basic concepts of interaction, giving all attention to "the other" and giving up the focus on self; these being the very spine of the style of improvisation described here.

**Medicine Ball**

Make circles of six to eight. In days long before the frisbee, it was the custom on beaches everywhere to stand in a circle like this and pass around a large, leather ball made heavy with stuffed rags. The game would start easily and slowly and as it speeded up, part of the fun was to throw the ball in unexpected directions.

We are going to "throw" sound/motions. One person starts by "throwing" a short, impulsive sound/motion in the direction of anyone in the circle. This direction must be unequivocally clear to the intended receiver. The receiver, without pause to reflect or evaluate, immediately repeats what was "thrown" back to the sender and then without any hesitation or pause, "throws" his.her own impulsive sound/motion to another in the circle. That other repeats the ritual of reflecting what was given to the giver and sends out a personal sound/motion immediately to a new person. In the act of reflecting, the goal is to truly mirror the sender, not diminishing what was given or augmenting it in volume or gesture. Never move closer to the receiver than half the distance between you because if you are mirrored truthfully, you will be knocked down. This receiving and giving continues until you hear, "OK, let it wind down."

What gives Medicine Ball life and reason for doing is to perform the two acts of reflecting and sending without any pause to reflect or to be "creative." The faster the exchanges go the better. Start slowly to get the flow and sequence of the actions and as you get more certain, build speed until you are all going as fast as you can. One person in each circle volunteer to start. Wait for the, "Go!"

Medicine Ball is much more difficult to do well than it must appear in these pages. Few find the flow easily. The ritual of returning the sound/motion to one and then giving a personal one to another without pause can be confusing and even unsettling to some. The ideal is an uncritical and immediate acceptance of what was given and an impulsive unplanned and uncontrolled release of a sound/motion, both rendered as a seamless whole. It is necessary for the director or teacher to catch the cautious evasions as they crop up and also to pick out mannered and controlled sound/motions. Few realize their lack of spontaneity or their own hesitations—even hairline hesitations—that slip in between receiving and reflecting or between reflecting and sending.

**Outrageous Travel**

Form yourselves into parallel lines of six to eight on one end of the studio and face the opposite end. Stand one behind the other. The first person (First Person) in line crosses the space doing the most outrageous sound/motion travel possible. The others in that line observe First Person. Then, the next person in line crosses the space "becoming" the First Person. This means not only duplicating what was visible—the appearance and motions of First Person, but finding the impulse behind the motions and the sounds. Then one at a time, everyone in that line assumes the identity of First Person. If what was originally done appears to be beyond your technical ability or strength to the degree that it might be physically dangerous for you, don't even try. Otherwise, throw yourself into it. Above all do not attempt to be more outrageous, sillier or funnier than First Person; just slip into his.her skin and become him.her.

First Person carefully observes all crossing the space. When the last person has performed the task, First Person awards an accolade to the one who comes closest to what was originally performed. The accolade is a gentle double tap on the top of the head and this person becomes the new First Person who now plays out the most outrageous possible sound/motion travel with the others, one by one, attempting to "become" what they observe. If no one has come really close to what was done, First Person puts hands on hips and says, "Tough," gives no one the accolade and makes, in the opposite direction, a new outrageous sound/motion travel for the others to observe and slip into.

The game continues for as long as the director chooses. In setting up Outrageous Travel, I start with one line doing it and the others observing. Wanting full energy from the dancers, I pick a First Person who from previous observation appears to be lively and uninhibited.

Sound/motion exercises of many varieties are used by numerous directors and teachers to get actors to explore movement. Most actors not only have a skill and freedom vocally —they love to sound off. Moving about terrifies and confuses many of them. Coupling motion with sound peels away their inhibitions. The effect on dancers is a mirror image of what happens with the actors. For them, injecting sound into motion is disorderly and by that token it suddenly becomes possible to indulge in messy motions, even wild motions, nothing like the neat, controlled actions which are the spine of their training and their ideal. Sound/motion for dancers is like being on a holiday or being a bit bad. Sound/motion exercises break down the narrow inhibiting walls of what is permissable. It is not wrong for a dancer, in an improvisation, to pour out neat, controlled actions, just so long as the moment cries out for neat, controlled motions. To really improvise, the dancer stands ready to do anything, in any style. In all of these exercises, games and structures, much freedom is gained by a mix of actors and dancers; both gain from the strengths of the other.

⌒

When I introduce improvisation for choreography workshops or classes, there is the need to deal with the mountain of excess baggage dancers always seem to bring into the studio. They come loaded with their self-defenses, their vanities, their expectations, their desire to please, their hostilities and whatnot. Something is needed to help shed the clutter and to bring them quickly into flesh contact with the moment at hand. The need is for what is present to become paramount in their minds. The following sequence is a way to bring this about.

| | |
|---|---|
| **Goldfish Bowl** | Sit in circles of six to eight. Close your eyes and clean out your head with your breath. In a while, I will say, "OK, go." You will then open your eyes, rise and whenever you are ready, walk to the center of the circle. The moment your body comes in contact with another body, close your eyes and you will become a goldfish in a very small bowl. You love to slither and slide among your fellows and above all you like finding yourself in the middle of all the others but, because you are gentle by nature, you would never force your way in. You only hope and wait for the opportunity to slip-slide into the center of all the others. Slithering and sliding is easier with the arms extended over head but that can get tiring. |
| **Blind Journey<sup>s</sup>** | After a while, I will say, "Go on a Blind Journey of curiosity." Leaving your goldfish bowl, pause, taking a moment to choose what it is in this space among the people and the objects you never really experience with your eyes open. When you know what that is, embark on this Blind Journey of curiosity to seek it out. Of course, move cautiously. A swift or violent move could injure you or another.

After a while, I will say, "Return to your goldfish bowl." With your eyes still closed, you attempt to locate the others with whom you shared a small space and resume what you love to do, slithering and sliding, particularly deep in the midst of the others. Is it important that you return to your original bowl? You decide that.

After a time at this, you will hear me say, "Go find a private place." When you get there, sit, and with your eyes still closed let your mind rove over what you just experienced. |

At this juncture, most groups will be in a wide open state and receptive to the next step, The Rhythm Series. The reader has probably noticed that the dancers are being asked to keep their eyes closed throughout this sequence. Most dancers find it strangely liberating; a few have difficulty with it. Those who wear contact lenses may experience a burning of the eyes. I tell them that they can open and shut their eyes a couple of times whenever there is an irritation. Some others just don't like moving about blind. I don't probe into their why. I tell them to open their eyes whenever they want, for as long as they want. I also tell them that when the eyes are open, the enormous flood of information and sensations coming through their eyes are distractions and dilutions of the work at hand.

With our eyes open, we are en garde, more deliberate and more aware of how we appear to other people, even if *their* eyes are closed. Ridiculous, but if we can't see, we tend to lose consciousness of being seen. Eyes open tends to be inhibiting. Eyes closed, we enter a space where the odd, the unexpected and the hidden that live inside us have the courage to venture forth and most of us become less self-conscious and freer—creatively. A wider range of possibilities and images becomes accessible. Moving about with eyes closed intensifies neglected senses and kicks off a slight sense of danger and adventure. The usual protective self-focus is diluted by the sheer necessity of finding others and touching the environment. Bodies bumping, as in Goldfish Bowl, set up an intimacy and sense of community with the other dancers without the watchful mentality that haunts most human relations.

Sometimes, the first time a group does Goldfish Bowl, at least one person will introduce an aggressive or rough energy that confuses and disturbs the others. Almost always, when the dancers return to the Goldfish Bowl, they are gentler and more sensitive to each other, having learned to be tentative in the Blind Journey. I'm sure there are occasional faint erotic flurries which are, in the context of the exercise, just that and nothing more— just part of the tapestry of life. The Blind Journey raises the awareness of every motion and passage through space to heightened level. Taking nothing for granted is not only a ground rule for a Blind Journey but for art. Not seeing, all the sensitivities are honed. "Eyes closed" and "working blind" will be used often throughout.

# 2 The Rhythm Series

**Breath Rhythm**[s]

This exercise and the next two—Pulse Rhythm and Inner Rhythm—comprise the center of The Rhythm Series. These three flow directly out of the Goldfish Bowl, Blind Journey, back to Goldfish Bowl and finding a private place. Then there is the readiness to embark on The Rhythm Series. To lay the ground for fuller energy, start each of The Rhythm Series exercises from a standing position rather than sitting or lying down.

> When you find your private place, remain standing with your eyes still closed. When everyone has found her.his private place, listen to the next sequence: with your eyes still closed, clear out your head with your breath. I am going to ask you to observe something that is easily altered. Odds are, the act of observing it will change it. Make an effort to observe it without changing.
>
> Observe your breath. Note its duration, rhythm, depth, texture, intensity. Note everything about your breath. When you are convinced that you have it, *become* your breath. Let your breath take full possession of your body. Let your body become the metaphor for your breath. Neither think nor imagine what your body will *look like* as you do this. Only do it. Become your breath. If what you become needs to cover space, open your eyes. Otherwise, all through this work keep your eyes closed.

There is no way to indicate precisely how long this or any particular exercise should last. My principles are: I give the dancers all the time they need to get saturated with the problem and time enough so that something happens. What is "something"? "Something" is a change, no matter how subtle. A change should be enough of a cue to move on. Whenever possible, I respect the timing of the "slowest" person in the group. All these principles are rattled badly by workshops and classes hemmed in by unreal, tight, academic schedules. When I sense that the group has "done" Breath Rhythm, I will say:

> Continue what you are doing. Without losing any part of your rhythm, neither its intensity nor its intent, continuously narrow the range of your movement. Every move will be smaller than the previous one. A time may come when you will appear to be still—but you will know that you are still moving.

## Pulse Rhythm[s]

When the group comes to an apparent halt, I continue:

> Now observe another rhythm in your body. This one is harder to detect. Sometimes when you are very quiet, you can actually become aware of your pulse at the base of your neck, or the tip of your nose, or your fingers. Try to sense that. If it doesn't work, try the usual technique of pressing the fingertips to the artery above the big bone in your wrist. Study your pulse: its tempo, rhythm, force, texture, intensity, intent. When you think you have it, study it a bit more because, unlike Breath Rhythm, once you begin to move, you will not be able to keep observing your pulse. You will have to keep it alive in your memory. As with Breath Rhythm, become your Pulse Rhythm. Let it take possession of your body. Let your body become a metaphor for your pulse.

When the dancers have "done" Pulse Rhythm, sometimes, rather than suggesting diminishing the range of movements, I will simply say,

> Taking all the time you need, let your Pulse Rhythm wind down.

## Inner Rhythm[s]

When there is stillness, I continue:

> You contain still another rhythm. Go into the space within you and in that silence, feel, sense, hear what you can. You may find a rhythm. You may sense the rhythm that drives you, that governs your eating, walking, talking, your doing. Your inner motor has similarities with what it was when you were ten, and it is in some way different than it was ten minutes ago. Seek out your Inner Rhythm. If you don't find it, do not make one up. You will find a value in listening to the silence. Sometimes, just shifting your position may help you feel it.

> When you find your Inner Rhythm, study it. When you feel permeated with what you have found, let it take possession of your body. Let your body become that rhythm. If it is complex, fine. Do it. If it is simple. Fine. Do it. If it isn't interesting. Fine. Do it, without trying to make it "interesting."

But what if it is too much, frightening or dangerous; a rhythm so violent you might hurt yourself attempting to realize it? Here, you have no choice. You cannot walk away from it. If you can't deal with all of it, deal with a part of it. Do its echo. Do its reverberation. Do what it feels like to observe it from a distance, but don't walk away from it. Make nothing up. Only deal with what you find and with what you can.

In the matter of finding an inner rhythm, be suspicious of what comes very quickly. It may be on the mark, but check it out, test it. Try the following. With your eyes closed, raise your arms. On my "Go," immediately let your arms slip into a repetitive rhythmic pattern. "Go." (After a bit): Continue what you're doing, open your eyes and look at the others. Call it an impulse rhythm.

You can get that from yourself or anyone at any time. You can say to a group of children, "Make up a rhythm," and everybody will do something. An impulse rhythm is easy—too easy to be of use in any venture to touch the core of your concerns. An inner rhythm is usually further down the hallway. Do not settle on the first thing you encounter. You may have to go into the basement, the attic or just get out of the house. It's not on the surface. Look at water. It glints, it reflects and it's lively. Chances are that what you're looking for is underwater. At the bottom? How deep is the bottom? You won't know unless you dive down. Whether it's found in the deep or in the shallow, and whether it's found quickly or after a long search, you arrive at a moment when you say, "This is it."

I've said that your inner rhythm is not on the surface, but in fact it may be. Our shelves are crowded with what's on the surface in terms of movement, answers, rhythms and solutions. And surprise! Sometimes what's on the surface is precisely what is needed. But unless you go to the bottom, you won't know what's there, and you will not have earned the right to choose what was there floating in front of you on the surface. Whether you are searching for the specific image or the inner rhythm, you will never know for sure what "it" is. All you have to depend upon is the intensity of your search and your sense of rightness.

**Dedicate Your Motion[s]**

This exercise can be used, on occasion, while the dancers are deep into Inner Rhythm. It jolts the dancers out of the premise that movement is motion is movement and nothing else. It is a deceptively simple ploy. I will call out:

Dedicate your motion to someone who is not present.

(Later) This can be a private exercise to be performed in your own time at your own discretion. Dedicate a whole class to someone who is not there. Or, as deliberately as you can, try to get someone's attention in class. Why? Just so that you might recognize that is what you may have been doing. Perhaps you're doing it all the time. What does it do to the texture and the tone of your body? In rehearsal, you might try to find the "audience" that will bring out the best way for you to do your role. In some of these attempts, you might be quite obnoxious, and in others you may discover a lovely way of dancing. Do this exercise in rehearsal or in class. If in rehearsal, the choreographer calls out, "And just what are you doing?" you know you have made an inappropriate dedication. A stage performance could be wrecked unless such a focus had been carefully thought out, chosen and rehearsed. You can dedicate your motion at any time: in class, in rehearsal, in performance, in creating a dance. Rather than to "someone," it can be to "an animal of which you are in awe," or to "a place of great beauty." Infinite variations are possible.

**Go Visiting**

After five to ten minutes of Inner Rhythm (the timing is a function of taste, style and a sensitivity to the moment), I say:

Continue what you are doing as I speak to you. When you hear me say, "OK, go," without losing one bit of the motion of your Inner Rhythm, go traveling, Go Visiting, and see what the others are doing. You must not lose one bit of your identity—the rhythm that is carrying you along—as you move among the others, observing them. OK, go!

After the dancers seem to have had a good tour of each other, I add:

Continue what you are doing and bring this question to the forefront of your mind. Who in this group interests you, positively or negatively? Either will do. Enter into the working area of that person and deepen your observation. After a while, you will become aware of one of several impulses. You may want to be influenced by that person, or you may want to change her.him in a specific way or just want to be in her.his area as you do your rhythm. Accept the possibility that the person who interests you may be focused on another. That should not alter your purpose. If and when you succeed in absorbing what you wanted to take away or in altering the other, or when you have had your enjoyment, you can leave the floor. If you fail (you are left alone), recognize that in movement and then leave the floor.

In all of this work, some people have difficulty finding an inner rhythm and, as a consequence, might feel ashamed because they seem to lack an essential talent or will become defensively hostile to the whole "stupid" idea. Almost always, these unhappy ones come out of the second or third session with shining faces, "I found it!"

Most groups being given Inner Rhythm for the first time approach it with uncertainty, and a few, with apprehension. Of late, when I sense a self-protective tension in the room, I have adopted a devious ploy. Instead of asking them to find their own rhythm, I take a side road:

> Is there someone with whom you are now dealing who rouses conflicting feelings in you? Is there a person who has qualities you admire, while at the same time he.she ticks you off? If there is such a one let's call her.him, "X". Now see "X" in your mind's eye. Take a good look from a distance. Then come as close as you dare and study "X" carefully. Walk all around "X", observing thoroughly. Now, look deep into "X", sense what is going on inside and try to feel the rhythm in her.his body. Can you hear "X's" inner motor? What is the rhythm that dominates her.his walking, talking, eating?

> When you find "X's" inner rhythm, study it. When you feel saturated with what you have found, let it take possession of your body. Let your body become that rhythm. If it is complex, fine. Do it. If it is simple. Fine. Do it. If it isn't interesting. Fine. Do it, without trying to make it "interesting," without exaggerating and without getting judgmental. Just do the rhythm you found in "X".

This exercise almost invariably gets quick and strong involvement from all, not infrequently tinged with caricature. The movement pours out freely. There doesn't seem to be any question that another person has a rhythm that dominates her.his every move. Having done this, it becomes a much easier leap to "do yourself."

## The Repetitions

The complete Rhythm Series is given only once. It has but one aim: to set the stage for an exercise and a process that functions as a meditation—a movement meditation, a way of getting into the body, getting it going, cutting loose from the mess of the outside, relaxing the militant control of the mind and, best of all, connecting with where you are at the moment. When Inner Rhythm is incorporated into later improvisation sessions its form is more precisely defined in one of two forms of repetition:

**True Repetition[s]**

> Go to the perimeter of the room. There is a place in this space that belongs to you. On the word "Go," roam the room until you find that spot. When you find it, stand on it, clean out your head with your breath and listen for, sense, find your inner rhythm. If

and when you find it, let it take possession of your body. Take all the time you need. It may appear bit by bit, like a chick chipping its way out of an eggshell. When you know it is complete, that it is being fully stated by your body, commit yourself to doing that phrase from that point on *and that phrase only*, with no changes for a hunk of time—plus or minus ten minutes. Change only if you sense that continuing will cause you physical harm or if you experience a fatigue that is threatening.

Otherwise, no changes at all.

## Evolving Repetition[S]

Start off exactly like True Repetition. When the rhythm finally emerges fully in the body, the intent is to do the rhythm as found. If a change happens, *allow* it to happen. If no change happens, do not force a change in the phrase. It is allowed to continue as it was. Radical or abrupt changes would be suspect because they would not be rooted in the rhythm that was originally found.

True Repetition acts like a movement meditation and draws dancers into an open, receptive and relaxed state. It is ideal for starting work sessions. Evolving Repetition is a more "athletic" and adventurous structure and certainly more interesting to watch. The Workgroup often opened programs with an Evolving Repetition. Whenever the dancers do not need Gifts because they are warmed and ready to dance, I have set up a ritual in which, as they enter the studio, they go in their own time into the space, clear their heads, find their own inner rhythm and slip directly into either True Repetition or Evolving Repetition for at least ten minutes.

## Spinning[S]

Another classic and ancient way of clearing the mind for work is Spinning. Members of a sect of Muslim Sufis use whirling as a way of achieving an ecstatic trance. For dancers, it acts like an emotional and intellectual centrifuge, throwing off distractions and leaving a clean center from which to begin the work of improvising. It can be used to precede Internal Rhythm.

Spin in place, at any tempo, for as long as you can. Pause, and then spin in the opposite direction for as long as you can. Then, in the stillness, find your internal rhythm. Those of you who know the secret of spinning interminably without getting dizzy may be interrupted by my asking you to bring it to a close.

# 3 Uncovering Sources of Movement

## THE FIRST STEPS

Each of the following exercises introduces important principles and ways of working that pave the way for more complex exercises.

**Circles[S]**

With your eyes closed, listen to the sequence of the next exercise. You will hear better with your eyes closed. First, you will hear music. After a while, I will say, "Someone or something is doing something." I may choose any verb: flying, loving, hunting, planting, destroying, shielding, ad infinitum. Let us pick an example at random, "Someone or something is running to or from someone or something." The "someone or something" can come from any part of your mind: books you have read, films, history, TV, friends, your own life. When you know who or what that someone or something is, with your eyes still closed, stand. Be certain that the someone or something is a specific. Is the runner a woman, a lion, a bird, a raindrop running down a window pane? If it is a woman, what is the color of her hair? Does she have a name? Do you know her? In other words, you must find in your mind a specific running man or woman or bird or lion or whatever, and never, ever, the generic idea of a woman, a man or a bird.

While you are standing, waiting for the others, use your time to learn all you can about "X". "X" is what we will call the someone or something known only to you. Look at "X" from all sides, from close up and far away. Does an odor come off of "X"? The more specifics you learn about "X", the richer and more personal will be the movement that emerges from this work.

The images of running may range from the literal, like the time you broke your nasty neighbor's window and fled the scene, to the metaphoric, like the memory of a raindrop running down a window pane last week. You might recall the Greek myth of Atalanta, the princess who would only marry the man who could beat her in a foot race. If he lost, he also lost his head. A crafty suitor, Hippomenes, hid three golden apples in his tunic, throwing them in her path one by one. He thus won the race and married the princess. You may choose anything—yourself fleeing, a raindrop, Atalanta or Hippomenes—so long as it is a specific and not a generalization or an abstraction.

When everyone is standing, I will stop the music and rewind the tape to the beginning. As I am doing this, each of you should sit, stand, kneel or lie down, whichever is an appropriate place from which to become "X". Above all, know that it is *you who are taking this position and not "X". Do not for a moment try at this stage to "become" or look like your "X"*. It is too soon, because there is too little you know of "X". To do so will shape all you do into a chain of clichés. When you finish Circles you may be surprised by all you have discovered about "X".

When you hear the music, something that may appear strange will be asked of you: let your scalp, your ears, your brows, your eyes become "X" running. Do not question the logic or the feasibility of brows running. At the center of what we do as dancers is the use of the body and its parts as metaphors for the whole world. If running is the action of "X", then run with your scalp, your ears, your brows and your eyes. If it is appropriate to "X" that your eyes remain closed, fine. If open is true to this moment for "X", then open let them be.

After a while, I will say, "Whenever you are ready, become "X" running with your jaw, your nose, your lips, your tongue." If you are still deeply involved with the first action, finish it before going on to the mouth. When you do go on, *do not lose what you have done*. That continues.

In time, I will say, "Whenever you are ready, with your neck, become "X" running."

Then ". . . with your chest, become "X" running."

Then ". . . with your shoulders, become "X" running."

Then ". . . with your elbows, become "X" running."

Then ". . . with your hands, become "X" running," and as you go on, lose nothing of what you have been doing. You are constantly accumulating, though at each stage your action is being led by that new part of the body.

Then ". . . with your waist, belly, voice, become "X" running."

Then ". . . with your pelvis, become "X" running."

Then ". . . with your thighs, knees become "X" running."

Then ". . . with your feet, become "X" running."

Then "Whenever you are ready, with all of you, with your totality, become "X" running."

In this last stage, a time will come when you will have *become* "X". When you sense that transformation, celebrate it and then leave the floor.

Two negatives: (1) This is not an exercise in isolations, but rather, the entire body supports the action of the individual part of the body. (2) This is not an exercise in exploring the range of movement that is possible, say, of your mouth or your hands. The motions are governed strictly by the image and action being fulfilled. Sticking to the specific action of a specific someone or something will create rich movement. Isolations or variation games will convert the entire exercise into an academic excursion irrelevant to our work and intention.

Because Circles is more complex than the previous exercises, it would be well to give a quick summary and then open the space to questions before actually starting.

Timing the intervals between calling out the parts of the body is a delicate matter ideally done by feel and not by the clock. A section can be a minute, two or three. The conductor of the exercise needs only to pay close attention to the flow of energy in the group. Inviting the use of the voice is a risky choice that may work best with a small group. If the group is large, and heated up, the din may be such that the subsequent directions will be inaudible and for some will be violently intrusive.

Whenever a group was ready to work on the ritual of becoming someone or something, I would first introduce Circles, making it clear that it would be done only once and that thereafter we would do its variant, Each Alone.

**Each Alone**[5]

Each Alone begins exactly the same as Circles. From a seated position, you will hear music and then I will give you "Someone or something is doing something." When that someone or something arrives in your mind, stand. When everyone is standing, I will stop the music and rewind the tape to the beginning. As I am doing this, each of you should sit, stand, kneel or lie down as before.

The variation begins here: When the music starts up again from its beginning call up the vision of "X" doing what "X" does *and immediately without plan,* allow the impulse for *any* part of your body to perform that act as "X". In time, you will feel as if you "have done" that part, that it has become "X" doing what "X" does and you will be ready to move on. Without planning or thinking, another part will have the impulse to do this. Taking all the time that is needed, you will proceed in whatever sequence your body tells you. Try to retain what you have done as Each Alone evolves. Symmetry is possible but not necessary: the focus of activity might be the shoulders or only the right shoulder. Discard the rigorous logic of Circles and instead follow the dictates of your body. Sequence and timing are governed by your impulses. You may never get to body parts mentioned in Circles and you may become absorbed in an area untouched by Circles. There will come a moment when all the pieces come together and you will be "X" doing what "X" does. Celebrate that becoming and then leave the floor.

Without the constant intrusion and interruptions from me and with the concentration of permitting the action of "X" to flow through the body undirected, the dancers are able to go much more deeply into the life of "X," discovering surprising movement metaphors and best of all, moving in an imagined context with conviction and freedom. If anything could describe the goal of creative movement, "moving in an imagined context with conviction and freedom," certainly touches the center. In the work of choreographing, Each Alone has the possibility of becoming a potent tool in finding movement that is not only surprising but precisely shaped to needs of the work involved. One becomes another in order to be, think, act and *dance* as another. No matter how personal the context of a dance work is, who or what is dancing is *another*.

Circles and Each Alone accomplish two things: they are sources of creative movement. In introducing these two exercises one never asks for an emotion or a mood. That is the direct highway to banality. One always asks for an *action* on the assumption that the specific "who" doing a specific action in a specific context will generate a truthful emotion or mood. To ask parts of your body to become in turn a fine-boned, young, red, female fox fleeing the hounds in a driving rain would in time produce a gut emotion of unquestioned intensity, a genuine feeling in the body of the dancer and some fascinating movement. The second value is that these exercises become profound lessons in the metaphoric possibilities of the various parts of the body. Without this awareness and a mastery of poetic dance metaphors, the entire way of working that is presented here would degenerate into one continuous flow of literal movement, which is the last thing we want from dancers. In dance, a strategic moment of literal movement has been the strongest part of some of our best dance works and the key to some ostensibly abstract dances. As an extended mode of expression, the literal becomes acting and negates the meaning and point of the dance art.

One both unexpected and yet obvious note: in at least one of the various stages of Circles or Each Alone, the dancer may come across a part of the body which translates into a literal action. Say the image is Hippomenes, the man in the myth, racing the princess Atalanta for her hand in marriage. Comes the moment when the focus is on feet, the dancer may find him.herself dashing through the studio. It may prove to be not only literal but dull or, conversely, the most exhilarating of all the segments. More, if most of what had gone before was retained, the running may be like no running that had ever been done since this literal movement is an island within a circle of metaphors for the same action.

You never know anything until it happens. It is very important in all improvisation not to look ahead, not to anticipate. Anticipation and, even worse, planning, cut out the heart and meaning of improvisation. Improvisation starts with a set of givens, rules and wishes, and from then on, one deals with the immediate present, never knowing what will happen until it does happen. By its open-ended nature, improvisation is an ideal tool to discover fresh and personal movement expression. Performing an action, one part of the body at a time, is a way of freeing it imaginatively. The improvisations are usually full of surprises. In the little talks after a workshop or class session, time and again, a dancer will say, "I never did anything like that." "I never moved like that." "I was completely into that." "I forgot the studio—all the others." "I didn't know I was dancing."

## Backdoor[5]

Everything up to this point moves dancers into deeper levels of consciousness but by that very token, a protectiveness of old ways can lead to shallow and impersonal choices that are clichéd, obvious or, worst of all, evasive. For these pitfalls, there are two meditations or mind trips that can open up the most unexpected doors:

> With your breath, empty your head. (Pause.) In a little while I am going to say a word or short phrase. The moment you hear the word or phrase allow a smell, a sound, an image, a word, anything, to appear in the center of your mind. With the next breath— or sooner—whatever is in the focus of your mind must change to something else. This process is continuous: a change in your mind with every breath, or sooner. Continuous change is the only control you are to exert on the process. Above all, don't try to impose any overall conception of how one thing should follow the other. You don't try to make a logical flow or conversely, try to create surrealist or strange connections. You simply attempt to observe passively whatever will emerge, logically or illogically. There is only one compulsion: whatever occupies your mind must change with every breath or sooner.

After about five minutes, I ask people to let it wind down, and when it has, to open their eyes. When everyone's eyes are open, I ask:

Is there anything remarkable, special, unusual, confusing or interesting about what took place? I am not asking about your specific sensations and images, which I am sure are interesting. I am rather curious about what, if anything, you found interesting in the structure or the process of what you were just doing.

Sooner or later, what emerges in any group of ten or more people is the following pattern: a large number of people had a recurrent image. Of these, some find that recurrent image logical, and others find that image rather unexpected and surprising. Again, some find that image rather attractive and interesting, while others find it kept recurring even though they didn't like it. Not a few experience a strong image they had never seen before. Almost everyone answered affirmatively upon being asked, "Is there some image that even now stands out beyond all the others?

**Hub Meditation**[s]

Immediately upon giving, doing and discussing Backdoor another exercise is given:

Close your eyes and clean your head out with your breath. In a little while I will say, "Someone or something is doing something." It will be a simple verb. Picking one as an example: "Someone or something is rising and falling." From here on, let your mind roam and search for everything in your experience of rising and falling—in nature, in history, in films, TV, the people you know, your own life—a piece of bleached driftwood in the surf, a child on a pogo-stick, a red autumn leaf in a cold wind, a close relation's struggle with an addiction, a graph of a sine wave, the breast of the woman who has just been crowned Miss America, a white line of paint running across a Jackson Pollock painting, the sound of the waves one evening when you were in Maui. Potentially the list is endless. Each of these will be for a moment in the center of your consciousness.

After a while, you may discover that regardless of what you come up with, the hub of your mind is occupied with one thing, even though you continue to raise up new images: there you are on that frightened horse being bounced up and down in the saddle as he gallops off the road into the desert away from the blaring horn of that monster white trailer truck.

Note everything mentioned was specific. Don't reach for anything as general and grandiose as the rise and fall of the Roman Empire. Avoid unspecific feelings like going from gaiety to sadness to gaiety. These will land you neck-deep into stencils, to steal a word from Stanislavski.

When you realize that the hub of your mind is occupied by one image regardless of whatever other images come up, accept that and move in to get a close look at what is there. Then open your eyes. You will have just done a Hub Meditation.

At this point I state a ground rule for this way of working in dance: the worst idea for a dance or the conception of a role is a "good" idea; the best idea is one that won't go away, whether you like it or not, like a nettle that sticks to your garments. I accept with a passion the statement by Ben Shahn, in *The Shape of Content:* "Whatever crosses the human mind may be fit content for art—in the right hands . . . it is the fullness of feeling with which the artist addresses himself to his theme that will determine, finally, its stature or its seriousness."[25]

The revelation that Backdoor and Hub Meditation bring is that, for most people, given enough time, the mind will find itself occupied with an image that dominates all others. It matters not whether the image is attractive or repulsive, whether the image is fascinating or on its surface quite dull, that is the image to work on and the one that probably will prove to be fertile.

A relevant story: I had a talented and devoted student who took a number of workshops in choreography with me. She always produced work that was personal, strong and unexpected but in the improvisation exercises involving imaging, she would resort to literal pantomime and dead-end repetitions. Finally I spoke up, "What gives, Sarah? Every time we get to this, you get lost." "Well, every time you give us a Hub Meditation, I see Archie Bunker." "So, did you ever do Archie Bunker?" "No! Of course not!" Too bad. She missed out on something that was perhaps more important to her than she was willing to realize. For her values and conscious mind, Archie Bunker *was not material worthy of dance or art.* This is precisely the self-inflicted snobbery that defeats many young artists and some mature artists. They keep under covers a passionate connection and knowledge of something that they fear is not "good" enough for "ART"—in favor of what? Better to spell "art" with small letters and learn to respect one's deepest feelings as the source and focus of the work.

The last thing one should do is to hunt for a "good image," a "creative image," an "exciting image" or worst of all, try to find an image which the dancer thinks will interest, excite, or please the teacher, the audience or the critics. The basic dictum of the work says, if it isn't personal, it isn't worth working on.

**Visualizations**

There are those people who are unhappy with the many problems that depend on visualization because they are convinced that they can't do it, or can't do it well. When I hear this, I throw out to the group:

Close your eyes and see the departure area of an airport with taxicabs, buses and limousines zipping by. A man is standing near the curb looking about. Can you see him? How is he dressed? Is he wearing a hat? Step up close to him and study his face. Walk around him and view him from the rear. Walk off to the side, still looking at him. Have you ever seen him before?

A suggestion to the reader: reread the above paragraph and then take the time to do what it suggests.

Have you ever seen that man before? In the many times I have given this simple setting, almost everyone discovered a man they had never seen. You too, probably created a man unknown to you. Your life of observation was the raw material—the encyclopedia from which he was shaped. Your memory, sense memory and imagination were the tools that worked for you without your control or supervision. The vision of that man did not just happen. Imagination stirs up the great soup of your many observations to create a specific man standing at an airport curb or a poem, a song or a dance. I have yet to find one of those, "I-can't-visualize" people who did not see that man on the departure curb. Something about that airport scene proves that they can.

## Gesture Permutations[s]

It is a given in modern dance that being literal is a no-no, and with justification. If our intention is to be specific and to have a specific identity at all times, what is to guard us against falling into this trap of the literal? The strongest substance has a vulnerability. An ancient vase of Venetian glass can gleam in its glory for centuries. One light tap of a metal hammer and we have a mess of shards. The plastic wrapping on four little cheese and peanut butter crackers will frustrate all efforts to tear it open until stabbed by the point of a nail file. Getting caught in the literal and the linear is the Achilles heel of our way of working.

What can shield us from the devastating question, "Why are you dancing? Why aren't you actors in a play and just speaking what you have on your mind?"

There is an answer. *Never flee the literal but never get stuck in it.* Learn to bend it, stretch it, squeeze it, quicken it, transmute it to another body part, alter the "who"—all of which is to say, learn to make the literal a springboard to a metaphor—and in so doing make motion poems, which could easily be another name for dancing. The next two exercises contain strategies for transforming the literal into dance metaphors.

Pair off. If there is an odd number, make one a trio. Now, talk about what you really think about Arizona. (Any place will do, the closer the better. After several minutes:) Continue your discussion, but make no sound. Communicate only with gestures.

(After several minutes:) Now pause and between you, cull a short sequence of the silent gestures you both exchanged, six to be exact. Person A makes a gesture. B replies, A replies, B replies, A replies and B replies. Period. If you are a trio, keep it to six: A, then B, then C, then A, then B and then C. Once you have decided on the six gestures face me. (When all are finished and facing me:)

Now, facing each other, go through the sequence of the six gestures three times, and each time you make your gesture do it as if it were the first time you ever did it. Do it with the same conviction that you had before I stopped you.

- Now do the six gestures three times, as fast as you possibly can.
- Now do the six gestures one time, moving slower than you have ever moved in your life.
- You are a mammoth human made of lead and concrete. Do the six gestures.
- You are actors in a silent movie. Do the six gestures.
- You are underwater. Do the six gestures.
- You are an ambitious courtier in the court of Louis XIV. The monarch favors anyone who appears to be an elegant dancer.
- You are clowns in a circus.
- Do the six gestures in waltz time.
- You stammer and stutter painfully.
- You have no hands and no arms. Communicate the meaning of the six gestures with your torso.
- Communicate only with your shoulders.
- Only with your feet.
- All your gestures are made of porcelain. They have been dropped, broken and glued together this way and that but not logically. Communicate as best you can.
- Don't do any of the six gestures. Rather do what they feel like.

Manifestly, this list is potentially endless.

**Gesture Rondos**

Leave your partner or your trio, and in your own space and in your own mind, go over the gestures you have been doing. Decide which one you want to continue working with, for whatever reason. When I give you the "Go," you will do that gesture with as much truth and conviction as you did the first time and then, with no premeditation, allow *anything* to flow out of it, from the most obvious, literal banal association to the most esoteric muscular association. You may start on a physical impulse that leads to dramatic one that leads to whatever. Just let it happen and above all, avoid "good taste." Just go. If and when the energy runs down, come to a pause and repeat the original gesture as simply and honestly as possible, and again allow anything to flow for as long as it does until it stops. Then, for as many times as the flow stops, return to the original gesture and an improvisation that will flow out of that. Continue until I call out for this Gesture Rondo to end. Go!

After doing this sequence most dancers, instead of living in terror of the literal gesture by either sedulously avoiding it or feeling guilty of a bad taste sin doing one, discover that the literal gesture is a gold mine. The literal gesture becomes a source of a limitless range of movement. The infinitely small island of classroom moves which most dancers think contains the whole world of dance movement becomes only one rich and useful area *among many*. If one were to total a lexicon of moves found in any one dance technique: flamenco, ballet, modern, tap or Hawaiian, each one would reveal a small number of moves compared to all that the human body is capable of. Whatever we do and have done in our lives—from early morning to sleep and dreams and from the earliest remembered days to this morning—is waiting there to be used in our dances: bent, turned, twisted, turned inside out, shaved, smoothly carved, stretched, shrunk or magnified. All that we do is the treasure chest for our choreography.

# 4 Metaphor

1. Look up definitions and descriptions of metaphor. Try several dictionaries, Fowler's *Modern English Usage*, the *Encyclopedia Britannica* (look under "figures of speech") and any book that purports to deal with poetry and the making of poetry. Fill a few pages of your notebook with whatever strikes you and makes strong sense to you.

2. In your reading of newspapers or magazines, as well as poetry and novels, search out and underline metaphors.

3. Take note of the metaphors that appear in your own speech.

4. Make a list of literal human gestures (this may be more difficult than it appears) and make a series of variations for each of them.

5. Make a list of common human movement metaphors. Take a few of them and make a series of variations for each one. This would resemble the Gesture Permutations exercise.

# 5  Sense Memory Sources

**Faces**

Will everyone please get to a sink and thoroughly wash your hands? On the way, or returning, choose a partner. When you return, washed, sit facing each other cross-legged, knees a few inches apart, and close your eyes. When you sit, avoid touching the floor with your clean hands.

The bemused go to wash, return as partners and sit.

With your eyes closed, clear a space in your head with your breath. Anytime after I finish speaking and whenever you are ready, reach your hands forward to touch the face of the person in front of you. With your fingertips study this face—the varied textures of skin and hair, the shapes of bone and muscle. You will study not only to experience but to remember. When you think your hands have the memory of that face, place them in your lap. When your partner's hands leave your face, with your eyes still closed, turn a quarter of a circle away on your bottom. Now reach your hands forward into the air *as if that person is still in front of you*, and with your fingers, relive the entire experience of touching his.her face, not merely going through the motions of touching but feeling once again the skin, hair, muscle and bone.

Do not be disconcerted if you find areas whose sensory experience you cannot recall. In some places, the most you will have is the idea of moist skin or a hairline, not the sensation. Do not despair. Do as much of the face in the air as you can. Then swivel back to face in the original direction, with your eyes still closed, and reach out to once again study to remember the face of your partner.

If you encounter a shoulder instead of a face, your partner is still re-creating in the air. Drop your hands and wait until you sense your partner return to face you. Then resume your exploration, going specifically to the places where your memory failed you. Experience and study with your hands what eluded you, and when you think your hands have it, drop your hands once again. When both you and your partner have lowered your hands, having finished this second study, swivel a quarter turn away and go directly to the blank places and fill them in by experiencing the actual sensation of touching. When you have done all you can, drop your hands to your lap and wait until you hear an "OK," indicating that all are finished.

When all have done this, I add the following:

When I give you a "Go!," open your eyes and rise to find a private space for yourself. Once you are there, without planning, without waiting to think about what you will do, begin to dance what it *felt* like to do what you had just done. Don't *dance* what you did, but to repeat, dance what it *felt* like to do what you were doing. Sit when you are finished. Now go!

When everyone has done their private dance and is seated:

Now go to find your partner and each of you show the other what you just did. After you have danced for each other sit where you are, facing in my direction.

When all are finished:

Now all come here and answer a question: What was the difference between the dance you did first, when you had no awareness that you were going to do it for an audience, when you had no audience in fact, and the second dance, the second version of what you did, when you presented it to your partner?

The ensuing discussions always reveal a vast variety of attitudes towards the problems of choreographing, performance, truth and art itself. Some say they are heightened, energized, exhilarated and even gain a clarity of expression by the presence of an audience; other people become dismayed, disoriented and disappointed. Those having negative experiences claim to have lost spontaneity, become falsely theatrical, forgot some good moves and worst of all lost the feeling that enriched the private experience. I ask, "Did you leave out some material because you thought it might not be interesting or did you exaggerate some parts to make them more interesting?"

Almost all admit to having left out material and also to speeding up all they did. Most artists do, though there are Asian artists and a body of post-modernists who make a virtue of extended time. Dance, like music and theatre, are artifacts that exist in real time. The question confronting every artist who speaks in real time is how do I reveal the true time of what I am doing? Is it best seen, felt, experienced, impacted by compression, or its opposite, extension or in real time? There is no one answer and every artist must beware of becoming a passive victim of a style, either a style of his time or what he.she has come to regard as his.her style. Rather than a general rule of rightness, the time-life of each phrase or dance writes its own rules.

For some, the changes from the dance in the private session to the dance for the partner were in the interest of gaining a clarity of expression and intent. They feared that their solitary work was rambling, shapeless and unnecessarily obscure and thus needed shortening, editing, speeding up, altering emphases or the addition of "something interesting." Even in that one unrehearsed "performance" for the audience of one, the original private exploration was regarded as a sketch and the "performance" as a "painting."

On the matter of the loss of spontaneity—the loss of the feeling that enriched the private experience, this must be said: the climate of the creative process is turbulent and constantly subject to change. Those who feel they cannot function as artists unless they are always in full heat and flowing are in serious trouble. Similarly, those who constantly seek the cool, objective detachment that gives them complete control over all that pours out of them are unwilling to risk the surprises and full life of an artist. For most artists capable of expression, there are periods of work where an intoxication possesses them and the work flows like a mighty river. *These same artists are quite capable of slaving away for long periods of time in the cold tunnel of creation, remembering, recreating and laborious editing.* They willingly bear tedium and hours of detailed concentration that to an outsider would appear dealing with minutiae.

How many dancers have in the heat of improvisation felt that they had flown past the limits of gravity and in the cold moments that followed knew that they might never recapture that ecstasy and those elegant phrases? The artists that last, patiently and stubbornly pursue the elusive, the ineffable moment and in time, hammer out a shape that may not be precisely what they had lost but rather a lovely poem *about* it. The journey of artists is a gamble through the heat and ice of the creative process.

To tie it all together, I throw out a ruthless ethic about art: that the greatest mark of devotion to the audience is not to create what they would like or expect, but rather for the artist to give all his.her devotion to the vision as was found. That is the true gift to the audience—even though they might hate it.

| The Obstacle[s] | Put a folding chair into the middle of the space. Pick a dancer for whom appearance and charm are the ne plus ultra of dance, and of life. Tell him.her that you would like very much to see whether he.she can pass under the chair without moving it. Or, devise any task that will be so demanding that the dancer will for once think only of *doing* without *appearing* to be doing. |

**Passing Through a Physical Object**

Form a big circle. When I tap any one of you on the shoulder, go to the center of the circle and on the impulse of the moment take any position—standing, sitting or lying down. The next person in the circle does the same, only some part of his.her body must touch the first person's body. Person after person, going around the circle, adds his.her body to the structure of bodies until one person is left. This one positions him.herself at the point where the diameter of the group is the greatest and must now wend, crawl, wriggle his.her way through—never around—the group *without disturbing or forcing anyone to change his.her position.* Coming out on the other side, he.she taps a dancer who rises, permitting the first person to take his.her place, and now this second person takes on the same task of passing through the widest part of the conglomerate of bodies without disturbing or changing anyone's position. If any of you is tapped and has already made the "journey," convey that fact by not responding, which tells the person to try another.

After everyone has traversed the structure, I will call out: "Find a private area for yourself." Now alone, do what you did working your way through the others. Do exactly what you did with only the *memory* of the other bodies to guide you. Do it once alone, then find a partner and do it for him.her to critique, and then observe your partner critically, thus helping each other learn to make the imaginary tangible.

This works best for a group of six to fifteen people. An alternative is for the leader/teacher to assemble the entire group and call out the dancers, one by one, to do the imaginary traversal through the group and then give or call for a critique of the sense memory displayed. Many elements go into the doing of this exercise. It opens up the possibility of body contact, without which improvisation is impoverished. It relates to the challenge of The Obstacle, a task that is so demanding that self-preoccupation and self-decorativeness are improbable. It is an ideal sense-memory exercise for dancers because it uses the whole body. The usual actors' exercises, like sewing on a button or putting on a garment, place the strongest emphasis on the hands—which are physically the smartest part of the body. Though sense memory exercises are a staple of the actor's training and a skill, no choreographer can afford to neglect them. It means what it says: having a vivid, sensual memory of actions with a real object and the ability to recreate those actions without the object. In the exercise, or in performance the real object is imagined—remembered—sensed—whatever, just so long as the motion of the performer is determined by truth of the remembering. It is the essence of the theatre—pretending what is not *is*.

**Slalom**

This is a more athletic version of Passing Through a Physical Object and is exactly what it sounds like.

Everyone picks an observer-partner. All the observers stand aside to observe! The others, one by one, form a single line, all spaced one to two yards apart. This line can be arrow straight or chaotically crooked, it matters not. When the last person is in place, I will shout "Go!," and this last person will run full tilt, slalom style, to the other end of the line, letting out a shout upon arriving. This is the signal for the next person to do the same. When the last person has performed the run, all gather around the point where the line started. One by one, run from where you started, duplicating the slalom run as if all those dancers were still standing there. When the running group has done this, find your observer-partner and learn how vividly and accurately you repeated your run. The critique concluded, the second group repeats the ritual. Finally, repeat the entire sequence a second time, the running and the critiques.

As Picasso was so fond of iterating, "Art is a lie." There is so little on stage that is real, that without a rich and continuous infusion of imagination, the whole edifice of credibility collapses. Passing Through a Physical Object and Slalom, two highly physical sense-memory exercises, are essentially exercises in imagination. The muscles of imagination always need exercising.

# 6 Sources of Movement Material

## THE NEXT LEVEL

The first three exercises should be introduced singly, but later they work best flowing one into the other.

**The Mind-Wash**[s]

Start seated, cross-legged and facing a partner with your knees two or three inches apart. Close your eyes and clean out your head. Whenever you are ready, open your eyes to look at the tip of your nose. Unlike the classic yogis who spent a lifetime doing that only, whenever you've had enough of looking at the tip of your nose, let your gaze drop to high on your chest and gradually allow your eyes to travel down your body, across the floor, across your ankles, across the floor between you and your partner, across your partner's ankles, another bit of floor, and then travel up the body of your partner, across the face, over her.his head, to the wall beyond, the eyes climbing in a path as wide as your eyes, up the wall until they find the ceiling. Then traveling across the ceiling and finally as far back and behind as you can, without falling over backward. Take as much or as little time as you need for this visual journey.

Any number of dancers have told me that they have done The Mind-Wash alone as a meditation technique to clear their heads prior to choreographing. I have used it myself innumerable times when my head was too turbulent to move on to the next step.

**Not Naming**[s]

You can add a Taoist touch to The Mind-Wash. Not Naming is a lovely challenge which some dancers find quite helpful.

In the course of the eye journey, as your gaze travels down and up, devote your mind to seeing *without naming what you see.*

Most find this difficult, but some are able to achieve it intermittently and find it a transporting experience. To make it work, when first presenting this exercise, instead of saying, "Your eyes go down to your chest, then to the floor, across to your partner's body . . ." I simply pantomime with the tips of the fingers where the eyes should focus, from the tip of the nose to the upper part of the chest, and so on, thus indicating the eye journey *without naming anything.*

**The Other**

When The Mind-Wash is complete, return to look upon the face of your partner, and when your partner meets your gaze begin The Other. Its title defines it. You are looking at this other to see what you can see. This is a rare moment when your bare face is exposed to another whose face is there gazing at you. What is there to see other than eyes, lips, hair, etc.? If you have the patience and the desire, you will begin to see things you never noticed, no matter how long you have known this other. Why do we go into this? Shortly you will be dancing with, to, for and about this other. Knowing more of the other allows for more sensitivity.

**A Duet**

Some of my first explorations into improvisation took place in 1969 at the University of Texas in Austin. During a lull in the second week of the workshop, I asked whether anyone had a game along the lines of the work we were doing. The best dancer spoke up:

> Back home in Connecticut, I have a big basement in which my friend and I would practice whenever we could and one of the things we loved to do best was to put on a piece of music we both liked and then we danced looking at each other. It was as if I was dancing about her and she was dancing about me. I don't mean "about" as "around." I mean that she and what she was doing was the subject of my dance and vice versa. We could do this all afternoon.

It sounded good if not sensational. I said, "Fine," and asked her to explain once again to everyone what they were to do. People paired off and I put on an ideal piece of music for an extended improvisation, Stravinsky's *Le Sacre du Printemps.* It turned out quite well. Not only did the energy flow right through its entire length of thirty-five minutes, but the actors and the dancers appeared to lose self-consciousness with a full absorption in each other. They were playful, teasing and serious in turn. This was a useful form. It involved everyone, built up a good dance heat and best of all, it asked for and seemed to get exactly the frame of mind I was seeking: a loss of focus upon self, replaced by focus on the task at hand and/or the other—the other person. To repeat her description of A Duet:

> Everyone pair off. (If there is an odd number, there can be either a trio or one person can drop out to observe.) When the music starts, you dance looking at your partner and dancing about your partner, about his.her motions, hair, clothing, personality traits, eyes—anything that gets your attention. Duplicating your partner's movements is only one of an infinite number of choices. Along the way, try to make something happen, either to you or your partner or both. When it happens, leave the floor. If your partner leaves first, dance a recognition of being left and then leave.

## The Duet as a Structure

There is a confusion possible when A Duet is repeated in different contexts. Calling one "A Duet" and the other "The Duet as a Structure" doesn't really help very much, but will have to do. Suffice to say, "A Duet" is the simpler form which I learned in that Austin workshop and "The Duet as a Structure" is what developed from that one simple exercise. This sequence is the centerpiece of all the improvisations in this book. It includes five exercises given previously: The Mind-Wash, The Other, The Hub Meditation, Each Alone and finally The Duet as a Structure itself.

From working through The Duet as a Structure can flow an understanding of self, the other, a way of dancing, a way of improvising and a way of creating choreography. It is ideal for studio work. Inevitably, on the first reading, The Duet as a Structure may appear to be overwhelmingly complex, but it is bound together by an internal logic. Approach it step by step and clarity will emerge. The Duet as a Structure can be mastered bit by bit, solidifying each part before attempting to put it all together. Once that happens, the dancer, the student, the teacher, the choreographer will have at hand a tool to practice this matter of becoming another and performing the metaphoric task that ignites the inner powers and sensibilities of the dancer. To describe the entire sequence, there will be, of necessity, some repetition of what has just gone before.

For The Duet as a Structure it is well to have about twenty-five minutes of music, preferably a single composition that does not have radical changes. Shorter pieces will work if they are bound together with a single, coherent style.

> Sit cross-legged, facing your partner, knees a few inches apart, close your eyes and clear a space in your head with your breath. (Pause.) First you will hear music. After a while, you will hear me say, "Someone or something is doing something to or with or for someone or something." Put this statement on a shelf of your mind to be dealt with later.

Should you, the reader, wish to follow this sequence with a specific image in mind, make one up now or choose one from the following:

- Someone always has to have his.her own way. You are that person or you are dealing with that person.

- Someone needs to live in a neat, orderly, predictable world. You are that person or you are dealing with that person.

- Someone is a protector, shielding another from anything potentially dangerous or negative. You are the person being protected.

- Someone is leaving. You are leaving or you are being left.

- Someone is always busy and in a hurry and the other is laid back.

- Someone is always on the lookout for funning, joking and clowning. You are that person or dealing with that person.

Now do The Mind-Wash, followed by The Other. Your partner is now "the other," the person with whom you are going to enter a complex world made by both of you. It may be the first time you have worked together or the twentieth, there will always be something new to be observed. What can you glean just by looking and looking? The moment will come when you have learned what you can for now and you are ready to take the "Someone . . . something . . ." statement off the shelf of your mind and do a Hub Meditation with it. Let your mind roam through literature, films, TV, your own life, until one statement dominates. All this time, you are looking at your partner. These two actions, looking at your partner and looking for what will occupy the hub of your mind may seem too far apart. Wait. You may find that they reinforce each other or lead you into unexpected paths. If and when you find the specific someone-something, you have a decision to make. Which role will you play?

After knowing which one, ask yourself the critical question: If you are so-and-so, *what is your task?* What do you need to do with, to or for this other person? Once you know your task, you need to find in your mind a movement metaphor for this task. It is here that your imagination has its greatest challenge: finding a poetic movement metaphor rather than a literal action. One way you will be dancing, whatever that elusive word means, the other way you might just as well speak like an actor rather than go through the motions of an inefficient dumb-show. A degree of patience will serve here. Allow for "near misses" or "failures" the first few times you do The Duet as a Structure. In time, finding the movement metaphor that charges your dance energy and communicates to your partner will become a part of your craft in this work.

Once you have determined your role and your task, you are ready for the next phase of The Duet as a Structure. When you are ready, indicate that to your partner by turning your palms up and resting your hands on your knees. When the other is ready, she.he clasps the upturned palms and both rise and separate, each to find a private place. Here you will prepare your self to become "X", the person you found in your Hub Meditation, and to be geared up to accomplish the task you have chosen. You do this through the structure called Each Alone. This is the development of Circles in which the entire structure becomes open-ended, with each dancer deciding the order, when and how long to work on the body parts.

Once in your private place, you will begin Each Alone, on your own. Call up the vision of "X" doing what "X" does and immediately allow one part of your body to perform that act, as "X". When you feel as if that part has become "X" doing what "X" does, you will be ready to move on. Taking all the time that is needed, you will continue in whatever sequence your body tells you, body part by body part. As you do this, try to retain what you have done. Symmetry is possible but not necessary: the focus of activity might be the shoulders or only the right shoulder. Discard the rigorous logic of Circles and follow instead the dictates of your body and your feelings. Let them control sequence and timing. You may never get to body parts mentioned in Circles and you may become absorbed in an area untouched by Circles. There will come a moment when all the body parts will become a unity and you will be "X" doing what "X" does.

You are now ready to engage with your partner, with the other. Without losing any of the character you have become, and deep within the danced truth of "X", approach the other person who, for simplicity's sake, we will dub "Y". Here you may face a decision. If "Y" is ready to engage, then each of you will proceed to do what you have to do—in dance. If "Y" is not ready, would "X" wait or barge right in? Would "Y" be pliant or resist by continuing with Each Alone until finished? This is the beginning of making choices as the person each of you has become. Whatever the outcome, sooner or later the two of you will engage in the attempt to make something happen. There should be no terror of the literal, only of getting stuck in it. The literal can be welcomed but only as an arrow leading toward a danced metaphor.

By now the questions arise: "How does each know what role the other has taken?" Neither knows, no more than we do in "real life." If this is true in life, then why should it not be so here in this duet?

Second question: "What if both take the same role—the same side of the implied dichotomy?" How many times are two united in a power struggle, each determined to dominate or each longing to find someone to lean upon? The complementary relationship of opposites is not a necessary condition. It probably happens as often as similar types try to relate.

If, as the duet progresses, you are having difficulty realizing your goal, be as flexible and resourceful as your "X" is—or as rigid, depending on who "X" is. It may even make sense to change your intent because of what you are experiencing as "X". If you achieve your task, celebrate that and leave the floor. If your partner does this before you, then dance out your recognition of failure and leave the floor. If nothing you do brings you any closer to success, you, still as "X", may give up and dance your acceptance of that failure and leave.

As noted earlier, anyone coming across this material for the first time may groan, "How complex! It's like a novel. How can anyone follow such a detailed and torturous path— and dance?" Answer: It is constructed out of a series of exercises, each of which should be known and practiced separately before being drawn together into this shape. A summary of The Duet as a Structure would go like this:

- Sitting facing your partner, you will hear "Someone . . . something. . . ." Do nothing about it except to save it on the shelf of your mind.
- Do The Mind-Wash and when finished, contemplate your partner, The Other.
- When you have done that, turn your attention to the "Someone . . . something . . ." and do a Hub Meditation.
- When you have found the dominating image, decide on your role and your task.
- When you and your partner both indicate readiness, both seek separate areas in which to do Each Alone.
- When you have become "X" through the work in Each Alone, find and engage with your partner.
- If you succeed in your task, celebrate that and leave the floor.
- If you fail, recognize that—in dance—and leave the floor.
- If your partner chooses to leave, recognize that and what it means—in dance— and leave.

Even reading this condensed version may still be confusing and perhaps it would help to review the mental process through which I went in a duet with Ara Fitzgerald, a member of the Workgroup. What was given:

Someone is favored in almost every way: looks, health, wealth, position—the works. You are that person or someone dealing with that person.

As I sat there looking at the sweet, clear-browed face of Ara, she became very wealthy and I became very ugly and poor. I found, from some dark corner of my mind, a very powerful man—physically powerful—who had spent time in jail for theft and assault. A resentful man with a violent temper. I had achieved a notoriety by writing of my childhood and history of violence. I was now a minor literary celebrity. Ara and I were guests at a country estate. I was determined that she should come to love me and because of that love, let me push her about and dominate her. Once she accepted my treatment of her, I would have all I wanted and could leave. I would have a victory over a "rich bitch."

Ara had found her role and task quite a bit of time before I did and her palms lay up and open, waiting for my grasp—for my decisions. She sat there gazing simply and directly into my face. Finally, when I was clear, I grasped her hands and we went off to separate parts of the studio.

When I found my "private place," I realized, as I stood there that it was a cell—a prison cell. The first place in my body that became active was my lower abdominal muscles which seemed to be writhing with all of their power as I was pacing the cell. It was as if I were being led by those muscles up and down the brief length of my space. In my mind, my feet were bare, though I was dancing with shoes. My attention then shifted to my feet which worked harshly into the cold, damp concrete as if they held the angry claws of a predatory animal. That action slowly flowed into the thighs which bulged with the muscles of a weight lifter. The power allowed me to perform sudden squats to a stillness as if waiting to spring. All this time, I was intermittently pacing my cramped space like a caged animal. Without warning, my mouth became alive—a stretched gash across my face which I constantly tried to make smaller by turning my lips inward. This, in time activated my whole face which was always on the verge of exploding out of control as I kept trying to keep it in rein, all the while pacing the cell. Then the attention shifted to the shoulders which felt massive and writhing like the abdominals. This action gradually flowed down the arms to the hands which wanted to flail about but were always caught by fisting and lowering the arms so that they would be quiet for a while. Lastly, the back came into play and its wish was to crouch, to duck, to avoid blows from somewhere but the wish had to be concealed so the crouch was spasmodically evident but mostly suppressed.

I had "become 'X.'" As I looked over to where Ara was, I saw her lightly flinging her arms about as if they were little flags pressed into the wind. I realized that I had to put on a well-tailored tweed suit over my anger and my ugliness. I did everything I had been doing but one could barely see what I was doing except that I was walking towards her with a slow held step followed by quick ones which were almost out of control. It resembled an erratic rhumba. The moment I approached Ara, she turned to me and circled me as if to observe me on all sides and to be observed by me on all of her sides. Pretending a cool, I alternately observed her closely and looked away as if there were other items of interest to me. There was a slide almost to the ground which I stopped with some show-off pushups into a sudden squat and then erect trying to tower above her.

Ara moved closer to me. "This was going to be easy!" Looking away, I reached to her, pulling her to me into a ballroom stance and leading with definite power guided her about the floor as if on a dance floor. She followed as if we had done this many times before, once releasing herself from my grasp to do the circling back into my arms. The more we danced, the more brutal I became until I was sweeping her down to the floor, pushing her away and pulling her back, each time going further and further from her, pretending an interest elsewhere, not unlike the way cats will play with a cricket or a mouse.

Finally, I went to the far end of the studio, confident that she would be waiting for me, so sure was I of my power. I was ready to leave the floor after "celebrating" my success, the achievement of my task. While I was strutting about, I glanced back to Ara and instead of that flighty arm-flinging, she was pacing back and forth in a limited space with a strangely familiar contorted body. *It was as if she was going through the same agony I had suffered in my cell.* The similarity was so great, I was shocked into the most unexpected compassion and concern for her. Uncertain, I wavered there, not knowing my next move and found myself drawn to her. Confused, I approached her cautiously and slowly began a dance of protection and cradling and loving—which Ara accepted and reciprocated. We ended with a fierce, yet tender love duet which finally settled into a moment of emotional exhaustion and we left the floor together.

I have no idea whether Ara achieved the task she found during the Hub Meditation or whether it changed as the dance progressed. What shook me was that for the first time I had set out in an improvisation with a clear direction and because of what I had experienced, I not only took an entirely unexpected path, but went through a profound change in character. To sum up these last few pages, The Duet as a Structure is the most fertile, challenging and exciting improvisation of all.

# 7  Finding Gold in "Bad" Habits

**Cliché Rondo[s]**

The Workgroup had the good fortune to experience several sessions conducted by the renowned theatre director and founder of the Open Theatre, Joseph Chaikin. Perhaps the most valuable insight gained from him was his suggestion to work through the cliché. This was a startling challenge. Traditionally, artists of every calling are ever en garde against any mannerism or cliché. We are forever checking and being checked by our "best friends and critics" from repeating gestures, phrases and solutions to which we habitually resort.

Anyone in the arts or observing the arts is aware of artists who grow unself-critical and get caught in the ruts of their own clichés. Chaikin's remark, ". . . work through your cliché," made us recognize that the cliché is important! It is a sign, a flag, a metaphor, a door to something that is vital to the artist. The task is never to flee from the cliché but to plunge deeply into it in all of its ramifications, associations and history—conscious and unconscious. If the prime responsibility of the artist is to make contact with what is deeply vital on a personal level, then the cliché is a door that must be pried open to reveal what is behind it. This observation blossomed into Cliché Rondo.

Ideally, each dancer should work alone with a piece of music he.she finds irresistible. Working with a group, a leader will use music that hopefully most of the group will find compelling. Something contagiously rhythmic and short is best.

First, find all the joy and pleasure you can in what you will now hear. (The tape is played and then rewound.)

This second time around, pretend that you are not in a room full of other dancers, but rather alone, and do what you usually do when you're listening to music that makes you dance. Disregard how you look or how "good" the movement is. You are not interested in choreography, interesting moves or virtuosity, only what you always do when dancing for the fun of it and when no one is looking. (The tape is played and then rewound.)

This third time, make a phrase of movement that will resemble a string of beads. In any order, string together two, three or four of the moves and phrases you just did in one phrase of sixteen beats or counts. (The leader should be clear about what is meant by this, pausing to play the music and count out the length of music asked for.) To repeat: we are not interested in choreography, interesting moves or virtuosity, only what you always do when dancing for the fun of it and when no one is looking. Link your moves into a sixteen count phrase. When you know it well enough to repeat it three times without stopping, leave the floor.

With most groups of any size, it will take two or even three playings of the selection until everyone has put together sixteen counts which they can remember and dance. This had better be a charming, "dancey" piece of music for it will be played many times as this sequence evolves. When all have stepped off the floor:

You are now going to dance a rondo. For those of you who are unfamiliar with that musical form, a theme is stated and then developed only to return to the same theme and then developed in a different direction and so on. If the theme is A and the developments are B, C, D, E, etc., the structure would be AB, AC, AD, AE, etc. "Development" will be whatever you improvise. When you run out of steam or at any time you have the inclination, you can return to A, dancing it once through and then going off to a new improvisation and so on until the music runs out. (The tape is played and then rewound.)

All sit, close your eyes and clear out your head with your breath. I am going to throw some premises at you. For the time of this exercise, assume they are correct. Afterward, you can reject them all.

Every move in your dance phrase is a thrust to be somewhere else and to become what you are not. Now, go to the dark of your mind, look at the sixteen count phrase you made. What is its itch? What is its longing? Where does it want to go? What does it want to become? Are your moves a metaphor for something? When you know, rise. When all are standing, the music will start and you will do the rondo, AB, AC, AD, AE, etc., only this time you will use all of the moves of the theme and variations to one end, to go where the moves want to go and to become what they are pointing towards.

Still another line of pursuit can be:

Use the Cliché Rondo to play with your original phrase's shapes and rhythms: bending, stretching, elevating, turning, pounding, caressing them to find out all that they contain. The surprise of all of this is how much gold lies hidden in our despised clichés. In fact, some dancers have used this structure both to choreograph and/or to perform as an improvisation. If there is an audience for a Cliché Rondo, in order to give the viewers a hint of what is going on, it is a good idea to state the A theme twice when starting. Thus the ideal structure would be AAB, AC, AD, AE, etc.

## Your Familiar[s]

Since the whole person of the dancer will be out there under the lights in front of all those people, some degree of self-awareness, sooner or later—and better sooner—becomes an integral part of the performer's preparation. The next three exercises raise to the surface —to consciousness—what should be known.

If working alone, choose several tracks of your favorite moving music. If working with a group, find something infectious enough to move almost everyone. During the first selection, have a good time, get loose and easy. Launch into the second piece and be on the watch for a position that is all too familiar. When it happens, freeze. What is the feeling of that position? What does it want to do or become? Stay with that position for a long time, until it is *impossible not to move*, and then go. The movement that follows should take its impetus from what is felt and implied by that same "familiar." When that plays itself out, return to the "familiar" and again hold the position for as long as you can, allowing all of its implications and all the feelings it provokes fill you until *you must move* once again. Keep this up until the music runs out or you run out of energy or, better still, until you have wrung that "familiar" dry. That will be the time to leave the floor. In the rest time that follows, let your mind run over what happened and what it means to you.

A variation of Your Familiar starts the same way: You halt at encountering a "familiar" and finally release the hold to continue improvising. But you stop when you encounter a *different* "familiar," freezing there until that one boils over into a further improvisation and so on. Question: was there a connection between the different "familiars"? In seeking the answers to these questions, there is no crying need that you be able to verbalize them clearly. In our business, some things are known even though they are never neatly wrapped up in words. Knowing without words and knowing with words are equally valuable.

Some choreographers get caught up in one or more manneristic expressions. A favorite of too many is what I unkindly call the "tushy roll" (a fall into a rolling sit and swift rise up to the feet). A marvelous Brazilian company performed here recently with a fantastic variety of moves, consistently punctuated by unmotivated double pirouettes finishing with a triumphant fourth position. One of our best choreographers has never quite freed himself from the image of Shiva tilted and balanced on one leg.

Most of us have one or more mannerisms that cling to us like barnacles. They are irrelevant and attract attention precisely because they usually are not pertinent to what we are doing.

While seated, close your eyes. Clear your head with your breath. In the empty space that ensues, ask the question, "Is there a movement or phrase that slips into my work regardless of the context? If the answer is no, open your eyes and leave the floor. If yes, see yourself performing this mannerism in your mind's eye. When it appears clearly and vividly, open your eyes, rise to do it and, whenever you are ready, travel among the others to find one to whom you will show this mannerism. If there are an odd number of you on the floor, the last person can go to one of the dancers who has chosen to leave the floor or join a pair to make a trio.

There will be five stages for this exercise:

- Stage one: Each of you in turn, demonstrate to your partner the mannerism you just recalled.

- Stage two: Separate and find your own space where you visualize the mannerism and, as you do this, begin to sense its inner rhythm, the motor that drives it. Once the rhythm is established, let it flood your body, let it move your body. Now, with this base, improvise a dance about the mannerism. Do it fully and consciously; do it in different ways, in parts of the body where it is never done; do it to show it to the world like a flag; conceal it while still doing it; sense what the mannerism is trying to say or do. Dance to, for, about and against your mannerism. The only music for this exercise will be the inner rhythm you found.

- Stage three: When you have done this improvisation, and you will know when you are done, find your partner, and if necessary, wait until he.she is finished. Now, taking turns, improvise for your partner the mannerism dance you did in private.

- Stage four: When both have danced for each other, rest and talk to each other about what you saw in the other and what you learned about your mannerism and, if it is not too private, what you learned about yourself.

- Stage five: Wait until you are next alone in a studio to do Possessed by a Mannerism again. In this private space and time, you may be able to delve deeper into what is really going on, where the mannerism came from and what it is really about. Habits do not need harsh criticism either from teachers or the self. Habits can use conscious and constructive attention. They are potentially fertile, for they signal something that is important to you.

Much of what is brought forward in the previous pages about clichés, "your familiar" and mannerisms has earlier been contradicted by remarks about the justification for repeating material from previous dances. We are caught in the embarrassment of mannerisms only when the repeated appearance of dance material is there for the reassuring comfort of its familiarity but inappropriate to its new context.

# 8 Music Sources of Movement

**Ambient Sound<sup>s</sup>**

Sit or stand and listen. Take whatever you hear and become that sound; let that sound take over your entire body.

**Rhythm Circle**

This exercise heightens rhythmic sensitivity and creativeness. Five to seven dancers sit or stand in a circle. One person starts by beating out, on impulse, any rhythm that rises up out of the moment, clapping, beating on the floor, the body or fingers snapping. Use all the time needed to settle into a rhythm until it can be repeated again and again with confidence. When that rhythm is under control, look at the person to your left and nod. That's the sign for the next person to learn what the first person has just found. The second person in the circle will try to duplicate the rhythm. The giver must stay with the learner until the rhythm is done accurately. If the learner is missing some part of it, the teacher can make a special emphasis to clarify.

When the teacher thinks the learner has it, she.he can stop but comes right back in if an error crops up when the learner is doing it alone. When the teacher is certain that the learner has it, she.he nods in assent. The learner then takes a time to "show off" his.her ability to go it alone. After this "graduation ceremony," the learner gradually modulates this rhythm, with no abrupt changes, to a new and personal rhythm. When that rhythm settles into a repeatable groove, the process is repeated. The new teacher will then look to the person on the left and nod, indicating that the rhythm is ready to be learned and the third person in the circle becomes a learner, absorbing the second person's phrase until finally getting the "go ahead" from the teacher. This third person continues the pattern until the whole circle has learned and taught a rhythm. If anyone finds a rhythm too difficult, she.he has the option of saying "I pass," to the teacher upon which the teacher shifts his.her attention to the next person over who becomes the learner. Those in the circle who are waiting their turn or have already gone can also learn each new rhythm but must beat it out soundlessly so as not to interfere with the master-disciple work. Vocalizations are not used.

When the last person in the circle begins to evolve her.his own rhythm, she.he turns to the one who started it all, teaching it to the first teacher. When that one learns it, she.he nods to the rest of the circle and all learn to do that same last rhythm. Rhythm Circle ends when the first teacher ends it.

## Before, After, and On[s]

No choreographer can afford to be unaware of this aspect of dance performance. An inappropriate use of the beat, either within a phrase or in the pervasive style of a work, can skew the entire focus in a contradiction to the choreographer's intention.

This exercise addresses the technical mastery of dancing at will, before, after and on the beat; the individual proclivity of the dancer in relation to rhythmic music; and the organic rhythmic relation to the music in the context of The Six Questions, the "Who or What is doing what?"

Problem 1: Find some infectious walking music: a paso doble, a Sousa march, a Dixieland march. To the walking music do the simplest of walking step phrases: one step on each beat. "Strutting" would be a better designation than "walking." I will call out, "Strut square on the beat." Then, "Strut a hair ahead of the beat." Then, "Step a hair behind the beat." When you have done that a few times, gather in groups of three. One of you calls out the commands, "Before! After! On the beat!" as one dances. The observer will tell you how successful you are—or not. Then the other two take their turns. Repeat the entire exercise to a moderate tempo waltz.

This is not an idle exercise, and if it is proffered to professionals, they should forego deriding it as childish. For all the world to see, there is a video of Rudolf Nureyev accompanied by a highly skilled woman who is usually behind the beat, sometimes on the beat, and never quickens when he so brilliantly chooses to. If you are good at this and do know what you are doing musically, congratulations—enjoy the exercise. Your help will be needed.

Problem 2: A highly rhythmic piece of music will be played. Go off by yourself and design an eight-count module of movement that can be repeated consistently. It is more important that you be sure of it than that you create a complex masterpiece. When you have it under control, get off the floor. When all of you are off the floor, re-assemble in groups of three. The music will again be played. One by one, dance for each other and observe each other with a view to characterizing each dancer's tendency—if there is one. You can challenge each other to go before, after or on.

The first exercise covers this ground but something extra will be revealed because each dancer will be creating her.his own phrase, thus revealing a more personal inclination.

## Who or What Is Alive in the Music?[s]

Michelangelo would go to the quarries and spend hours contemplating the great blocks of raw marble until he could see who or what was alive inside. Find your place in the room, sit, close your eyes and clean out your head with your breath. When you hear the music, seek who or what is alive inside it. Your quest is for a specific—never for a generalization. When you find the who or what is there, let your attention move in close and learn all you can about "X". Most of all, what is the inner rhythm that lives in "X"? The motor that drives "X"? How does that rhythm coexist and live within the rhythm of the music? The last question that needs an answer is *how long is this rhythmic phrase*? You may hear a four count or a six count or a nine count phrase. It matters not as long as that is what you feel but before you go on, you have to make a conscious analysis and know its length. It would not be acceptable at this point to mush along with an indeterminate phrase length. Miles Davis was permitted, not you, not yet. If and when the inner rhythm of that person in the music emerges full and clear, let it take possession of your entire body. Let it move you where it will.

When you hear the music, rise and find a repetitive phrase for your "X". Once you can repeat it with security, leave the floor. When all have left the floor and the music is restarted, all return to do your step precisely on the beat. When you see me rotate my hands quickly, do your step a hairsbreadth *ahead* of the beat. When I make a slow spreading motion, drag it so that you almost don't make the beat. When I make an up and down chopping motion with my hands, drive clean down on the center of the center of the beat. I will randomly redirect your attitude towards the beat. When I drop my hands, *do the phrase as you feel it should be done*. This may mean that it starts off behind the beat, quickens in the middle to be ahead of the beat and ends square on it. Find your own structure which may be all of one thing or rhythmically mixed.

## Riff Cactus[s]

To the same music and the same phrase which you are declaring comes out of "X", start to do it "forever," meaning that you have no intention of changing it or developing it in any way. It just continues on its way *until it changes itself.* You could say this is a Taoist exercise. Well, it is. I use the word cactus because as I think of how this happens, it is just the way a beaver-tail cactus will send out a bit of a bud that will grow into something like what it came from but not quite the same. Try to find steps that happen to you.

**Using Music for Improvisation**[s]

For a group, a leader can choose a strongly moving piece of music and call out at random the following instructions. For an individual working alone, improvise to a piece of music that makes you move with one of the following instructions in mind. Or you can keep two of them in your mind, alternating them on your own impulse. The last two of these will only work for a group.

1. Isolate and work only one part of the body keeping precisely with the basic rhythm.

2. With the entire body, follow or counterpoint the melody of the music.

3. With the entire body, follow or counterpoint the rhythm of the music.

4. With the entire body, follow or counterpoint the dynamics of the music.

5. Sense and do the inner action of the music.

6. Draw out of the music a short movement riff and do a rondo.

7. Give yourself a challenge of taking any of the above as a guide, while improvising to music that is rhythmically challenging.

8. While doing any of the above, add technical challenges of turning, balancing, endurance tests, high speed or moving in slow motion.

9. If you find something special, save it, work on it and if you want, teach it to all.

10. Move . . . dance . . . listen for the sheer delight of it without taking mental notes or for any "useful" purpose.

11. Don't dance and instead watch the others.

12. Work with a partner, sharing a problem. One of you dances. The other observes, takes notes and gives you suggestions and criticisms. Then change roles.

# 9  Words and Movement

| | |
|---|---|
| **Words**[S] | Make a study for each of the following: |

*Creating Words*[S]

What motions can you do that will explode or germinate words?

*Being Created by Words*[S]

Find words that can move you as fully as music.

*Becoming Words*[S]

What words/movements are wrapped so closely around each other that they can properly be conceived as one?

| | |
|---|---|
| **Prison**[S] | For this exercise you will need to construct, in your work space, separate enclosures or cells about six feet by four feet. Use cushions, chairs, tape—whatever is available. Step inside the space furthest from where you are now. When you arrive, you have only one thing to deal with, the word *prison*. Whatever that word means to you and whatever flows from or away from that word, is what happens. |

When I did this with the Workgroup, it provoked some of the most profound and complex improvisations I had ever seen. The dancers used that word the way an oyster uses a grain of sand, taking it in internally and growing something significant around it.

Make your own setting and try it with any word you choose: drop "forest" into to your mind, let it roam about for a while and odds are you will find yourself in a dense and active world, possibly as vivid as an actual forest. In a dry time, playing with one or more words as germinating seeds may loosen the creative forces.

**Poems**[S]        Long before the Workgroup and long after, a collection of spare and evocative poems have been seeds for some of the most creative work in my classes. In a book of essays by Kenneth Rexroth, titled *Assays*, I came across a collection of Native American poems that were gathered by Frances Densmore.[26] I was caught up by their elliptic power and a brevity like that of haiku. I immediately sensed that they belonged to dance. At the time, I had the good fortune to have at my disposal the services of a young actor with a typewriter. At the rate of $1.50 an hour, Dustin Hoffman typed out forty or so index cards which I have been using in classes ever since. At that time, the class was a group of young actors gathered up by Dustin. Here are six of the poems that most provoked their imaginations:

**Chippewa**

Strike you
Our land
With curved horns.

⇜

In form like a bird,
it appears.[27]

⇜

Sometimes
I go about pitying
Myself,
While I am carried by the wind
Across the sky.

⇜

The odor of death,
I discern the odor of death
In front of my body.

⇜

**Pawnee**

He said, Unreal the buffalo is standing.
These are his sayings.
Unreal the buffalo is standing.
Unreal he stands in the open space.
Unreal he is standing.

∽

**Teton Sioux**

A voice,
I will send.
Hear me!
The land
All over,
A voice
I am sending!
Hear me!
I will live!

For the Workgroup, I tacked the cards on the studio walls saying:

Take a trip around the studio to read what is there. When and if you find one that gets to you, one that stings you, one that changes your breath, learn it, drop it into your body and let the words come to life.

For about two weeks in the early days of the first Workgroup, the pillars and walls were decorated with about twenty of these. The dancers would, in their warmups, in breaks, while lunching, during an extended improvisation, pause to glance at them and then sometimes we would make them the focus of our work.

While writing this passage, I checked back to Rexroth's paperback and was struck by these lines:

The intense aesthetic realization which precedes the poem is a realization of identity with a beneficent environment. Often this is focused in a dream or vision, waking or sleeping, after long, lonely fast and vigil in the forest or desert. An aspect of the environment, an animal or a natural object or force, appears to the Indian, waiting in a trance state, and gives him the song, which remains his most precious possession and the pivot of his life forever after.[28]

Despite the vast differences between the men and women who created those poems and Dustin's friends and the dancers of the Workgroup, I was and am constantly trying to make the same creative process happen. Our contemporary environment is, in many ways, other than "beneficent" but that is our life and our world. I present dancers with the creative paradox: lose yourself as you observe and interact with the world, with the other, with the object and in that "abandonment" of self, allow the poem to well up out of your inner being.

The work on the Native American poems was never performed by the Workgroup, though the time spent strengthened all of our subsequent work. In retrospect, the Native American poem time was the most valuable of all. We learned from those poets how to find metaphors that invigorated our vision, poeticized our dance and provoked the imagination of our audience.

# 10 More

**Why Do You Dance?**[s]   Answer the question without words. Try this alone and with an audience. It is not a bad idea to repeat this exercise over the years. You may find that the answers change and that most times they will, in some respect, surprise you.

**Props Fantasy**[s]   One can fire up the imagination to find, create and become using a prop or a costume. It really doesn't matter from where you start, just so long as you ultimately plunge in deep enough to get your eyelashes wet with the magic "if."

Set out in the space anything that is available: a wine bottle, chairs, a table, a book, a pillow, etc. One or two of you enter the space and begin to deal with what you find there. Beginning on a literal level is fine. Where and when does the literal spin away into fantasy and metaphor?

**Inside the Outside**[s]   This exercise requires at least three days of work. The beginning assumes that the dancers are not only physically warm but have achieved a psychic looseness with a Repetition, Spinning or any physical meditation.

Day one: Sit with your hands clasped. Close your eyes. Clean out your head with your breath. When you achieve some clarity, unclasp your hands. (When all unclasp their hands:) First you will hear music and then you are going to embark on a Hub Meditation. The question is: "What is male?" When you find the specific image at the hub of your mind, pause to learn all you can about it. Observe it from all sides. Step a bit closer. When you have finished your observation, go to an initial starting position—sitting, standing, kneeling or lying down—that would be appropriate for you to work at becoming "X". In that initial position, you are you, not "X".

When you hear music, without planning or anticipating, become "X" bit by bit, as in Each Alone. If and when your Each Alone is finished, do Go Visiting, as the "X" you have become, to see who the others are and what they appear to be doing. In time, gravitate toward the person who interests you the most, positively or negatively. What do you want? Do you want to change that person? Be changed by that person? Or just be in his.her company for a time? When you get what you want, celebrate that and leave the floor. If you fail in what you wish, dance the recognition of that and leave the floor. Take time to absorb what happened.

Day two: Everything is the same except that for the Hub Meditation, the question is, "What is female?" (Best to leave this question for day two. The women will not mind exploring "What is male?" on that first day while the men, having "had their day," will more easily accept the adventure of answering the question of "What is female?")

Day three: Yesterday, you did a Hub Meditation on "What is female?" The day before, you did one on "What is male?" Recapture the specific images of each in your mind's eye, first one and then the other. Now mesh them into one body and wait to see what will happen. What do you see? Is one image visible and the other present but not visible? Is one on the outside and one on the inside? Are both visible but is one dominant? So many possibilities.

When the male/female structure is clear to you, go to work on whichever is on the inside, using the technique of Each Alone to become that image. When you have finished, you are ready for the second stage. As "X", go through another Each Alone, this time putting on the other image *on the outside*. We can call this outside image "Y". "Y" is what "X" shows to the world.

When you have finished this double task, you are ready again to do Go Visiting. Look about you and take in the "world" in which you find yourself. You have one more question to answer before you go on. What do you as the complexity of "X" clothed as "Y" want to do—need to do—for, to or against the world in which you find yourself? Are there individuals out there with whom you need to interact? To avoid? Do you have a task in relation to that entire community? To one or to a few individuals? Are you a hermit? Once you have answers, retaining the full sense and presence of both "X" and "Y", find the danced metaphors that contain this action. Now you are ready to do whatever you have to do, with or without others. If you succeed in your task, celebrate that and leave the floor. If you fail, dance the recognition of that and leave the floor.

I offered this structure fully only once, at The University of California at San Diego. It covered the three days and it worked. There were many dancers, men and women, attending this workshop. Large numbers often make for freedom because the dancers quite accurately assume that they will be less conspicuous among so many. There was no problem from any of the men when the question went out, "What is female?" The dancing was varied, animated and quirky. Duets and trios went on for a long time and *things happened*—people changed as they danced. The talk afterwards was full of a wonderment at how completely they were caught up and how the many emotional and intellectual surprises jolted them.

There's always a risk when the space is opened to deep and often conflicted feelings. Over the years, I've given out these two questions, "What is male?" and "What is female?" to about eight different groups. Be warned. This one is, as they say, "heavy." In the Appendix of *Dance and the Specific Image: Improvisation* (195–203), there appears a dialogue between some dancers at a University of Hawaii workshop and myself. It was kicked off by some who were upset because they had wept during a male/female improvisation. The discussion touched upon some of the fundamental attitudes that go to shape art.

Most of the dancers in the workshop were excited that they could be dancing *and* actually dealing with what really mattered to them. How sophisticated and how mature should the dancers be to attempt this? I have no answer. I only know this stuff is dynamite in the bodies and minds of dancers who are open and willing to look at each other and themselves.

| **Body Contact** | Pair off and face each other, hands raised shoulder height and palms touching. Sooner or later one of you will begin to move one or both hands in the same or different directions. All movement should be slow in this exercise. Whoever starts the moving has a commitment: Once started in a specific direction, there can be no wavering, curving or change of direction. Continue the motion until it is not possible to move any further in that direction. Whoever is being moved has an equally important but more subtle commitment: The pressure of the mover must be answered by pressure from the moved one, i.e., the moved one maintains an answer life *all* through the slow thrust of the mover but *never with the intention of stopping or hindering that thrust at any point.* When the mover has reached the full length of his.her thrust and is not able to go any further, the moved one becomes the mover and initiates with the pressure of hands the next thrust, which similarly is unwavering in a straight line |

until no further progress is possible. The feet never move until they must. Little convenient shifts of weight by foot movements are out. Stay with no sudden movements; all is slow.

When anyone tears away from these ground rules, it becomes immediately apparent as a betrayal of the commitment. When both stay with it and in the oft repeated cry of Tamiris, they "follow through," the experience of doing and of viewing it touches deep places. Body Contact is not easy to pull off at first but after some practice, exquisite and astonishing events can occur. Tamiris and I taught actors extensively and this was a particularly fertile exercise for them. They would slide into pelvic falls that would take months to teach them. Body Contact has many variations:

- Do it with three, four or many. (In *Dance for Walt Whitman*, Tamiris choreographed a whole chain of linked dancers using Body Contact.)
- Do it with the palms of the hands close to each other but not touching.
- Give secret and sometimes contradictory inner actions to each of the dancers. This is best with three or four dancers. Examples:
  - "Keep your distance from the others."
  - "Be protective and shelter the others."
  - "Tower above the others."

Note: In these examples, one can express one's will only when one's turn comes up. Each person must "give in," even though unwillingly, while the will of the other is being expressed through pressure of the hands.

## Seeing through the Eyes of Another[S]

Any number of dancers sit in a circle. Rotate in any direction and at any speed on your bottom. What you are really doing is observing the others in the circle with a view to pinning down who it is that interests you the most, positively or negatively. When you make this decision, learn all you can about this person while you continue the circling. During all this observation, you never let anyone catch your eye, particularly the one upon whom your full attention finally settles. Your observation remains covert. When you think you have absorbed all you can from this person, stop the rotation at any point, close your eyes and continue to observe and absorb what you see of that person—in your mind. When all stop, I will give the next direction.

(All have stopped rotating.) When I say, "Go," open your eyes, rise and find another place to sit in the circle, but not in the place of the person in your mind. (They do so.)

Now, close your eyes to mentally recapture that person. When you do, open your eyes and look out at everyone *through the eyes of that person*. Again, begin the rotation on your bottom and through the eyes of that person, observe all the others with a view to pinning down who is the person who that person would find the most interesting, positively or negatively. When the person is found, observe her.him closely and covertly. Repeat the rest of the sequence: ceasing to rotate when the person is absorbed, closing the eyes to continue the study of that person, rising when the "Go," is heard to find a new place in the circle, sitting, closing the eyes to recapture the person and then opening the eyes to look through the eyes of this person.

A brief summary of the above:

1. Find and observe the one who takes your interest.

2. Go to another place and look at rest of room as she.he would do.

3. Pick out someone else as she.he would do and take that person's place.

When does one call a halt to this process? Two or three times should be sufficient to underline the creative possibilities gained by "seeing through the eyes of another." Hidden within this simple and subtle little game is the possibility of a giant moral-ethical leap, but that is something for the reader to pursue in his.her own time, not here in this book. One person can perform this exercise in any assemblage of people where a close scrutiny can be carried on unobtrusively: a subway car, a restaurant, a dance class, etc.

## I Dare You[5]

When dancers work with each other day after day, inevitably they notice each other's style, strong points and limitations. I Dare You is all about limitations. It only works with a group that has been working together for some time and has a non-competitive spirit.

One person will leave the room and the others try to find the key limitation in the way that person has been working. Once there is a consensus on this, the challenge for the group is that the I Dare You has to be couched in a poetically specific and nondestructive way, a way that will stimulate the imagination of that dancer. A literal statement like "Improvise with a flowing, gentle quality," will come off as criticism and beg for a generalized response. Once there is agreement, the dancer is called back and the person who contributed the most to the formulated I Dare You gives it to the dancer, verbally. Time is left in the session for each to write down the exact wording of the challenge they received.

Allow a week for all the dancers to work on their I Dare You, finding a specific image, a rich movement metaphor and a loose construction around which to improvise. There is no pressure in this exercise to create a piece of choreography, though many have done just that. An improvisation that has been roughly sketched is just fine. The purpose is to encourage the dancer to enter a new room, to experience something in a new way. A week should be enough, and when the dancers meet again, they show what they have found. At best, this is a quality that was *there all the time* but was never previously exploited by the dancer. As part of the challenge, an appropriate, though makeshift costume could be helpful to slipping into "X". The group helps the dancer by commenting on how closely she.he met the challenge. Here are a few sample challenges from an actual class:

"Become a length of lavender silk thread that is being used to crochet a delicate rose." This was given to the strongest dancer of her class, tall and powerfully built. As exciting as she was to observe, these were the only qualities we ever saw her exhibit. Her study-improvisation was gossamer and yet strong as silk. Later, she built a piece of choreography around this study and performed it with success at the student concert.

"Become a monstrous, brutal piece of construction machinery used for road building." This was for a tall elegant man who had a narrow image of what constituted beauty in movement: fey and floating. I think the I Dare You made him furious, and that only added to the power of an awesome study that was the best and most exciting dance I ever saw him do.

"Become a hard-hearted, egotistical, cocky, smart-assed, macho stud who's on the rampage." This was given to an exceptionally attractive woman who tended to cling fiercely to a her idea of femininity in all that she did. Her study was a farcical, hilarious and outrageous blast climaxed by making violent love to the floor. She appeared to have a giddy relish in letting go of her girly-girl image, at least for the length of that improvisation.

Humorous challenges can be just as effective as profoundly poetic ones. I Dare You can also help dancers explore the matter of for whom they are dancing: "I dare you to dance for the spirit of José Limon." "I dare you to dance for a Hollywood casting agent." "I dare you to dance for the wild winds."

Can I Dare You be a solitary exercise? All it takes is a ruthless objectivity in self-observation. "What is it that I never do? Am I shying away from it out of fear of my inadequacy or is it completely beyond me? Would a shot at it open a door that I thought was closed to me—even a crack?" If you fail, who would know but you? That is the precious beauty of private time in the studio. Every failure is another brick in the tower you are building and every victory is a window in that tower. Go for it.

# Notes

1. Dr. Christena Schlundt, "Tamiris: A Chronicle of Her Dance Career, 1927–1955," in *Studies in Dance History* 1, no. 1 (fall/winter 1989–90): 128–129, 131. This is the most detailed and comprehensive survey of Tamiris's career in the period indicated.

2. Sedgewick, Maine, where Tamiris and I had summer workshops in 1961 and 1962. It had been, for years, a dance camp for young people owned and directed by Evelyn De Latour. She graciously invited us to use the place for our company and students.

3. The two classes Marion Scott refers to here are probably Pre-Classic Forms and Modern Dance Forms.

4. Caryn James, "The Arts Festival: 4 Directors in Seminar on Movies," *New York Times*, 23 June 1988,The Arts section, C17, C21.

5. W. I. B. Beveridge, *The Art of Scientific Investigation* (New York: Vintage Books, 1957).

6. Federico García Lorca, *The Poet in New York*, trans. Ben Belitt (New York: Grove Press, 1955): 154–166.

7. Ben Shahn, *The Shape of Content* (Cambridge: Harvard University Press, 1957). I have often recommended this book to students and friends.

8. Definitions for *abalienating*: a. transferring legal title, b. estranging, c. to cause a mental aberration.

9. Joseph Needham, *Science and Civilization in China*, vol. 2 (London: Cambridge University Press): 243.

10. Daniel Nagrin, *The Six Questions: Acting Technique for Dance Performance* (Pittsburgh: University of Pittsburgh Press, 1997): 38–39.

11. Oliver Sacks, "Neurology and the Soul," *The New York Review of Books*, 22 November 1990, 48.

12. Traditional lyrics.

13. Janet Cawley, "Playwright Nurtures New 'Baby': 'Heidi' Author Chronicles Life, Weighs Her Own," *Arizona Republic*, 13 March 1992, E2.

14. Lincoln Kirstein, *Dance: A Short History of Classic Theatrical Dancing* (G. P. Putnam's Sons: New York, 1935; reprint, Princeton: Dance Horizons, 1987): 195.

15. Kirstein, 195.

16. Ralph Gilbert was a dance accompanist for Martha Graham's school alongside of Louis Horst. He was also the husband of Iris Mabry, a dancer in Graham's company and a fascinating soloist. She had the cool elegance of a fashion model and created fresh, novel solos for which Ralph had composed music. It was at one of her concerts that I heard his music and decided to ask him to write a score for *Dance in the Sun*.

17. "Manifest" is an obsolete version of "manifesto." I never learned why she used that word.

18. Daniel Nagrin, *How to Dance Forever* (New York: William Morrow, 1988): 341–353.

19. Shahn, 22.

20. Francis Sparshott, *Off the Ground: First Steps to a Philosophical Consideration of Dance* (Princeton: Princeton University Press, 1988), 33–35.

21. Sparshott, 73.

22. John Richardson, "The Great Forgotten Modernist", *The New York Review of Books*, 27 March 1997, 31.

23. Martin Buber. *Ten Rungs: Hasidic Sayings* (New York: Schocken Books, 1947, 1962).

24. The most serious intellectual (and emotional) failure of most human beings is the conviction that for every question and every problem there is but one answer. Forget it.

25. Shahn, 72.

26. Kenneth Rexroth, *Assays* (New York: New Directions, 1961): 59–68. Another rich source of evocative poems ideal for dance is a collection of poems by peoples of Africa, America, Asia and Oceania, called *Technicians of the Sacred*, ed. Jerome Rothenberg (New York: Doubleday Anchor, 1968).

27. Robert Duvall, another young actor in the class, made a startling study for this one.

28. Rexroth, 58.

# Index